ALL ARMS
and
ELBOWS

New
Third Edition

Published by:
Mercian Manuals Limited
353 Kenilworth Road
Balsall Common
Coventry
West Midlands
England
CV7 7DL
+44 (0)1676 533304
www.mercianmanuals.co.uk

Distributed worldwide by the same.

© 2005

We would like to thank the following photographic agencies.

Zoë Mayho......................................LAT Photographic
Borris & Rainer Schlegemilch.......SCHLEGELMILCH Photography
Other images have been supplied by Innes's family.
Cover design....................................Richard Shimmell MM Ltd

First printed by Pelham Books Ltd, 1967
Second Edition Transport Bookman Publications Ltd, 1994
Third Edition Mercian Manuals Ltd, 2005

ISBN 1-903088-25-9

CONTENTS

This third edition of "All Arms an Elbows" some may think is an attempt to ring out a nearly dry rag, we believe this is not the case. This edition has been produced in a totally new layout, and includes information and photographs never before published.

Jean Ireland, who's co-operation in this project, and who owns the 'rights' to Innes's books has been most helpful in putting this document together, would like to share images and information with those who may be interested.

Being the archityple Scotsman, Innes found his way into motorsport by sheer guts and determination. His interest came at a time when two of Britains famous racing drivers died, one on the track at Nurburgring, Germany (Peter Collins) and the other (Mike Hawthorn, World Champion) on the Guildford bypass Surrey, England.

"Who was Innes Ireland?"

Most people have always thought of Innes Ireland as being the archetypal Scotsman, how wrong this is. Robert MacGregor Innes Ireland was born in Mytholmroyd in West Yorkshire on June 12th 1930. Innes's father William Alexander Ireland was a veterinary surgeon, his mother being Mary Margaret Ireland.

In his later years Innes had a reputation as a "Hellraiser", this belied the fact that he came from a Scottish Presbyterian background, with an uncle being a Church of Scotland minister, and a grandfather who lectured for a temperance organisation.

All this said, Innes was to be found in a Prep School in Chipping Campden, Gloucestershire until the beginning of the Second World War, which was when his family returned to Scotland. Innes was a great sportsman at school. While attending Kirkudbright High School he had much success in all the varying sports activities the school had to offer.

On leaving school in 1950, Innes entered an engineering apprenticeship at Rolls Royce Aero Division in Glasgow. After a period of time he was transferred to the Car Division in London. At long last he was in an environment that interested him greatly. Cars. Innes's interest in motorsport had been fired by Tim Birkin's escapades as one of the "Bentley Boys" before the war. It was around this time that he became involved with a 3½ litre Bentley. 1951 saw Innes attend his first serious motor racing event which was the Daily Express Trophy meeting at Silverstone. Much to his great jubilation he finally entered his first race in the Bentley at Borham in which he came fourth.

1953 saw Innes doing his National Service in which he enlisted in the Kings Own Scottish Borderers, soon being promoted to the rank of Lieutenant. Shortly after this, he was seconded to the First Parachute Regiment. It was during the "disturbances" in the Canal Zone in Egypt that some twelve members of Innes's Regiment were killed which did not do much for his enthusiasm for wanting to stay in the Army. He left soon after his return from the Middle East.

The purchase of a Brooklands Riley "9" eventually lead to Innes's contact with a certain public school boy, that being Jim Clark. Innes was to compete in the car on a number of occasions over the ensuing couple of years.

The 30th of October 1954 saw the wedding of Norma Thomas and Innes Ireland at Scalby Parish church in Yorkshire. After leaving the Army, Innes again rejoined Rolls Royce Cars Ltd. in London, but this was not for long as his interests were elsewhere. The garage trade beckoned, and with his friend John Mason, started repairing Rolls Royce and Bentley cars. During his free time at weekends not far away from Elstead where the garage was located was the Goodwood motor racing circuit. Whilst competing there, Innes had victories in both 1955 and 1956.

With the help of an ex Army colleague of his brothers, Major Rupert Robinson, Innes was able to purchase his first real modern racing car, a Lotus Eleven. The debut event was at Goodwood on the 22nd September 1956 where the result was a 2nd and a 4th place. This success was the start of a career in various forms that was to span some thirty years.

1957 saw Innes in numerous events such as winning at Goodwood in the Brooklands Memorial Trust race. July saw him win the US Airforces Trophy for Tommy Sopwith. After a telephone call from Colin Chapman, Innes had his first drive for Team Lotus at the Swedish Grand Prix in a World Sports Car event. There were more events of the same calibre that year which finally brought Innes into the public eye. The newly opened circuit of Clermont Ferrand witnessed Innes beating a host of Ferrari's in the Trophee d' Auvergne. Later that season he won several more races on UK circuits.

Innes made his Formula 1 debut at Zandvoort in 1959 at the Dutch Grand Prix of that year finishing fourth. The season was not one of the best, with cars being underpowered, unsafe and in some cases dangerous. By the end of the season Innes was on his own at Team Lotus, with Graham Hill leaving for pastures new.

1960 was a very good year with two wins over Stirling Moss at Goodwood. By the end of the season he finished fourth in the World Championship. With all this success, he moved from Surrey to a large house in mid Wales becoming the talk of the local area. 1961 was by comparison a bad year in as much as after a nasty crash in the tunnel at Monaco, Innes suffered serious injuries to his legs which took a long time to heal. He did however win three F1 races. By the end of the season though he was not wanted at Lotus. The reason for this was never clear, lots of speculation but nothing was ever confirmed.

Over the next three years, Innes drove in the British Racing Partnership alongside Stirling Moss. The team was the idea of the Moss family, with sponsorship from outside the sport. It was a new concept which was to be followed into the modern era. Some success along with some failures created an interesting and frustrating time for all concerned.

Tim Parnell in 1965 had an F1 Racing Team, but all types of problems inherent in participating in the sport, the team were always struggling to perform to the highest level required. At the Mexico Grand Prix in 1965 various things went wrong, none more frustrating than several drivers being late for their drive, one of them being Innes. This caused problems with drivers and their managers, and in Innes's case he lost his drive. After that experience, long distance endurance races beckoned without any great success. Innes was encouraged to drive in the 1967 Daytona 500 in which he was placed 7th before being forced to retire. Innes did drive in the 1968 London to Sydney rally. Various other competition activities such as World Cup Rallying, driving for Lancia and Endurance series with Stirling Moss. All took their toll on Innes's racing and rallying enthusiasm. His career finally came to and end 1985.

Over the ensuing years Innes had many different activities. He became one of the main Editors of Motor Sport and Autocar. He wrote his book on the London to Sydney Rally, this followed his first title which you are about to read "All Arms and Elbows". Innes returned to Scotland in 1970 to live in the village of Borgue, where he ran trawlers for a while. After several years, and no real profit, he found his way back again to England to get involved with cars. Then came the opportunity to write for "Road and Track" in the USA. An activity which he liked very much as his head was full of very many great interesting tales, as well as wonderfully amusing ones.

Innes had divorced his first wife, married again which also lead to a second divorce. In 1992 Innes was made President of the "British Racing Drivers Club" whose home is at Silverstone racing circuit which they own. Innes again married, this time to Jean Mander, who in her earlier days was Jean Howarth who was an ex model and ex fiancee of Mike Hawthorn at the time of his very untimely death. Innes had a daughter, Francis Christianne and a son, Jamie.

Around this time Innes was diagnosed with cancer, which finally took his life in October 1993.

Innes, apart from being the love of my life, was a remarkable man. There wasn't anything he couldn't do if he decided to turn his hand to it. He was a good racing driver, could sail a boat by the stars, could fly an aeroplane, was a good shot, wrote three books and became a journalist. He was very proud to be included in the Guild of Motoring Writers and he was also an extremely good after dinner speaker.

Innes was fearless, loyal and totally honest, he never let people down. When a deal was done he would stick by it even if the next day a better one came along. He was kind and generous, which unfortunately some took advantage of, hence he never had much money but that never stopped him from doing the things that mattered to him.

His motor racing brought him much happiness and sadness, he always was deeply affected whenever his compatriots were killed, but it didn't let it effect his dedication to his sport. Only once did I see him worried and that was when Jean Behra went over the top of the banking at Avus and he knew his Lotus would break sometime during the race, he just hoped it wouldn't break on the banking. It did break and on the banking!

Innes's quick wit got him out of trouble on many occasions with the police. He always drove flat out, never wore a seatbelt, but always kept an eye out, so wasn't ever caught, except once when we were driving to Dover, coming down the hill, a car in front was going far too slowly for Innes when he suddenly overtook him on double white lines, unfortunately Innes on this occasion didn't see the police behind him, who flagged him down and stopped us to ask what he thought he was doing, only to be told by Innes that the car in front had suddenly braked and he had swerved to avoid him! We were sent on our way with a wave and have a good holiday.

Innes was a wonderful character, fun loving, totally outrageous, smoked too much, drank to much on occasions, loved the girls, but underneath was a serious person who took his responsibilities seriously. He was immensely proud when his peers made him President of their club, the British Racing Drivers Club. He became a valued President and was sorely missed when he died in office.

Jean Ireland 2005

Foreword

What a splendid character we had in Innes Ireland! One of the great flamboyant personalities of motor racing who made his era of the sport a marvellous one for all of us who were lucky enough to be there with him.

Innes's exploits are legendary in the motor racing fraternity and you will enjoy reading some of these in this book although no doubt many of the best ones had to be left out!

Although always ready to party and have a good time, he took his motor racing very seriously and his contribution to the sport is enormous, a fact recognised and appreciated by fellow drivers and motor racing enthusiasts around the world.

Innes was held in high esteem by his peers. A wonderful companion, a good friend and a legend from a golden age in motor racing. He of course will always be missed, but the glorious memory of Innes magnificent in kilts, telling another outrageous story will bring a smile to many faces for a long, long time.

Jack Brabham O.B.E.
Sydney, 1994.

The author.

The following pictorial section are images of Innes in his early years learning his trade in some varied and interesting machines.

A

A young Innes in his 1926 Bentley (which he called Francis after the lady who left it to him) contemplating the forthcoming race, and his potential for the future.

At speed at Charterhall 1949. (Note the driving position also without seatbelts)

Driving a Works Lotus 11 (Le Mans) in very poor weather conditions.

Innes's own Lotus 11 in the paddock at Silverstone. Also on the left is the Ford Zephyr that pulled the cars to various meetings.

Driving a Tojero Jaguar (Larkhall)

Through the Esses's at Goodwood driving a Lister Jaguar.

Competing in a Cooper/Climax (Silverstone).

Mastering a Cooper/Climax exiting the Esses's at Goodwood.

Stirling Moss offering the best advise at Le Mans 1964.
(Stirling Moss was working as a comentator that year)

Innes performing very well (finishing 4th) in the BRM engined BRP MKI at Zandvoort in 1963.

Innes at the centre of attention in the "Hermitage" Monaco, where a new chair was required after a press gathering, 1969.

Listening to yet another hard luck story with Tony Maggs, Le Mans 1964.

Innes having won the 1961 US Grand Prix at Watkins Glen responding to a remark made by the photographer.

The last lap of the 1960 Grand Prix at Monaco saw Innes having to push his Lotus 18 up the last part of the hill from Sainte Devote due to engine failure. He new that if succesfull, he could roll the car from Casino Square all the way to the finishing line. This he did and was placed 7th.

Innes driving the Aston Martin (Project DP214) in the Tourist Trophy at Goodwood 1963.
He was placed 7th.

Driving an AC Cobra, partnered with Masten Gregory in the 1964 Targo Florio. They did not finish due to an accident. (A car he did not enjoy driving).

Innes Ireland Complete GP Results

Event	Pos.	No.	Entrant	Chassis	Engine	Laps	Results	Points	Grid
Dutch Grand Prix 1959	4	12	Team Lotus	Lotus 16	Climax	74	-	3	9
French Grand Prix 1959	R	34	Team Lotus	Lotus 16	Climax	14	Wheel Bearing	-	15
British Grand Prix 1959	DNS	15	Team Lotus	Lotus 16	Climax	-	Driver Ill Stacey Drove	-	-
German Grand Prix 1959	R	15	Team Lotus	Lotus 16	Climax	7	Gear Selection	-	13
Portuguese Grand Prix 1959	R	12	Team Lotus	Lotus 16	Climax	3	Gearbox	-	16
Italian Grand Prix 1959	R	20	Team Lotus	Lotus 16	Climax	14	Brakes	-	14
US Grand Prix 1959	5	10	Team Lotus	Lotus 16	Climax	39	-	2	9
Argentinian Grand Prix 1960	6	20	Team Lotus	Lotus 18	Climax	79	-	1	2
Monaco Grand Prix 1960	7	22	Team Lotus	Lotus 18	Climax	56	-	-	7
Dutch Grand Prix 1960	2	4	Team Lotus	Lotus 18	Climax	75	2h02m11.2s	6	3
Belgian Grand Prix 1960	R	14	Team Lotus	Lotus 18	Climax	13	Spun Off	-	8
French Grand Prix 1960	7	20	Team Lotus	Lotus 18	Climax	43	-	-	4
British Grand Prix 1960	3	7	Team Lotus	Lotus 18	Climax	77	2h05m54.2s	4	5
Portuguese Grand Prix 1960	6	16	Team Lotus	Lotus 18	Climax	48	-	1	7
US Grand Prix 1960	2	10	Team Lotus	Lotus 18	Climax	75	2h29m30.2s	6	7
Monaco Grand Prix 1961	DNS	30	Team Lotus	Lotus 21	Climax	-	Injured	-	19
Belgian Grand Prix 1961	R	32	Team Lotus	Lotus 21	Climax	9	Engine	-	18
French Grand Prix 1961	4	6	Team Lotus	Lotus 21	Climax	52	2h15m27.8s	3	10
British Grand Prix 1961	10	16	Team Lotus	Lotus 21	Climax	72	-	-	7
German Grand Prix 1961	R	15	Team Lotus	Lotus 21	Climax	1	Fire	-	16
Italian Grand Prix 1961	R	38	Team Lotus	Lotus 18/21	Climax	5	Chassis	-	9
US Grand Prix 1961	1	15	Team Lotus	Lotus 21	Climax	100	2h13m45.8s	9	8
Dutch Grand Prix 1962	R	9	UDT Laystall Racing Team	Lotus 24	Climax	61	Spun Off	-	6
Monaco Grand Prix 1962	R	34	UDT Laystall Racing Team	Lotus 24	Climax	64	Fuel Pump	-	8
Belgian Grand Prix 1962	R	20	UDT Laystall Racing Team	Lotus 24	Climax	9	Suspension	-	5
French Grand Prix 1962	R	36	UDT Laystall Racing Team	Lotus 24	Climax	1	Broken Wheel	-	8
British Grand Prix 1962	16	32	UDT Laystall Racing Team	Lotus 24	Climax	61	-	-	3
Italian Grand Prix 1962	R	40	UDT Laystall Racing Team	Lotus 24	Climax	45	Suspension	-	5
US Grand Prix 1962	8	15	UDT Laystall Racing Team	Lotus 24	Climax	96	-	-	16
South African Grand Prix 1962	5	11	UDT Laystall Racing Team	Lotus 24	Climax	81	-	2	4
Monaco Grand Prix 1963	R	14	British Racing Partnership	Lotus 24	BRM	40	Accident	-	5
Belgian Grand Prix 1963	R	4	British Racing Partnership	BRP Mk1	BRM	9	Gearbox	-	7
Dutch Grand Prix 1963	4	30	British Racing Partnership	BRP Mk1	BRM	79	-	3	7
French Grand Prix 1963	9	32	British Racing Partnership	BRP Mk1	BRM	49	-	-	9
British Grand Prix 1963	DQ	11	British Racing Partnership	BRP Mk1	BRM	26	Push Start	-	11
German Grand Prix 1963	R	14	British Racing Partnership	Lotus 24	BRM	1	Accident	-	11
Italian Grand Prix 1963	4	32	British Racing Partnership	BRP Mk1	BRM	84	Engine	3	10
Monaco Grand Prix 1964	DNS	14	British Racing Partnership	Lotus 24	BRM	-	Injured	-	17
Belgian Grand Prix 1964	10	3	British Racing Partnership	BRP Mk1	BRM	28	-	-	16
French Grand Prix 1964	R	16	British Racing Partnership	BRP Mk2	BRM	31	Spun Off	-	11
British Grand Prix 1964	10	11	British Racing Partnership	BRP Mk2	BRM	77	-	-	10
Austrian Grand Prix 1964	5	14	British Racing Partnership	BRP Mk2	BRM	102	-	2	11
Italian Grand Prix 1964	5	46	British Racing Partnership	BRP Mk2	BRM	77	-	2	13
US Grand Prix 1964	R	11	British Racing Partnership	BRP Mk2	BRM	2	Gear Lever	-	10
Mexican Grand Prix 1964	12	11	British Racing Partnership	BRP Mk2	BRM	61	-	-	16
Belgian Grand Prix 1965	13	22	Reg Parnell Racing	Lotus 25	BRM	27	-	-	16
French Grand Prix 1965	R	22	Reg Parnell Racing	Lotus 25	BRM	18	Gearbox	-	17
British Grand Prix 1965	R	23	Reg Parnell Racing	Lotus 25	BRM	41	Engine	-	15
Dutch Grand Prix 1965	10	38	Reg Parnell Racing	Lotus 25	BRM	78	-	-	13
Italian Grand Prix 1965	9	38	Reg Parnell Racing	Lotus 25	BRM	74	-	-	18
US Grand Prix 1965	R	22	Reg Parnell Racing	Lotus 25	BRM	9	Driver Ill	-	18
Mexican Grand Prix 1965	DNS	22	Reg Parnell Racing	Lotus 25	BRM	-	Driver Fired	-	13
US Grand Prix 1966	R	10	Bernard White Racing	BRM P261	BRM	96	Alternator	-	17
Mexican Grand Prix 1966	R	10	Bernard White Racing	BRM P261	BRM	28	Transmission	-	17

NC=Not classified	NT=No time set in qualifying	R=Retired	EX=Excluded from meeting W=Withdrawn
DQ=Disqualified	DNS=Did not start	DNQ=Did not qualify	DNPQ=Did not pre-qualify

Innes Ireland
All Arms and Elbows

B

First published in Great Britain by
PELHAM BOOKS LTD
26 Bloomsbury Street
London, W.C.1.
OCTOBER 1967
SECOND IMPRESSION DECEMBER 1967

For
T.O'C

1

For hour after hour, I watched the landscape of America slide beneath the wing of the big Boeing 707 as we flew steadily in brilliant sunshine towards San Francisco. Thousands of feet below, the rolling prairie of the Middle West gave way to the rippling foothills of the Rocky Mountains and I knew that in an hour or so we should be losing height and cruising in to land.

Normally, I would have felt glad. Air travel is rather tiresome most of the time and I knew that soon after landing in San Francisco, I would again be on my way to Seattle and another motor race in a new car, amongst old friends.

This time, however, it was different.

For no real reason, I felt uneasy.

Ever since we had left New York, I had had this odd feeling about the coming race. Suddenly I was convinced that something was going to happen to me. I suppose you might call it a premonition.

Now, on the last lap of the journey, I felt a terrible urge to get my thoughts down on paper.

I have spent many, many long hours on aeroplanes - sleeping, reading, drinking, eating but never before had I felt prompted to write a letter. This time, however, I was driven by an odd sense of urgency, so I called the stewardess and asked for notepaper and a pen.

I started writing and just went on and on. I can't remember clearly what I wrote, but it was all to the effect that I felt I was going to have an accident. I addressed the letter to a very close friend of mine in England, and handed it to the stewardess for mailing with a feeling of melancholia which I had never known before.

When I left the jet at San Francisco, I tried to shrug off the feeling. My travelling companion. Don Miles, a large and extremely strong fellow who formerly played baseball for the Brooklyn Dodgers, had slept throughout the journey and was now in his usual high spirits. I did my best to join him.

We were on our way to meet Don's father-in-law Tom O'Connor, a Texan cattle and oil millionaire who owned the Rosebud Racing Team for whom I was to drive in the North-West Pacific Grand Prix at Seattle. I very much liked being in their company for we were old friends. Furthermore, I have always regarded Tom as being one of the finest men alive, one whose judgement and common sense I have always trusted and respected. Being a cattle man at heart and a true man of the soil, he has a tremendous wealth of wisdom and I could listen to him talk in his soft Texas accent for hours. He has a wonderful sense of humour which is obviously part of his Irish heritage. Thinking that he might talk me out of my mood, I looked forward to meeting him again at the Hilton Hotel in San Francisco.

I was therefore somewhat taken aback when I met Tom and found that he was in a most peculiar mood. He seemed edgy, and when he called for drinks, I noticed that he had no sooner downed his first Martini than he ordered up another, which was most unusual for him.

Between cocktails, he began talking about the car. We were using a Lotus 19 specially fitted by the Rosebud mechanics with a powerful V-12 Ferrari engine. Tom himself had been working through the night with his men to get the car ready for the race. It was apparent that the thing was very much on his mind, since for him it was a very personal effort on which he had lavished a great deal of love and care, sweat and tears.

He also began to talk as if he, too, had some strange feeling about the race.

'I don't give a damn what happens to the car, Innes,' he said. 'I just want to hear it go round the track a couple of times and I'll be happy. The rest doesn't matter.'

He never said anything outright about being worried or having any odd premonition or anything like that, and in the circumstances, neither did I. It was pretty obvious, however, that he had been affected by something like the feeling I had experienced on the plane.

I myself had never been subject to anything like this in my life before. Plenty of times, I had had the odd thought that something might happen to me, but it was only in a vague and fleeting way. Of course, when things do go wrong, you only have a millisecond to realise it. Your experience tells you — some sixth sense warns you — that all is not well even before you actually know what it is.

8

Never before, however, had I known the feeling days in advance.

Then when I finally saw the car at Seattle. I felt perfectly relaxed. This Lotus was probably the best-prepared car I had ever seen. The care and workmanship which had gone into it were obvious. Everything was just so, the attention to detail was evident and it was easy to see that hundreds of loving hours had gone into the making of the car. It bore very little resemblance to the original car and when the chief mechanic Jock Ross started the engine, it produced the sweetest sound you have ever heard.

I did a couple of laps in it on the first practice day, which was a Friday, and stopped at the pits a few times to make running adjustments, although there were a couple of things amiss with the car which I knew could not be fixed in time for the race. One was the brakes which were juddering a good deal and the other was the suspension which was too hard for the circuit. I was confident, however, that I could learn to drive with them as they were, so we did not worry about them,

The car was, in fact, going fantastically well. It was exciting to drive, the engine made such a wonderful noise and the gear change was a dream. I was greatly impressed by the car and simply forgot my forebodings of the previous couple of days, particularly since I knocked a second off the overall lap record during my third outing in practice.

I decided to do one more lap — and that was when my premonitions caught up with me.

One section of the Seattle circuit consists of a hairpin bend, a slight hill, and then a fast left-hand corner, followed immediately by a tightish right-hander.

The way to take this section was to leave the hairpin, run up the right-hand side of the road and at the top of the hill, take this left-hander just as the car got all light and 'airy-fairy'. It all had to be pretty finely judged if you were to take the hill correctly for the left-hand bend and bring the car round again for the right-hander.

I thought I had it all fairly well worked out, but on this particular occasion, I must have been so excited at the way the car was going that I misjudged the whole thing. Anyway, I was going too fast when I swept over the brow of the hill and when I landed on the other side the car was just about to fly off the road to the left. I could feel as I got to the top of the hill that I had done it all wrong, but by then it was too late to do anything about it.

The car began to spin to the left. I tweaked the wheel round to try and get the car to spin away to the right where I knew

9

there was more open country, instead of the side of the hill which loomed up on the left.

At first, the car spun to the right as I had intended, but then started sliding towards the banking.

In the split second in which I was able to glance over my shoulder, I could see another hazard.

Standing in my path was a big 300 Mercedes car, parked on the trackside. (I've often thought I'd like to meet the chap who left it there.)

I hit the earth banking first, then bounced off and clouted the Mercedes right in the middle, pushed it along for about ten feet and stuffed it into the banking. My car flew off down the road and stopped.

I was trapped inside and hurting like merry hell.

I was also terrified in case the car caught fire, being quite unable to move. The crash had buckled the front of the car, trapping my feet behind the pedals; a lump of the windscreen had torn through my right arm and my shoulder hurt abominably. Although I did not realise it at the time, the severity of the impact had caved in the bulkhead of the chassis and, as it did so, had dislocated my right hip.

What I did know was that I was in worse pain than I had ever known through my years of racing and half a dozen other accidents.

I remember thinking, in the few seconds in which I sat there alone, what a stupid bastard I was. I had survived numerous accidents when wheels came off, cars broke up, brakes locked and almost every other sort of mishap happened.

'But you've done it now,' I thought, 'and it's all your own bloody stupid fault.'

10

2

It was a magnificent old 3-litre Bentley which began it all for me. I was in my early teens when I first got to know this car which belonged to an old lady who lived near my family in Scotland. Actually, I first befriended her chauffeur who looked after two of these monsters, although there was a war on at the time and both cars were laid up.

I used to go to the garage and just touch the cars, look at them and weave my own kind of dreams around them. I was fascinated by these pieces of silent machinery, by the hidden majesty of their works — even though I could only imagine the noise, the speed and the wind howling past me as I drove it in countless imaginary races.

Then, as a Christmas present, the dear old lady gave me a book by Tim Birkin called *Full Throttle.* It was all about Bentleys and the fabulous era when they won dozens of races. This, of course, inspired my dreams and I imagined myself doing the things Tim Birkin had done.

The result of all this was that I became filled with the desire to race, to drive at high speed and to become part of the fascinating sport of motor racing.

This was the spirit which filled me for years afterwards even when I began to race in Formula One. It was always, for me, the sport of the thing. When I broke into the top ranks of motor racing, it was never with any particular ambition to win the World Championship or anything like that, but simply to race motor-cars. Perhaps this is one of the faults in my make-up, for I have never had any particular ambitions — unless it has been to win the particular race in which I was engaged.

However, my first motorised transport was an old motor-bike, a machine on which I lavished many, many loving hours — and consequently devoting less and less time and enthusiasm to my scholastic studies at Kirkudbright Academy in Scotland. My father, a veterinary surgeon, had wanted me to follow in his footsteps but I think he realised that I could never buckle down to study for that profession and would probably not pass my exams in the end, so he compromised with the situation and enrolled me as an apprentice to Rolls-Royce in Glasgow.

I spent six years with that firm altogether. One of the jobs I had was in the aero engine testing house, but after a series of monumental explosions, one of which wrecked part of the test bed as well as a very expensive aircraft engine, I was transferred to the car repair workshops in London.

While living in the capital — on a converted motor torpedo boat in Chelsea basin — I saw my first motor race at Silverstone. This was in 1952 when that great champion of the sport, Reg Parnell, driving an Alfa Romeo, won the race when it was stopped after five laps or so because of the flooded track. It was a dripping wet day and I remember I got soaked, but it did nothing to dampen my ardour. I was hooked on motor racing.

By now, I had acquired the Bentley I loved so much. Incredibly, the old lady had left it to me in her will, and I devoted myself to that car with a love that only a Bentley knows. Unfortunately, it didn't go down too well at work, when some people frowned on the idea of a Rolls apprentice coming to work .in a Bentley.

My association with Rolls ended, temporarily, when I was conscripted for National Service into the Army and went for training with the Kings Own Scottish Borders in Berwick-on-Tweed. Only one little drama intervened in the routine life of my officer cadet training and that was when I went absent for a day to take part in a Bentley Owners' Club rally nearby. My absence would, in fact, have been entirely unnoticed, so carefully did I lay my plans, except that I won the class for 3-litre cars. The result was printed in a local paper and the Commanding Officer saw it and hauled me in front of him to explain myself. I got away with it by taking him for ride in the Bentley.

After being given a commission, I was seconded to the Parachute Regiment with whom I spent several months in Egypt.

I very much enjoyed my time in the Army. The intense pride of the Parachute Regiment and the men in it fostered a marvellous spirit of comradeship which I have rarely found elsewhere. Furthermore, the things I learned about hitting the ground without injuring myself came in very useful later on when I spilled out of motor-cars with such regularity!

When I came out of the Army in 1955, I started racing my Bentley in club meetings in the South of England. I had a garage

12

business in Surrey by this time and I also acquired a very speedy little Riley in which I won a few races.

But the first real racing car I owned was a little Lotus Eleven, which was christened 'Chloe'. I sold the Riley to buy the Lotus in kit form and assembled it with loving care, finishing it half-way through the 1956 season, just a week before a British Automobile Racing Club meeting at Goodwood, for which I had entered myself.

Official practice was allowed on the Saturday before the race and I trundled the Lotus down to Sussex full of high hopes and determination.

Incidentally, this club system whereby members are entitled to take their cars down to a circuit like Goodwood and thrash around for a few laps is one of the reasons, I think, why this country produces so many good drivers.

Anyway, I discovered that the little Lotus went very quickly — a great deal more quickly than anything else I had ever handled.

I was flashing round and round Goodwood, going faster and faster, until I flew off the road at Madgwick corner. Then I flew off at Woodcote, and again at Madgwick, and I kept on doing this. I remember at that time, they were growing wheat in the middle of the circuit — it was almost harvest time and so the corn was standing very high. On one occasion I flew off the road so far at Madgwick that when I belted into the corn, I couldn't see where I was because the corn was higher than the car. The only way I could get back on the track was to back the along the swaithe of flattened corn I had made.

Halfway through the afternoon, however, I was asked to go to the official enclosure and I was hauled up before Mr Dickson Cade, then the assistant secretary of the BARC — and by the time he had finished with me, I thought my racing days were over.

He told me in no uncertain terms that I hadn't got the first idea what I was doing and that if I continued to behave like this and fly off the road every five minutes, I most certainly would not get anywhere in any other race meeting.

Finally, knowing that I was entered for the club meeting the following week-end, he said: 'If you so much as put a wheel on the grass in practice next week-end, we shan't let you race.

I left the office feeling very shaky and as if I had just left the headmaster's study after a sound thrashing.

I spent a very dejected week before it was time to go down to Goodwood again for practice the next Saturday. I was absolutely determined not to do anything foolish, but once I got the car out on the circuit I couldn't resist pressing on a bit — and sure enough, I spun off again at Woodcote.

13

I was quite sure that this time I had had it. I would be barred from every circuit in the country or something, my career as a racing driver in ruins. Fortunately, by some wonderful chance, no one spotted me sitting the wrong way round on the grass verge, and I got going again to finish practice.

I don't think I distinguished myself too brilliantly in that particular race, but I did win a few more club events in 1956 and by the following season, was beginning to make headway in sports car racing. My entry was accepted for the Easter Monday meeting at Goodwood where I was to drive the Lotus in a 26-lap event over a distance of 75 miles, competing against all the big names of the sport. I remember Team Lotus had a couple of cars entered, driven by Alan Stacey and Keith Hall. This was a big event for me — and I damned near won it.

Except that, half a lap from the end, when in the lead, the camshaft of my engine broke in pieces and wrecked everything.

It became a big thing with me to try to beat the Team Lotus boys, with their works-prepared cars and this I managed to do a number of times, although just as often I flew off the road in my own impetuous fashion.

I remember one of the motoring magazines making the observation that Ireland was a very quick driver and would probably win a lot of races if only he could stay on the road.

Yet, I was learning my craft.

Late in 1957, I was recruited to race for Team Lotus at the occasional meeting both in this country and abroad, and in 1958 I began to do fewer club meetings and more international racing. I drove for Tommy Sopwith a few times in his Formula Two Cooper, which broadened my experience tremendously, and also for Ecurie Ecosse in their big, powerful D-Type Jaguars.

In 1958, in fact, I won my first really big sports car race, at Clermont-Ferrand when, for once, everything worked smoothly and kept on working, and I managed to beat a whole field of Ferraris and other hairy motor-cars driven by some of the real top men in the sport. That was a tremendous thrill, for the French crowd rose to my David and Goliath performance en masse and at the end, I was mobbed by hundreds of people.

Not only was it tremendously satisfying, but it put me into the running for a works team contract.

Without question, the thing which brought me near to the top in motor racing was luck. I was lucky to have the opportunities — coupled with a gift of some sort for driving cars.

I was lucky in that during my first year, in 1957, I won quite a number of races which although unimportant, got me noticed by the scouts of motor racing who must have thought I had ability.

14

Towards the end of that season I was asked to drive a sports car for Colin Chapman in the Swedish Grand Prix, which that year was a long distance race for sports cars.

I was to share the drive with Cliff Allison, and this being my first continental race, I was carried away by the thought that I had been asked to drive for a works team — although the works constituted a very small business at that stage, and the name Lotus did not have the significance which it has today.

We finished ninth overall, having put up a fairly good account of ourselves, and I was asked again to drive for Lotus, this time in Belgium.

Naturally, I was quite well pleased with myself and the things I had done in 1957 and at the end of the season, I went off quite happily hunting in the Highlands with my brother. While I was there, I received a 'phone call from David Murray, of Ecurie Ecosse, asking me down to Silverstone to test one or two of their cars.

It only goes to demonstrate my incredible lack of ambition that I turned down the offer.

Now, at that time, Ecurie Ecosse was a magic name in motor racing. They had won Le Mans in 1956 and 1957 and they raced those most marvellous D-Type Jaguars which had always fascinated me. I was very thrilled, naturally, at being asked to go and test their cars, but my love of the Highlands and my love of hunting combined to make me turn down the offer.

I suppose in my own stupid way, I didn't see the opportunity that was being offered to me, and it was, in fact, my brother Allan who made me see the light. When he asked me who had been on the telephone and what had been said, he roundly denounced me as a bloody fool and eventually he persuaded me to go down to Silverstone.

I shall always remember what a tremendous thrill it was to get into one of those D-Types. Those were real sports cars with lots and lots of power and the noise from the exhaust was the thing my dreams were made of — remember, I had only been driving little 1100 cc and 1500 cc cars — and driving the D-Type was a fantastic experience. They were beautiful cars, and, of course, for quite a long time that day I couldn't drive my car properly because I had to learn an entirely different technique. But I thoroughly enjoyed myself.

At the end of the day, we all repaired to the Saracen's Head in Towcester — myself, my brother Allan, David Murray, his chief mechanic 'Wilkie' Wilkinson and the rest of the crew.

We had a tremendous evening there.

I remember that after a very hilarious meal, I decided to do

15

one of my party pieces — a highly explosive trick with two metal cigar tubes, and a great many match-heads. The thing to do is to cram one tube with non-safety match beads, then ram the other tube into the first. Then you heat the bottom end of the loaded tube and after a while — the suspense is terrible — there is an enormous explosion and the projectile tube shoots off at high speed and burning match heads fly all over the place.

It was all fairly safe, since the floor of the old pub was stone and so on, but I didn't realise that the lady who owned it had two highly nervous poodle dogs. At the sound of this terrific bang, they fled in all directions, followed at a high rate of knots by their mistress.

It took her quite a long time to find these dogs, for in the meantime, 'Wilkie' Wilkinson, who was as full of wine and high spirits as myself, challenged me to repeat the trick, betting me that I couldn't hit a target which happened to be a piece of armour, a breast-plate or something, hanging over the bar door. So I loaded up a really devastating charge in two more cigar tubes and aimed it at the door.

Exactly on cue, just as this shattering explosion went off, the door opened and in walked the landlady with both dogs under her arm. The chaos was unbelievable! Both dogs shot out, yelping, the woman screamed and there were cigar tubes and burning match-heads flying everywhere.

We were practically thrown out of the place there and then. It was thanks to David Murray's tact that we had a bed that night.

However, I can't remember whether I hit the breast-plate or not. I feel I must try again some day.

The following day, Allan and I went back to the Highlands to continue our shooting holiday. I did, in fact, drive for Ecurie Ecosse on four occasions in the 1958 season and acquitted myself not too badly, I think. I scraped the corners off one or two of their beautiful D-Types, perhaps, but I thoroughly enjoyed driving for my National Stable and a great friendship grew between us.

At that time, I had my own small garage business where I spent a lot of time tuning up other people's motor-cars for racing. This occupied a lot of my life then, tweaking up cars, transporting them to various circuits and then, after the race, picking up the bits, taking them back and starting all over again. Oddly enough, I never used to tune my own cars. Somehow, I never wanted to. I always preferred other people to do that. I only liked to drive them, although I am an engineer.

By now, though, I was beginning to break in round the edges of the big-time motor racing scene. I bad raced abroad once or

(Photo: *Charles Dunn*)

Above: Innes Ireland driving a Riley 9 in the B.A.R.C. Twentieth Members' Sports Car Meeting at Goodwood, September 1955. Helater traded this car for his first Lotus.

Below: The author winning the Brooklands Memorial Trophy from Chris Bristow and Keith Green. Goodwood 1957.

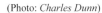

(Photo: *Charles Dunn*)

(Photo: *Charles Dunn*)

Above: One of the author's favourite cars - Ecurie Ecosse Jaguar.
September 1958.

Below: Innes Ireland passing Stirling Moss. Goodwood 1960.

(Photo: *Patrick Benjafield*)

The author (*left*) talking to Alan Stacey and Bruce Mclaren. Sebring 1959.

(Photo: *Charles A.Lytle*)

As the Duke of Edinburgh said: 'It's all a question of getting your fingers out gentleman!'

(Photo: *Desmond O'Neil*)

The author with his old mate Alan Stacey at Aintree.

(Photo: *A. Whittington*)

Alan Stacey with opposite lock in an 'Electra'. 'These Electras don't half understeer,' he's saying.

twice and since I quite enjoy going places, I was fairly well content.

Actually, my first trip abroad was quite amusing.

Colin Chapman was sending me to drive a Lotus in Sweden, at a place called Kristianstad. He had only the vaguest idea where this place was and when I asked him how I should get there, he simply told me to get a plane to Gothenburg and take a taxi.

However, when I arrived in Gothenburg, I quickly learned that Kristianstad was about 300 miles away and I would have to take a train. I got one going in the right direction at about midnight, but found that I had to change somewhere at around five in the morning and would have to wait an hour for the connection.

I am never at my very best in the morning, though, and I think perhaps I may have dozed off in the restaurant of that station where I changed. At any rate, I came to just in time to see my train disappearing down the track. I don't speak Swedish, of course, but by dint of a great deal of pointing and jumping up and down, I discovered that this was indeed the train I should have caught and everyone was very sorry.

But I must say that the porter fellow I had been gesticulating at was a resourceful chap. He grabbed me by the arm and quickly rushed me over to the signal box where the man in charge spoke a little English. He also had the right idea, for when I explained how much I wanted to get to Kristianstad, he announced: 'I stop the train.'

Then he led me out to a taxi, gave the driver some instructions in Swedish and we set off in a state of high excitement.

Not that the excitement fired the taxi driver because he drove the whole way at a miserably slow rate and I spent my entire time leaping up and down making 'go faster' signals.

However, we trundled on and finally turned off the main road on to a dirt track until we crossed a railway bridge and there, standing in the tiniest of stations, was this damned great express train — waiting for me!

In the race Cliff Allison and I were going very well until the starter motor kept jamming and every time we came into the pits we spent about half an hour trying to get the wretched thing started again.

This was my first introduction to the really big names in motor racing — men like Mike Hawthorn, Peter Collins, Harry Schell, Fangio and Stirling Moss. They were all driving these great big hairy cars, big noisy Ferraris, Maseratis, and Jaguars, and I got the feeling that at least I was in good company. I felt terribly small and insignificant in their company and wandered about looking at people in awe, hardly able to believe, I suppose, that I was actually driving in the same race.

For although I began racing just for the fun of it, preparing my old cars and thrashing them to the limit and generally enjoying myself, I quickly began to think in terms of bigger, better and faster machines.

I was gaining a great deal of experience now, racing against the big boys of the sport, and I felt I had enough talent to acquit myself well in Grand Prix racing. This, I suppose, was one of my few ambitions.

My break into this class of racing, this Formula One stuff, was a lucky one. In 1959, immediately after the Monaco Grand Prix, Team Lotus found itself a driver short. Their team drivers for the season were to have been Graham Hill and an American driver, Pete Lovely. However, after Monaco, Pete Lovely decided that he could no longer afford to spend so much of his time away from his business interests in America and he quit the team.

I have since learned that when this happened, a considerable debate took place' at the Lotus factory about who should be asked to fill his place. Colin Chapman himself wanted me, but the other chap concerned at that time with Team Lotus, a very fine fellow named Mike Costin, (who later parted company with Chapman) was in favour of Alan 'Stacey. I was fortunate in that Chapman had the final word in the matter, and I was asked to sign up with the team on a three-year contract.

I suppose Mike may have been influenced by the fact that I was always flying off 'the road, whereas Chapman thought I might get over this phase and, if I lived, make a decent driver!

Anyway, here it was. I signed for Team Lotus.

18

3

My first ever Grande Epreuve was at Zandvoort in 1959, where Lotus had the 2½-litre, front-engined cars. Those machines looked lovely. They were very pretty cars, but I was always rather disturbed at the awkward and cramped cockpit. It had the propeller shaft housing running diagonally across the cockpit, so that you sat half on it with your left leg cocked across it in order to reach the clutch. I always remember feeling distinctly nervous about that sitting position in case the prop shaft ever came loose and did me a terrible mischief. It was a constant source of worry to me, especially as something similar had happened to me shortly before, while racing a 1500 Lotus sports car at Silverstone. The centre bearing on the prop shaft came loose during the race and the whole issue began thrashing around me, making the most awful din and I became so alarmed that I just leapt up on the seat!

Anyway we got to Zandvoort and I really felt that I had arrived on the racing scene, a works driver at last. My joy was made complete, I remember, when Stirling Moss spoke to me during some reception or other before the race. I know that sounds rather starry-eyed, but one must remember that I still felt like the new boy in this sort of company. Yet, when Stirling chatted to me — I think he asked me to play golf the next morning — I felt accepted, as it were, as an equal professional.

On the day of the race, I felt more than usually tense. For one thing, I had a deceptively flattering position on the grid. The position in which a driver and his car are placed for the start of a Formula One race depends on the time he has put up in practice. The fastest has the pole position at the front, the next best alongside him and the rest in lines of two and three down the track. Naturally, the nearer the front you are, the better chance you have in the race.

And I found myself well up the front — through no effort of my own.

What had happened was this. During practice, I had indeed put up a good time — 1 min. 40 secs or something of that order — and at one time Graham Hill wanted to take my car out to see what he could do with it. He did, and clipped a couple of seconds off my time. Somehow or other, the timekeepers attributed this to me.

Right from the start of the race, I was fairly well placed. I think at no time was I lower down the field than sixth and I whistled along very happily in my first-ever really big race. At one time, I became almost mesmerised by a combination of my own efforts and the exhaust fumes of Jean Behra's big Ferrari. I was slip-streaming him, knowing that I probably did not have the speed to overtake him — and feeling, in any case, that it might be cheeky of me to try!

The noise of Behra's car was unimaginable. In those days, in 1959, the Ferraris were front-engined cars, big, hairy, monsters which made a noise Like a banshee wail. I can remember sitting right behind him, staring at his exhaust pipes, being absolutely deafened. I couldn't hear my own engine, had very little idea what was going on in my own car and was, in fact, being quietly asphyxiated by Behra's exhaust fumes. What woke me up, as it were, was a glance at my water temperature gauge, which was giving some astronomical reading because I wasn't getting any air to my radiator in that tight slipstream position.

I dropped back a bit to cool down, but noticed that I kept closing on the Ferrari. At last I thought: 'Hell's teeth, perhaps I can get past him!' After all, it was a motor race, Behra was a nice fellow, and surely he wouldn't think me too cheeky if I did so. So I showed my nose one side of him and then the other and I think maybe this upset him a bit, for eventually he lost it on one of the corners and, though no expertise on my part, I slipped past him. This put me in fourth position in my first Grand Prix and in fact that is where I ended the race.

A week or so later, I had my introduction to the fabulous Nurburgring where I had never raced before. I was due to drive a GT Aston Martin. I did not actually race, though, thanks to some technical disqualification of the Aston — but I managed to scare the daylights out of myself and my co-drivers.

I was due to share the drive with Jonathan Seiff and during practice, purely out of interest, he asked me to take him round

20

the circuit, I suppose to see how I did things. Now, at one point on the Nurburgring Circuit, there is a long straight it the end of which there is a hump-back section with a bridge over it, followed by a sharpish left-hand downhill bend, and, as we approached the hump, I was really letting the Aston go. Of course, I couldn't see over the hump and at the same time I didn't notice that it had been raining. As I tore over the brow of this hump, I was alarmed to find a car with its rear end hanging out of the hedge across my side of the road.

I banged the wheel over and the Aston went into all sorts of gyrations; the hedges on either side flashed past me in turn and the corner loomed up very quickly. All my guardian angels were out in force that day, I think, pushing me out of the way of the hedges and round the corners. But whatever it was that kept me on the road, I did manage it. When I finally straightened myself out, I found Seiffy bundled under the dashboard, looking at me with an expression which clearly showed he thought I was a dangerous lunatic. Anyway, he vowed he would never come in a car with me again and as far as I can recall, he never did.

The following day, another driver, Keith Greene asked to come round with me, despite having heard Seiffy recount the previous day's drama!

We set out one day after practice, not trying too hard but quick enough to be interesting. It so happened that my crash helmet was lying in the back of the Aston and by the time I had gone halfway round the bumpy, twisting circuit, I had had enough of it rolling and banging about in the back, so I stopped the car and put it on, unstrapped. Keith's face when I did this was a masterpiece of apprehension and it grew even more pained when I again stopped to do up the straps which I had found bothersome.

As he said afterwards, he wondered what the hell I was getting all prepared for, and really began to think that perhaps Seiffy had been right in calling me 'a bloody lunatic'!

However, I know Keith has dined out on that story a few times since then.

Anyway, as I say, we did not actually race the Aston because it was barred from the meeting over some regulation oversight. I was pretty busy all the same, since I not only raced Team Lotus's own cars, but entered my own 1500 Lotus and F2 Lotus in various races under the team colours. Why I did that, I don't quite know, except out of enthusiasm perhaps, but I know I paid for the maintenance, transport and everything else. However...

21

One of the races I entered my own car for under Team Lotus colours was a sports car race at Rouen. I thought I had a fair chance here, for I had been driving quite well that season and managing to stay on the road more often.

I had also brought my own F2 Lotus and entered it in a later race the same day. That was a terrible mistake!

From the start, until my untimely finish, it was a most eventful day's racing.

I did not start well, though — for when the flag dropped in the sports car event, I was left on the line with a jammed starter motor. You are not allowed to push-start cars in this type of race, but after about thirty seconds or so I did manage to get the thing going and tore off in pursuit of the rest of the pack. That day, the 1500 was going like the clappers and after about sixteen laps I found myself passing Alan Stacey in the bigger, 2-litre Lotus. Delighted with myself, I pressed on as hard as I could until some laps later, I noticed from my pit signals that I was catching up fast with Stirling Moss in his very new 2-litre Maserati — gaining on him, in fact, to the tune of about two seconds a lap. The crowd was obviously wise to what was happening and they rose to their feet, I remember, as I flashed down the long hill past the pits, and I felt terrific.

I didn't feel terrific for too long though because a couple of laps later, I found myself running out of brakes. Indeed, I didn't have any back brakes at all and the front ones were acting strangely, jumping on and off wildly with the result that I was locking the front wheels left, right and centre. Every time I went round a corner I could smell my tyres burning off.

Of course, I was having to take it a little more easily and Moss slipped out of catching distance. I was bitterly disappointed and, to cap it all, I was literally within sight of the finishing line when Alan Stacey in the 2-litre Lotus whipped past me with a big grin on his face and two fingers up in the air!

Still, I easily won my class and it was, I suppose, good for the record that the 2-litre Lotus should get home before me.

When I had a look at my front wheels after the race, I found that one tyre had a patch so badly worn that the inner tube was just showing through! I kept that tyre for years after.

Despite the luck of old 'Ireland' in that race, I felt in a competitive mood for the Formula Two race later in the day. But the car was motoring like a bowl of soup and I was getting nowhere. However, I gave the thing a terrific thrashing particularly on the braking, was pressing on in the middle

22

of the pack somewhere, when I made one of those appalling discoveries.

It was my brakes again — but this time there was absolutely nothing there at all!

I was in fact, accelerating hard uphill at about 100 m.p.h. towards a sharp left-hand corner when I found that the brake pedal went straight into the floorboards without the slightest effect whatever.

This, indeed, was not my day.

Ahead of me lay a ramp-like banking and sure enough I headed straight for it.

I was travelling so quickly, in fact, that — according to an eyewitness — I ran up the banking and took off, clearing a car parked behind the bank by eight or ten feet. Beyond the banking, and about fifty yards on, there was a steep ravine fringed with trees.

By the time 12 hit the trees, I was at an altitude of about 25 feet! I went through the trees and the nose of the car caught in the branches and the whole thing started tumbling down the ravine end over end with me still in the driver's seat. It then finished up about 150 feet down the ravine on its nose at the bottom of a tree and with the tail caught in the branches above. Of course, when it stopped suddenly in this position, I was catapulted out, still travelling downhill and bouncing from tree to tree.

The various impacts had been so violent that I discovered afterwards that the whole of one side of my crash helmet had been ripped off.

Oddly enough, I was still alive and conscious. When I picked myself up, I clambered up to the car. It was completely destroyed — but was still ticking over beautifully. I can remember thinking quite the most ludicrous thought, namely that my mechanic Brit seemed to have got the slow-running going pretty well!

However, I started climbing back up the ravine, increasingly conscious of a shocking pain in my leg.

By this time, the race officials had sent out word that a car had completely disappeared from the circuit and an ambulance hurried round the perimeter, since anyone who was last seen flying a car into a ravine was bound to be a stretcher case. Apparently, however, the ambulance crew had taken a quick look over the banking, seen nothing and toddled off back again.

So when I crawled up to the top of the banking, there was nothing for me to do but sit there until the end of the race which went on for at least another hour!

By then, thank Heavens, Stirling Moss spotted me and came

23

along to give me a lift back to the pits on the other side of the circuit.

The ambulance never turned up again, and I suppose it was just as well I wasn't too badly hurt or I might have ended my days down that awful ravine.

The next big race was Le Mans, for which I had been engaged by Ecurie Ecosse to drive one of their D-Types, as co-driver to Masten Gregory. The D-Type was an absolute gem of a car, ideally suited to the fast Le Mans circuit. It had good cornering, wonderfully efficient brakes and was very quick on the straights — it reached about 175 rn.p.h. at its peak. If the car had been entirely reliable, I think we might well have won the race. The only reservation I had beforehand, though, was that the engine had had to be scaled down to three litres in accordance with the 1959 regulations.

It was still a joy to drive. I had been to Le Mans before, with Team Lotus, and just to give an indication of how much faster the Jaguar was, compare the lap times I got with the two cars. With the Lotus, I was getting about 5 mins or something of that order, and I thought I was going pretty quickly. The first lap I put in with the Jag took only 4 mins 18 secs — and when I really tried, I got down to 4 mins 6 secs.

However, I always seemed to have some kind of drama whenever I got behind the wheel of a car, and in due course it happened with the D-Type. During practice, I asked Masten where he was doing his braking on the approach to the S-bends just after the Dunlop Bridge. He said he was anchoring up at around the 200-yard mark, and this seemed to me to be cutting it a bit fine. However, I was determined to try it out, and the next time I took the Jaguar round, I kept my foot off the brake until the 200-yard marker was alongside me — way past my normal braking spot.

Cutting it fine was the understatement of the year. I damned near did not get the car slowed at all, and I had it all locked up, crossed up and sideways before I got it back under control in time to take the Esses. After this, I pulled into the pits and climbed out a little shakily. I explained to Masten what had happened and said that if he wanted to wait until the 200-yard mark, he was welcome, because I certainly wasn't about to try it again.

'Oh,' he replied affably. 'I didn't meant the 200-yard marker, I meant the big boarding at the top of the slope.'

I could have killed him! This was exactly where I had been doing my braking. I remember thinking that one really ought to be more careful when explaining brake markers to one's co-driver!

24

The start of the race proper was a very good one for me, Stirling Moss was the master of Le Mans-type starts, where you stand across the other side of the road from your car, rush across when the flag falls, leap in, start and tear away. Naturally, the quicker you can do this, the better chance you have to get motoring without being bogged down in a scrum of cars. I was standing next to Stirling in the line and when the flag came down, we dashed across together and in fact I got away a fraction behind him.

The amusing thing was that shortly after the 1959 Le Mans, Stirling bought out a book on the race, in which he emphasised the vital importance of a good start and said that it required hours of practice with any particular car to achieve it. And, in theory, he is perfectly right. Yet my own start practice with the D-Type had been very sharply curtailed.

Some days before leaving for France, I had gone to the Works and tried this 'leaping in and starting' business, by running across the Works yard and vaulting into the Jaguar over the windscreen.

I was in the act of doing this for the third time when the Ecurie Ecosse chief mechanic, a big burly Scot by the name of Sandy, came across to me with an expression of absolute ferocity on his face.

'What the hell do you think you're doing?' he roared.

I explained a bit sheepishly that I was only trying out the Le Mans start, but he brushed all that aside.

'All you'll do is break the bloody windscreen. Now be off with you.

Boy, those mechanics really love their cars to such an extent that I often think they resent anyone driving them. But Sandy was not really the sort of chap you can argue with anyway, and I quit. So much for hours of practice!

The race itself was tremendous fun. At the end of the first lap, I was lying sixth and feeling extremely happy. For several laps, I had a light-hearted dice with Roy Salvadori in his Aston — he was the eventual winner — and all in all I had high hopes.

I did fly off the road once, without doing any damage or even losing much time, although the aftermath to this little incident, when it came the following day, left me rather red-faced. Handing over the car to Masten at about 6.30 p.m. on the first day, I was checking through my lap-times with the Ecurie Ecosse team manager and he was curious to know why one lap had taken some fifteen or twenty seconds longer than the rest.

I knew full well that it was because I had flown off the circuit, down an escape road and had had to push the car back on to the track — those were the rules — before I could get started again.

However, I did not think this would sound too good, so I made up some story about being terribly baulked at one corner by a lot of slower cars and so on.

Imagine my horror next day, when one newspaper reporting the progress of the race, carried a large, prominent photograph of Ireland pushing his D-Type on an escape road criss-cross with his own tyre marks. There were a great many raised eyebrows in the Ecosse pit that morning and I felt about half an inch tall. Ever since then, I have always been candid about my own foolishness!

However, by the time this all came out, we were out of the race. Taking over from Masten again at about 11 o'clock on the first night, I found we were in second place, and I motored on in high spirits. My hopes of winning Le Mans, however, were shattered along with the D-Type's engine when it threw a connecting rod with a great big bang and a clatter. I shed most of my oil, and in fact, spun on it, finding myself gyrating perilously close to a large brick wall. I remember praying that I wouldn't hit the wall, not because I was in fear of my own safety, but because I thought no one would believe my story about the con-rod if the Jaguar ended up in a crumpled heap against the wall. However, I did not hit it, but that was the end of the 1959 Le Mans for me.

A fortnight later, I was back in a Formula One car for the French Grand Prix at Rheims. And still the incredible series of mishaps with the Lotuses went on.

This time, the front right-hand wheel suddenly came adrift.

I had noticed that this wheel was locking and making a terrible mess of the tyre every time I went into a corner and, of course, the tyre gave off great clouds of smoke each time. Naturally, the car didn't steer very well, but it was all very exciting. The crunch came just as I was approaching the pits at something like 130 m.p.h., when quite suddenly, the wheel collapsed. The top end fell in towards the bonnet, the bottom end fell out and the car made a great dive over to the right. This un-heralded manoeuvre very nearly put paid to Toto Roche, the legendary French race starter, who is noted for his antics (personally, I think it is just a question of time before somebody does run him over)! This time, however, I narrowly missed him, but the sight of that rather round gentleman hopping and skipping out of the way must have been very amusing. Anyway, that was the end of another race.

When Team Lotus went to Oporto in 1959, ten minutes before

the race was due to start I walked out to my car in the normal way, but as I approached it, I had a funny feeling that it didn't look quite right.

When I had a closer look at the front suspension, I found a complete break in the main chassis tube — the big one that held the front suspension on!

I could not believe my eyes!

So I got hold of one of the mechanics and pointed out to him that I was about to race a car on which the chassis was broken, and that I really didn't feel like it any more.

He looked at the chassis for a moment and said: 'Oh, yes, so it is. Never mind, we'll get it welded.' This was literally about ten minutes before the race was due to start!

I must confess I was in something of a daze while they whistled up from somewhere a welding kit and a couple of acetylene bottles on a trolley, wheeled it all out on to the grid and started welding my car together.

Of course, this inspired me with no-confidence and [thought to myself: 'This is going to be a great race, Ireland, and it may be your last.'

Fortunately for me, perhaps, something else on the car blew up very shortly after the start of the race and .1 retired gracefully enough.

By the time we arrived at Monza in 1959, however, I was beginning to feel that, for my part, I was getting the hang of the Lotus. I was getting it to move quickly and getting the back end hung out a bit on the corners so that I was getting everything out of it that I could. What I couldn't get, what no one would get, was reliability.

I remember I was very satisfied with myself as long as the cars kept going, particularly with the way I was getting round the corners, which is the very essence of racing driving.

All in all, I was learning a lot about the business of Formula One driving.

My confidence, however, kept getting badly shaken by the series of mechanical mishaps which occurred in the team.

I remember at Monza, one day after practice, I wandered down to the circuit workshops to have a look at my car. I found it in the workshop surrounded by mechanics, welding furiously. I went over to see what they were welding and said to Stan Elsworth, the chief mechanic: 'What's the trouble, Stan?'

'Oh,' he said, 'there is just a little crack in the chassis.'

I had a look for myself, and sure enough they were welding up this wee crack in the chassis.

The result of all these incidents was that I never really had complete confidence in the cars and without that you cannot really drive at the maximum. How can you, when you are constantly expecting something to break? — and relieved when it does!

At the time, though, I didn't say anything. I still felt very much the junior officer in the mess and I reckoned myself lucky to be part of a Grand Prix outfit like Team Lotus.

Because of this, I was always willing to help out in any way I could. Chapman, himself, did not have the equipment to transport his racing cars properly, for instance, and on one occasion I drove the two racing cars to Monza on my own double decked trailer, followed by the Team Lotus spares truck, which was almost as unreliable as the ears themselves.

I shall never forget the time we were on the way to Monza with these two vehicles. At the point where we came to the Swiss-Italian border customs post I had come screaming down the pass — it was a rather steep hill — with the loaded trailer hitched to my own Ford Zephyr. I waited at the customs post for the Lotus truck to arrive. This heavily-burdened machine came whistling down the hill just then with four columns of smoke belching from the brake drums and rapidly running out of brakes. In order to avoid diving straight through the customs barrier, the poor driver had locked everything on and was busy steering into the side of the road every two yards in an attempt to slow down. Finally, myself and another chap in my car had to run back up the road and throw rocks under the wheels of the Lotus truck before it would stop.

By the time the truck came to rest, you could hear the brakes just sizzling like bacon in a pan.

Such was the Team Lotus equipment in those early days of trials and tribulations.

Actually, on that same trip, I had the unusual experience of seeing one of the wheels of my 4-wheeled trailer overtaking me along the road! The thing had just come adrift and bowled along for a bit before bouncing off the autostrada and into the fields. While we were searching for the wretched thing, a squad of police drew up and damned near gave me a ticket for parking on the road.

Towards the end of 1959, I went to America for the first time to take part in the American Grand Prix at Sebring — the first ever American Grand Prix to count towards the World Championship. Graham Hill did not come with us. Alan Stacey was the other Team Lotus driver for that race. Unknown to me at the time, Graham had already decided for himself that racing for Team

28

Lotus was no longer for him. In fact he left the team at the end of the year.

Alan Stacey I always found to be a tremendous fellow. He must have been to drive a Formula One car with one tin leg. He had a marvellous sense of fun and always thoroughly enjoyed his motor racing and life in general. Not everyone appreciated his idea of fun, though. I particularly remember the captain of an America jet airline who got most starchy with us both.

On the way to Sebring, Alan and I stayed a couple of days in New York, at the end of which we had to fly to Miami. At Idlewilde airport, we walked out to our aircraft and boarded it' but found not another soul inside — no passengers, no hostesses, no crew. So after a bit, we went to take a look at the sharp end. Sitting in the drivers' seats, we began fooling around with the control columns — not doing anything stupid like pressing buttons, though — imagining how the big Electra would handle on full opposite lock. Like a couple of kids.

When the skipper of the aircraft walked in he very nearly had a fit. He was going to have us arrested there and then. I believe he thought we were a couple of lunatics and he all but had the aircraft searched for bombs — they are always a bit neurotic over there about bombs!

I don't remember too much about the Sebring race, except that my gearbox went adrift and I motored through half the race with only fourth gear and managed, despite this, to get fifth place at the end.

The most amusing thing about that particular Grande Epreuve concerned Harry Schell, who was driving a 2-litre Cooper. On the second day of practice, everyone was absolutely staggered to find that Harry had done the fastest practice time — with half a litre less than the rest of us with Formula One cars. Harry, full of gamesmanship, as he always was, complained bitterly to the organisers that he had been placed two or three rows back on the grid and demanded to be moved up in view of his practice lap time.

It was not until a very long time after that race, that Harry revealed how he had managed to put up so fast a time.

Apparently, away out on the back of the Sebring circuit Harry had found a little service road where he could turn off the track, take the service road and cut out a mile or more of the circuit. Harry had obviously worked this out well in advance, for he turned in a time that was just credible. Had he simply used the service road and hared off down the shortened circuit, his time would not have been believed. As it was, he got away with a time fractionally quicker than Stirling Moss.

This was just about the end of the 1959 season. I now found myself the No. 1 driver of Team Lotus, at a time when I thought that things in the Lotus stable might just sort themselves out. Unfortunately, they did not quite work out as well as I had hoped, but nonetheless, 1960 was to be quite a season for me, one way and another.

30

4

At the end of 1959, Colin Chapman asked if I would prefer to drive a different type of car to the 2½-litre front-engined car with which we had battled throughout the year. What he had in mind was the first of the rear-engined Lotuses, for which he had made advanced designs. He asked if I would rather persevere with the old car, or change to the new. Personally, I always preferred the front-engined car because — for so long as it kept motoring — I had got it mastered. It handled well, it went quickly and, let's face it, any car looks right with the engine at the front.

I expressed the opinion that the front-engined car could be made into a good one if it was redesigned and properly built, but came to the conclusion, albeit reluctantly, that having the engine in the back end was going to be the thing. I don't, for one moment, believe that Chapman weighed my words very seriously. He obviously had his own ideas and was probably sounding me out for my opinion to see if I had enough intelligence to see what was happening in motor racing.

Until early in 1960, everyone at the Lotus factory worked like mad on this new project and literally days before the Argentine Grand Prix — the first of the season — the car was ready.

There was actually only time for the new Lotus to be run up and down the road outside the factory for half a mile or so — just to see if the brakes, clutch and throttle worked — before the car was shipped out to Argentina. That was where I first saw this odd-looking thing with its engine nestling at the back of my head.

Tremendous interest was shown in Colin Chapman's latest product because it had a great many novel ideas — as always, Chapman's design thinking was good — and it was of great technical fascination. I can remember being rather overawed by being

31

thrust suddenly from the position of rather junior second driver to No. 1 driver in charge of this entirely new car. I didn't think, to be perfectly honest, that I was ready for this big new responsibility, but I was more than willing to have a go.

In the first trials of the car, in practice, I found immediately that one needed a completely new technique to drive it, and this took a bit of time to get used to. Otherwise, for such a brand new car, it was remarkably free from troubles. This is something which nearly always happens to Chapman-designed cars — he designs them, thinks them out and builds them and they are really good.

In 1960, he started off very well, looking personally to the development and preparation of the cars, but halfway through the season the preparation of the cars appeared to suffer.

One of the annoying things that happened concerned the gearbox on the Lotus. All through 1959, things had kept going wrong with the thing. It was beautifully designed - by Chapman himself — but I think it was far too complicated to work consistently. I suggested to him that in 1960, we had a new kind of gearbox and I was assured that the gearbox would be redesigned to work efficiently.

All that went by the board. In the very first race — the Argentine GP — with the new rear-engined car, sure enough the damned box broke.

What made it all the more infuriating was that when it broke, I was leading the race and the car was behaving beautifully. But I only managed to do a couple of laps when, trying to change down into a low gear, it jammed and I had to spin the car to stop. From then on, it got worse and worse and I never knew when I was going to get a gear.

In practice, though, the car had been really going frightfully well: in the race, I got off the line like a rocket. But, after the gears had jammed I had to back off a bit and then, to cap it all, a couple of bolts sheered off the steering ann and broke a hole in one of the disc brakes with a monumental bang.

I was left with only one gear, and one front wheel in such a mangled condition that it would hardly steer, but, because I was terribly conscious of being the Team Lotus No. 1 and 'all that', I pressed on. I remember that every time I passed the pits, I had to back off, in case anyone black-flagged me for having one wheel shaking in the breeze.

The most alarming thing was the front wheel wobbling about and only steering in a vague sort of way after half a turn of the steering wheel. Anyway, everything held in place and I finished my first Grande Epreuve as Team Lotus leader in sixth position.

32

'You should have seen the one that got away!' Marineland of the
pacific, 1960.

(Photo: *Bernard Cahier*)

That memorable race at Solitude in 1961, with Bonnier and Gurney in close attendance.

Had we been spared mechanical defects I could have won the race with ease.

Apart from the racing itself, a number of quite bizarre things happened on that trip to South America. I recall that after the GP we all went over to Cordoba for another Formula One race.

We flew from Buenos Aires in the most dreadful old rattletrap of an aeroplane that I have ever been in. It was first of all held up for eight hours on the ground because of technical troubles — I can easily imagine that the engine might have fallen off, or something equally ridiculous. Eventually, we staggered off into the air and flew for half an hour or so, after which the pilot did a complete turn and headed back the way we had come. Pretty soon, one of the engines packed up and we limped back to Buenos Aires, where the pilot did a quick landing, jammed on the brakes, switched off the engines and left it to an airport tender to tow us back to the main buildings. And if *he* was glad to get that aeroplane landed it was nothing to *my* delight on finding we were back on the ground again.

The later flight back was, if anything, even worse. I shall always have the mental picture of Harry Schell, who loathed flying, sitting in his scat with a look of absolute horror on his face from the first moment to the last.

And on that trip, he had something to look horrified about. We took off from Cordoba and flew smack into an electrical storm which made the plane buck and leap about in phenomenal style. Then it started raining. I know it was raining because the water started dripping in through the roof. A few minutes later, it was pouring in and we all got literally soaked. I shall always remember seeing someone — I forget who it was — who had won a trophy in the races, holding the trophy over his head, catching the water as it gushed into the plane.

In Cordoba, we had, of course, taken part in the Formula 1 race, and had then been invited to the ranch of a very rich and respected polo-playing landowner who gave us the most fabulous party. All the girls there were absolute dreams, I seem to remember. During dinner, the whole company had been somewhat startled when the dining-room door burst open with a terrible crash to reveal a man standing on the threshold with a tommy gun in his hands. I thought immediately of Castro and the Mafia, but this chap turned out to be the landowner's son. He, apparently, had a fetish about guns and used to blast off from his bedroom window whenever he felt like it. This is one of the least likeable South American customs, I think; certainly, bringing a hobby like this to the dinner table does nothing to aid the digestion.

33

However, the old man dealt with the matter by screaming something or other at his son, and we all went back to our soup. -

I imagine I must have been born with a penchant for getting into trouble with the law, but I must say in my own defence that very often I am the innocent victim of circumstances — such as ignorance of the local customs and regulations.

Such a case brought me into personal contact with the police in Buenos Aires, whose guest I became for several nerve-racking hours early in 1960.

Apart from the heat — which made motor racing an exercise in slow cooking — I was enjoying my first Visit to South America. The social life was pretty good, especially since one of the people travelling with the team, a chap named Edgar Keoh, had relatives in the city. Including a most attractive niece.

Driving in a strange, foreign city is always a little bit touch-and-go, of course, and one particular afternoon, when I went to this girl's flat to see Edgar — he was staying there with his relatives I found that I had approached it from the wrong direction. So I made a U-turn in order to face the car I was driving towards the city centre again.

Just as I parked the car and got Out, two very large and rather villainous looking policemen appeared. My experiences with the law have somehow sharpened my instincts towards their particular kind of trouble and I had that old feeling that these two were interested in me — although I had not the slightest idea why they should be.

As they approached, I hurried across the pavement to the entrance to the apartment building, where one had to press the appropriate apartment button and speak to the occupier in order to get into the building.

Feeling increasingly ill at ease, I pressed the girl's apartment button and yelled: 'For God's sake come down quickly, I think I'm going to be arrested.'

By this time, I was surrounded by the two big policemen and was trying to remain aloof as they grunted at me in Argentinian, or Spanish, or whatever it was. In response to my alarm call, the girl came whistling down to intervene in this one-way argument and managed to convince the police that I was a good sort. Apparently, U-turns are punishable offences in Buenos Aires and the policemen were very reluctant to let an arrest go by.

After a torrent of high-speed Spanish and much wagging of fingers, they grudgingly walked away. That evening, I took Edgar and his niece out to dinner and afterwards ran them home. I was very careful not to make the same mistake and approached her flat from a different direction, arrived at the near-by junction,

34

turned left and pulled up outside the building. I left the young lady at the door, and walked back to the car.

Just as I did so, these two lads appeared again — one certainly had to admire their patience!

It turned out that one is not supposed to make left turns, either, for some unknown reason, and as quick as a flash I found myself being bundled into the back of my own car.

What's more, they grabbed some poor innocent bystander off the street and made him drive my car to the police station.

The four of us ended up at police headquarters in the middle of Buenos Aires where I was thrown into a cell while this other fellow went off with my two friends.

After half an hour, which I found was time enough to start getting a little worried, I was wheeled out and presented in front of some swarthy inspector or other. I can't describe the incredible pandemonium that ensued when at least five policemen started shouting at each other in Spanish, while I added my own curses and recriminations in English. Ten minutes' later, they all gave up, shrugged and marched me back to my cell again.

This performance was repeated twice more, each time at a different office in front of a different police officer, until finally I was brought in front of the Chief of Police himself.

I was getting a bit tarty by this time and when I found that the Chief could muster a little English. I launched into a terrible tirade, demanding that the British Ambassador be brought to the station and heaven knows what else. In fact, I made a great big noise.

Now, whether the Chief was impressed by me, or whether the British Ambassador was a peppery old gent who would make trouble if disturbed at three in the morning. I can't say. But the effect was immediate.

After giving me a short lecture on the traffic regulations in Buenos Aires, the Chief said he would be able to let me go.

At that moment, they produced this poor little chap whom they had snatched off the pavement and made him sign an enormous form on which they had filled in my particulars. Naturally, I was a little perturbed at this and asked why the devil this complete stranger was putting his name to this questionnaire.

The Police Chief explained: 'I am making him sign it so that he will be responsible for your behaviour for the rest of the time you are in the Argentine.'

Poor little chap! I never saw him again after that night, but I bet he sweated a bit. I always imagined him desperately reading the papers to see when I left the country.

Actually, we very nearly didn't get away at all.

I remember that on the day we left to catch our plane, Colin Chapman was driving our hired car out to the airport. As usual we were late, since we had had a tremendous drama at the hotel. They had lost half my kit somewhere or other and we immediately knocked ten pounds off the bill, which we refused to pay. So we left the hotel not only much later than we should have done, but pursued by the screams of the manager shouting — as always — for the police.

We shot through Buenos Aires in a cloud of dust, hell-bent on getting to the airport and out of more trouble.

I think I was more nervous than anyone, and my heart sank with a deadly thud when I saw a police car turn in the road and begin to follow us. The only thing I could think of doing was to lean out of the window and make signs pointing to the front wheel of the police car to indicate the tyre was flat.

Miraculously, it worked. The police car slowed, then pulled into the side and we lost it in no time. More drama followed, however, when Chapman, who was cutting up the other traffic in fine fashion made a fractional misjudgement and tore the front bumper off a large, shabby black motor-car.

And that, too was full of policemen!

I think I began saying my prayers at that moment. Why they weren't shooting at us I could not imagine.

The effect on Chapman of this last incident was to make him drive even faster, but I think we could only have been saved from summary execution by the fact that this last police car was unable to move because the front bumper bar was hanging off.

At the airport, we scrambled out of the car, shifted our gear into the airport building, then drove to the other side of the airport and dumped the vehicle.

I need hardly add that waiting for our aircraft to take off was complete agony, and I was never more pleased to get away from any place in my life.

5

From a practical point of view, the trip to South America was of great value. We learned a lot about the rear-engined cars and, as a result, a number of modifications were carried out. More were being built and, in fact, by the time I got back to England, I had both a Formula 1 and a Formula 2 model. Chapman appeared to be putting in a lot of hard work on the cars in preparation for the European season.

I took the opportunity to acquaint myself with the F2 car by racing it at that most beautiful of English racing circuits, Oulton Park. To my delight, the car behaved itself perfectly.

It was about this time that I first came across John Surtees. He had a Cooper in the race and I remember that I had got off to a pretty good start and was lying third as I went down to Cascades Corner. At the beginning of a race, of course, everyone is trying to get themselves sorted out and normally one takes it fairly cautiously. I had just finished my braking and was about to turn into this particular corner when a car came by on the inside, all crossed up and going sideways. I had to brake damned hard to avoid hitting him because he had slewed across the nose of my Lotus.

This was Surtees — World Champion — in his early days.

Despite this early incident I won the race — the first ever win for a Lotus single-seater. I did not have to do much more than sit there and keep on the road. The car went like a dream.

This was one of the relatively few occasions when the Lotus gearbox worked perfectly and the way the car moved was altogether very encouraging. I thought we had had at last got things sorted out at Lotus.

And it was in that mood that we went to Goodwood for the Easter Monday meeting in 1960.

I went to that meeting to drive two cars in two races — Formula 1 and Formula 2.

What happened that day though became the subject of a tremendous amount of hoo-hah, which, as far as I was concerned, got really quite out of hand.

The records show that on Easter Monday, 1960, I beat Stirling Moss twice in a day. This was certainly true. I did win both races while Stirling tried very hard to catch me. What the records do not show — and nobody at the time bothered to point out — was that in both cases my cars were superior to Stirling's.

The Press went quite mad over it all. The popular press didn't look further than the ends of their noses. They just saw it as a good story, I suppose, and they gave their readers this big thing about a brilliant new driver who thrashed Moss not once, but twice in a single day and so on and so on.

The result was that I became a sort of three-day wonder.

I had literally hordes of journalists phoning me and coming up to my home in Radnorshire wanting interviews. Of course, I let it happen. In a way I was flattered by it, although the effect on me personally was very much tempered by my own knowledge of the facts. I didn't subscribe to all the stuff that was written about me then, but I suppose I went along with it because it was publicity and it would be no bad thing for me in my career —which, remember, had began seriously in Grand Prix racing only twelve months previously.

I must make it quite clear that I did not believe all the horse manure that was written. But it is a funny thing about the press. Later, when I left Team Lotus at the end of 1961, they revived all this stuff and began writing stories saying, in effect, that I had failed to live up to the fantastic promise I had shown the previous year, etc. etc. Maybe I had not lived up to their expectations, but these were based on a false promise. I had lived up to my own expectations. Never in my wildest dreams had I ever thought I was in the same street as Stirling Moss, but it was by this standard that they had judged me.

This went for well-known and respected motoring writers who ought, in my view, to have known better. It was even suggested that I had been carried away by all the bull that was written and that I had grown too big for my hat. I deny this absolutely.
I do think the press can do an enormous amount of damage to a young driver — if he believes what is written.

I can think of one or two people I knew who did get carried away by the glowing reports which appeared about them in the press.
One doesn't, perhaps, like to speak of the dead, but I certainly

38

think that Chris Bristow was a case in point, I am sure he was affected by the tremendous write-ups he got. Whether that had anything to do with his subsequent death in a crash at Spa, I wouldn't like to swear, but I do think that the adulation of the motoring correspondents when he first broke into big-time racing may have exaggerated his style of driving.

Chris Bristow was undoubtedly a very talented driver, and he had got an enormous amount of courage, but he was only a comparative youngster and a newcomer to the game when he was suddenly lionised as a brilliant pilot of GP cars. He died having a real ding-dong with Willy Mairesse during the Belgian Grand Prix, and he simply over-did it.

Had this anything to do with a belief in his own publicity? One cannot say for certain. But for me, the suspicion is there.

A slightly different case of a man suddenly attracting the spotlight and the big build-up is Peter Arundel. During the 1964 season all sorts of glowing things were said about him. It was his first season in Formula One, yet Peter had been driving racing cars for almost as long as I have. A good driver and a safe one, I always thought.

Yet he got the hot blast of the press on him and within two or three months, he had this tremendous shunt at Reims which put him in hospital for months.

Once again, I would not like to swear to the fact that his accident can be attributed to this over-enthusiastic press acclaim, but I can see that it might well be the case.

Where I think all this is very dangerous is in the situation which arose in '64 and '65 where a number of quite unknown drivers were being recruited as second-strings in the top Formula One teams.

Mike Spence, I think, was and is a very competent driver. What's more, he is very sensible; he has his head screwed on properly. But as early on as the beginning of 1965 in the South African Grand Prix, where he drove a good race in close company with Jim Clark, until he lost it on a bend near the finish, Mike has been sorted out for some of this 'boy wonder' treatment.

In my own case, I believe I might well have been affected by it all. But by the time it happened, I was near the thirty mark and had perhaps got a bit more sense — sense enough to realise the truth of the matter, which was that I beat Stirling Moss only because I had a superior car.

I had the new, rear-engined Lotuses and at that time they were both superb motor-cars. They had better suspension than anyone else, better traction; they were lighter and had superior acceleration.

Everything, in fact, was in my favour; I could get round the corners and out of the corners more quickly, and that is where motor races are won.

About the only thing one can say in my favour as a driver was that I didn't make any howling mistakes and I kept on the road until the end of the race!

I don't think for one moment that if the positions had been reversed — if Stirling had had my cars and I his — I would have got near him in either race. The only difference I think is that he would have made my cars go quicker.

I hope I do not sound too wide-eyed when I talk about Stirling Moss, but one cannot but acknowledge that he was a better driver than anyone in motor racing at the time. If I had to summarise the difference between myself and Moss as racing drivers, I would say that it added up to the different degree of concentration that we both gave to any particular race. He was able to concentrate for longer periods and more intensely over any given time. I can concentrate, of course — obviously you have to when you are motor racing or you would never live to talk about it — but never to the same degree as Moss.

Everything he did was absolutely at maximum — all the time. If the race lasted for thirty minutes, he concentrated on it at maximum for thirty minutes. If it was three hours, he blanked everything else out of his mind for three hours.

I never could. I would find myself in the middle of a race, thinking about the party we would have that night.

I would not be thinking about it for a couple of laps, of course, but just momentarily my mind would stray to something like that. And then I'd find myself arriving at a corner sideways or something bloody stupid like that, or I would have passed my braking point by a couple of yards and that would bring me back to the matter in hand.

I never actually got into bad trouble on the track because of this, but undoubtedly my mind would take off at a tangent during a long race.

This, of course, is bad. It is the sort of thing that Stirling would not do. Whereas I might take a corner a little bit sloppily — take it at a hundred revs slower than usual, Moss never would. If he was taking a corner at 6,500 revs, he would go round that corner at 6,500 every time.

But he also had something else — an uncanny ability to get the best out of any motor-car he stepped into. This is what stamps him as being so very much different from the fellows racing today. He could beat very good drivers, top-rank men, even with an inferior car. He would just out-drive them. Two outstanding

40

examples of Stirling's superior ability were at Monaco in 1961 and also at Nurburgring that same year.

This was when Ferrari had the V-6 engine, much more powerful than the four-cylinder Climaxes used by the British cars. Even so, Moss won, driving a 1960-type Lotus, which had put him at a very serious disadvantage to the Ferraris.

Earlier, in Monaco, he had the whole might of the Ferrari team pounding after him the whole time, pressing him fiercely in very much better cars. Stirling just drove the wheels off them. He only won the race by a few seconds and throughout most of the race he had either Richie Ginther or Phil Hill right up his exhaust pipe, yet he just kept on going and going and going.

This, to my way of thinking, is the greatness of a driver like Moss, that he can do something like that even when he is up against the most difficult circumstances. Naturally, he could not do it all the time, but where there was a driver's circuit, Moss was very often able to finish in front, when in theory he should have been well behind.

In both cases I have quoted, his driving outstripped the machinery, but that sort of thing just does not happen in this day and age.

If a driver today is a hundred revs adrift on a corner, he's a hundred revs adrift. So what? But that kind of standard was never good enough for Moss. And if a car today is not entirely up to scratch, it comes out as a reason why the driver did not do well, instead of a reason why he might have tried a little harder at the sheer driving of the thing.

What exactly it was that made Moss the best driver I ever raced with, is a little tricky to define. Concentration, certainly; the ability and the will to fight, certainly; but also I think, this mystic quality of being able to get the best out of any car he climbed into. I am sure he got more out of the cars he drove than even the designer thought it possessed, or indeed intended it to possess.

If a car was meant to go round a corner at 100 m.p.h., Moss would get it round at 101 m.p.h. — while the rest of us would make it at 99 m.p.h.

Belligerence, determination, coupled with a remarkably fine sense of balance enabled Moss to do what others would not.

In effect, Stirling was as much a machine as the car he was driving. This is why he was so successful in every branch of motor racing. He applied exactly the same technique to whatever car he handled, be it Formula One, GT, sports or whatever. And let's face it, a machine can do the job better, if you want to reproduce the same article time after time, than a craftsman can.

Anyway, that was Goodwood. A bit of a hollow victory for me, in the circumstances, but a victory nonetheless. And I felt even more strongly that now, with Team Lotus, I could look forward to a good season with a good car. I had high hopes when we set off for the next meeting of the season, at Silverstone, for the Daily Express Trophy meeting.

But at that meeting began a series of tragedies which, for me, made the 1960 season an unhappy one.

First, Harry Schell was killed during practice at Silverstone and motor racing was robbed of one of its last really colourful characters, a man who thoroughly enjoyed life and raced for the fun of the thing first and foremost.

Silverstone during that practice day was at its worst. It had rained hard and the track was full of puddles.

Both Alan Stacey and I, in Team Lotus cars, spun on our way round. I found the rear-engined car a beast to handle in the wet. Up until this time, I had disliked driving in the rain. Now, I found it slightly terrifying.

I was in the pits when I heard that Harry Schell had been killed. It seemed that in taking the very fast Abbey curve, he had lost the car on one of the puddles, hit a little wall on the left-hand side of the road and been thrown out of the car. He died instantly. It put a tremendous damper on the whole proceedings.

Soon after the accident, I made up my mind to go out again and get the whole thing off my mind by trying to master the conditions. I went round a couple of times but in going into Woodcote
— the scene of one of my more spectacular spins a few years later
— I hit one of the puddles, over-corrected the steering for it, and shot over a small barrier wall at the entrance to the paddock area and finished up ramming an embankment further on. It all happened at fairly high speed and this shunt pretty well wrecked the whole car. Naturally, this put me in a fairly average kind of deep depression since the race was the following day.

I must say the Lotus mechanics really were a good bunch of chaps. They must have been cursing me to hell and back when they came round to collect my sorry-looking mess of a car.

Jim Endruweit, the chief mechanic, just shook his head rather sadly and started to pick up the bits. They loaded the whole thing on the transporter and took off back to London -. and that, I thought, was me out of the Silverstone race.

But not a bit of it. That night the Lotus mechanics worked like Trojans without a wink of sleep to make good the damage.

Back at the factory, they got hold of a new chassis which had just been built and cut it in half. Then they took a blowtorch to my vehicle and cut the front end right off and fitted the two halves together. It was a remarkable effort on their part that they had

42

fitted new suspension, new controls, steering and everything into that mongrel of a car by the following morning.

An hour before the race was due to begin, I was jumping up and down with anxiety, feeling sure that I would have nothing to drive that day, when up rolled the transporter with what looked like a brand-new Lotus on board. I could have hugged them.

Thanks to the botch I had made in practice, I had a fairly low place on the grid, but at least my prayers had been answered with regard to the weather, and it was a dry day. From the start, the Lotus motored extremely well — much better than one could have hoped, considering the car was half new and half old — and I worked my way steadily through the field until I came in sight of the master himself— Stirling Moss. He was leading the race and the first time I caught sight of him he was just in the braking area at the far end of the straight as I entered it.

It became tremendously thrilling then, because at the end of every lap, I was getting signals telling me I was closing on him all the time, and I could see myself gaining on him mile by mile.

Once again, it was a repetition of the Goodwood performance: me in a better car and Stirling motoring to the limit with his last year's Cooper. Nevertheless, I became exhilarated with the thought of catching him. I must have really been concentrating on what I was doing that day, because in the course of chasing Moss I set up a new lap record for Silverstone which was not broken for four years.

Eventually, I did catch him, and we motored round in very close company. Then — I couldn't believe my eyes! — Stirling waved me past. So I went by. I was absolutely staggered. If I had thought about it a little more carefully, I would have realised that Stirling's plan was to sit on my tail and see what happened. It is always a good idea to do this if you are being closely followed —just to see how the other chap makes out with you pressing him. Anyway, I went into the lead, and stayed there for a couple of laps.

Now Moss tried a little bit of gamesmanship. He pulled up with me — I think I must have slowed fractionally since I always drive better when I'm chasing than when I'm being pressed — and kept pointing at my car.

I did not know what the devil he was trying to say and I tried to ignore it. However, he passed me, still pointing. Unfortunately, for Stirling, a couple of laps later as he was going into the corner just after the pits, I think it was, I saw his car give a funny little wiggle and he did not appear to be going round the corner the right way. In fact, his front suspension had collapsed.

This put me in the lead, where I stayed until the end, although

43

it was not quite as easy as that. With Jack Brabham closing on my heels, I found that I was not going as well as I wanted. One of my spark plugs kept misfiring on low revs, so that I had difficulty getting away from corners, and I found that Jack was steadily and surely gaining ground on me. I worked it out that if I kept going at the rate I was proceeding, I would just about make it, so I pressed on, cursing the makers of my sparking plugs all the time, and swept over the line less than three seconds, I think, ahead of Brabham. Much closer, indeed, than one would have liked.

I was quite pleased with that race. My only regret was that Stirling fell out. We were having a tremendous ding-dong together and I was sorry that it did not continue until the end. For one thing, I might have learned a lot — especially about his tactics in letting me by and then passing me again.

With Silverstone over, I packed my bags for the first of the Continental Grands Prix, which that year was at Monaco.

Just before going to Monaco, however, Alan Stacey and I drove to Nurburgring, stopping off on the way at the Belgian circuit Spa. Alan had never ever been there before and we knew we should be driving there early in the summer when it was to be the venue of the Belgian Grand Prix.

I took Alan around the circuit in my own Lotus Elite, imparting to him what little knowledge I had of the course, which is a tremendously fast and rather frightening one.

We went round a couple of times and I gave Alan a kind of commentary on what I was doing as I went. He asked a few questions and we pulled off.

'That's a bloody fast circuit,' Alan said. 'I don't reckon it much.'

I agreed. I said that it scared me, too the first time, but later you get to like it. Then he said: 'I think I'll stick to learning the circuit this year and just take it easy. Next year I'll race on it.'

I said I thought that was pretty wise. I never thought that his words were soon to be proved so terribly, tragically wrong.

On the way back from Germany, we again stopped off at Spa and did a couple more laps. We then set course for the South of France and the Monaco Grand Prix.

I had never been to Monaco before, since I had joined Team Lotus after Monaco the previous year.

One of the things about this race was that the organisers allowed only the sixteen fastest cars in practice to take part in the race it-self. At least, they did at that time, although I believe that has now been changed. Monaco is a round-the-houses course and a tricky one to get to know; on my first day's practice I found that I was simply not quick enough to qualify for the race at all. Things were really hotting up and I would be out of the race unless I was very lucky.

I was lucky — lucky to have Stirling Moss to help me! During practice, Moss asked me to have a drive in his car — an identical Lotus to my own this time, having just bought it from Chapman. I did so and we had a chat about the car, during which I complained about my own inability to make a fast time round the Monaco course. So he offered to help.

'Stick close to me next time I go round,' he said, 'and maybe I can give you a few pointers.'

I must say that was the finest driving lesson I ever had. Before then, I was a bit at sea. It was the first time I had ever driven in a round-the-houses race and I suppose the sight of all the concrete, masonry, lamp-posts, harbours and things was a little off-putting. Anyway, I followed Moss while he went round quicker and quicker. Through out the whole time, he was pointing to places —where to keep tight to the kerb and where to take it wide, braking points and so forth. In following him, I put up a very respectable practice time, second-row of the grid sort of stuff. Thanks to Moss, I was very much in the race again.

I think this shows the spirit which existed in motor racing in those days, particularly between Moss and people like myself as he must have known at the time that I was a bit upset to learn that he had the same car as I had with Team Lotus,

Moss, of course, was driving for a private entrant, Rob Walker, and when I found that he had exactly the same car as myself I must confess I was more than bewildered.

I explained to Chapman that I was a little concerned at seeing Stirling with an identical car to mine, since it seemed to me that Team Lotus had a pretty good chance of going places with the car, and that it appeared to me to be an odd move to let Moss have one for himself.

However, Chapman replied that he wanted more than anything to win the Manufacturers' Championship that year, and with one of his cars in the hands of someone like Moss, his chances rose considerably. I was quite satisfied with that answer. As I saw things then, the team was the thing and if we won the Championship with the help of Stirling Moss, so much the better.

So we got that sorted out, and I got myself sorted out on the circuit and the race duly started.

I can tell you that was the most exhausting race I ever took part in!

For a long time during the race. I was lying in sixth or seventh position — nothing spectacular, but I was at least getting the hang of the thing and quite enjoying it. So much, in fact, that I was most surprised when, going up the hill just past the pits, the engine suddenly quit dead and the car very quickly stopped. It felt to me as if the car was just out of fuel on one of the tanks and I thought it would be worth pushing it up the hill, past the Casino, to coast down the other side and get going again — for, remember, in those days, we had no self-starter.

So I pushed the car all the way up that frightfully steep hill, and damned near broke my back doing it.

If I had known how steep the hill was, I would never have tried it. I've been back since and I can barely walk up it on my own, never mind pushing a racing car.

However, there I was, like a half-wit, pushing my guts out to get the car to the top; when I finally got there I was absolutely on my knees. I can't tell you how completely exhausted I was. All the way up, of course, I had a track marshal walking alongside me making sure than none of the crowd gave me a hand, since that would have meant automatic disqualification. I must say my efforts brought the crowd to its feet with delight and I was much encouraged, but even so I could only push the Lotus a couple of yards at a time, then I'd almost have to lie down under the back wheel to stop the thing rolling back down again. I must confess —with eternal gratitude — that the marshal slipped me a chunk of rock halfway up the hill to jam under the back wheel whenever I stopped!

The other thing which kept me going was the voice of a chap named John Dalton, a fellow who used to drive and who is very often around at race meetings. He happened to be at a point on the circuit near where I stopped and kept alongside me all the way up the hill, shouting encouragement and abuse throughout.

Every time I collapsed and lay down, he would shout: 'Come on, Ireland, you lazy hound. Get to your feet. Push, man! Push!'

I remember him dancing up and down waving 'the flag', doing his utmost to keep me going. I could cheerfully have slaughtered him at some points, but it was largely due to him that I did eventually get to the top amid a great round of applause.

Gratefully, I leapt into the machine, switched the fuel tanks over, let in the clutch — and nothing happened. Not a spark of life could I get from it. I limped down to the seafront and rolled to a halt again. Maybe it was the heat or something that was driving me mad, but I began to think of pushing the car round the rest of the circuit, waiting at the finishing line until the race was over, then pushing the Lotus across to qualify as a finisher.

Whether it was the heat, or love of the marque I wouldn't like to say, but push it to the line I did.

46

There were only about seven cars running in the race by then, and it seemed worth finishing even last among that lot.

The first hazard I came to was the tunnel leading down to the harbour. It was pitch dark in there as near as dammit and when I considered pushing the car through there with other cars whizzing around, I thought to myself: 'This is going to be bloody dangerous.

However, I had by then got the picture of the race and figured that I had 'x' number of seconds to get through the tunnel after the last car had passed through. So I waited until the right moment and heaved the dead Lotus forward.

I scampered through that tunnel, literally running with the car, while marshals were shouting and screaming and waving yellow flags and heaven knows what. I ignored them and trundled down to the harbour. Now there is a gentle rise up to the corner at the Tobacconist's Kiosk, and that very nearly killed me. It was only about thirty yards long, but I can't tell you the agony that was. Once again I had to push it bit by bit and then jam my feet against the railing at the side of the road and hold the car while I gasped for breath. More than once I damned near gave up and let the bloody thing roll back into the harbour, but somehow or other I did manage to reach the finish. I waited there for the chequered flag and gently pushed the car over the line, in a pool of sweat.

Incidentally, Monaco in 1960 saw the brief introduction of the Scarab cars, the Formula One vehicles built by Lance Reventlow, the American Woolworth Millionaire.

I have always felt that it was a tremendous pity about Lance and the Scarabs. They really were the most beautiful motor-cars. The trouble with them was that by the time they had been de-signed, developed and built, they were two years out of date. Had they appeared in 1958, they would have been real opposition. As it was, they hardly stood a chance. At Monaco, they were in all sorts of trouble. The cars simply would not go quickly, and added to that, their driver, Chuck Daigh, had never been to Monaco before.

I remember though, that the obvious effort which Lance and his team had put into the Scarabs brought out the best in everyone else. When the Reventlow team were scampering round looking for new springs, fresh suspension units and other bits and pieces to try and improve their performance, everyone helped. John Cooper, I recall, was most helpful to them really and everyone wanted to see them do well.

I don't think anyone has ever given Reventlow credit for what he tried to do. I am sure the American public did not appreciate what it was like for an American sportsman to try to break into

47

the European racing scene with something so totally different from anything ever made in America before. In my book, he deserves full marks for a good try — albeit an expensive and unsuccessful one.

At Monaco, they had a most discouraging time. It is not a circuit where you can, fairly, hand over a brand new car to a new driver strange to the surroundings. Poor Chuck didn't know whether he was coming or going.

Furthermore, he couldn't tell whether his slow times were due to his unfamiliarity with the course or whether it was the car. Once, in desperation, Lance asked Stirling to have a drive in the Scarab. I must say that within two or three laps, he was thundering round at a tremendous pace, but really that only demonstrated Moss's ability to get into a car and motor to the limit almost immediately.

They did eventually get the car to go quite well, but the machine was never competitive. It was a great pity.

Anyway, that was Monaco.

In the next race on the calendar — the Dutch GP at Zandvoort — it was again bad news for Stirling Moss. This time he was lying second to Jack Brabham, with me in third position, when a stone thrown up by Jack's car hit Moss's front wheel and burst a tyre. He pulled in to change it, so letting me into second place, and we finished in that order.

Once again, I was pretty well pleased with myself and the Lotus. I had at least finished in every outing so far that season — even if I did have to walk home at Monaco — and one thing which pleased me no end was to see Chapman actively engaged in making the Lotus work, and work properly. In passing, I think this must have been terribly galling to poor Graham Hill, who had left Lotus at the start of that season to go to BRM. For while he was struggling with the BRM his former No. 2 at Lotus — myself — was in charge of a car which, at last, looked like getting places.

Pretty soon, however, my confident outlook was shattered — demolished by the incredible accidents and final tragedy at Spa.

6

The Belgian Grand Prix at Spa in 1960 was a disaster, and for me, a personal tragedy.

Two men were killed, two badly injured, — one of them Stirling Moss — and I narrowly missed being added to the casualty list myself. By the end of the meeting, I was absolutely shattered...

But let's start at the beginning.

When we got to Francorchamps I was given a new Lotus. The car that I had first used in Buenos Aires had been sold, under the new policy that Chapman had set, to a very promising young driver named Michael Taylor. He appeared with this prototype for the first time in a Grande Epreuve at Spa.

For Team Lotus, there was myself, Alan Stacey and Jim Clark, who joined the team at the start of the season along with John Surtees, who was engaged to ride for Chapman whenever his motor cycle commitments would allow. Alan was new to Monaco and did not put up a very good practice time. As a result he was worried, particularly as he felt that unless he got out and went more quickly, his car might be given to Surtees.

The mental effect of this on a driver, to my way of thinking, is not only appallingly worrying, but downright bloody dangerous,

By the time we got to Spa, Alan was worried about the situation — especially since he did not like the Belgian circuit with its extremely high speeds and highly unnerving surroundings. If you go off the road at speed in Spa, the chances are that you will not get away with it, since all around are trees, houses, ravines and suchlike,

On the first day's practice, there were two pretty bad accidents concerning Lotus cars which were not calculated to jack up our spirits.

The first happened to Stirling Moss. He was taking the very fast curve at Burneville — a downhill right-hander which one takes at about 135 m.p.h. or thereabouts — when his back wheel fell off. It transpired that the hub had sheared off. Anyway, I was one of the first drivers to stop at the scene and I raced across to find Stirling in a pretty bad way. After the ambulance had taken Moss away, I went back to the pits and related what had happened. I had had a look at Moss's car beforehand and I could see that this particular hub had broken. I told Chapman.

'Right,' he said. 'I'll take your car and go and look for myself … in the meantime, none of you are to take your cars out.'

In the pits, moral slumped to zero. When such a terrible accident happens through no fault of the driver, people seem to feel it more. It is one of those times when you realise that a similar thing could happen to you, and it goes quite deep down. For a time, nobody feels like having much of a go.

Almost immediately, amid all the pandemonium of Moss's accident, we heard that Michael Taylor, in my old Lotus, had gone off the road. This too happened on a fast corner, another 130-odd m.p.h. affair. Instead of taking the right-hand curve as he meant to do, he just went sailing straight on; how he was not killed, I can't imagine. The car went across a damned great ditch, shot into the air, hit a tree which it completely uprooted and finished up smack into another tree. Somehow or other he came out of it with only a few broken bones, although he had a neck injury which gave him trouble for some months after.

When I visited Michael in hospital shortly after the crash and asked him what had happened, he said: 'The steering broke. I turned the wheel and nothing happened.'

Indeed, this was the case. The steering column had sheared off, and I must say it gave me a few uncomfortable moments when I realised how long I had been driving that car.

Meanwhile, when the panic of the accidents had died down somewhat, the Lotuses of Stacey, Clark and myself were wheeled off to the circuit garage to have their hubs examined for any fault similar to the one which had developed in Stirling's car.

The results were just terrifying. Clark's was uncracked, Stacey's was cracked halfway round the hub; and mine was all but sheared off! I suppose it was a gauge of how hard the cars were being driven at the time. Moss obviously drove his car harder than any of the rest of us and his hub went first. It is long odds that if he had not, in fact, crashed, I certainly would have done within a very few laps.

I was, for once, quite speechless.

However, Chapman explained that a fault had been found in

50

one of the machine processes at the works. He had new hubs flown out from England and they were fitted on to our three cars. I can't say, however, that I was filled with confidence when I got to the starting line at this particular meeting.

After all the drama of practice, I was not well placed on the grid, and when the flag went down, I tucked myself in behind Jack Brabham, who took the lead, and then held on tight to him. He had the faster car, the Cooper, on the straight, but I knew that the Lotus's superior roadholding would always get me round and away from corners quicker. I hung on to his slipstream all the way down the straight every time, planning to wait until the last lap, then pull past him on the uphill section after the straight and nip home ahead of him. I was very happy with this situation until, after about six laps, my clutch began to slip badly and I had to go into the pits for an adjustment.

I came out again and got going once more only to find the clutch slipping again, necessitating a further pit stop. Out I trotted for the second time, determined, still, to get back in the race and I really started to press on. Shortly afterwards I passed both Clark and Alan Stacey who were in close company; as I did so I clearly recall thinking: 'Well, old Alan is doing what he said he would, just motoring gently round and not trying to be clever.'

Perhaps I should have been thinking more about myself, though, for shortly afterwards, coming through the double left-hander before La Source hairpin, I lost it. I was going at a hell of a rate of knots and the car spun five times through 360 degrees, all the way down the middle of the track. I left great black marks on the road like some gigantic doodle which were still there the following year, I think.

This monumental spin ended with me pointing in the right direction with my engine still running but my right wheels on the grass on the right-hand side of the road. I was quite happy to have got out of it so fortunately and decided that since I and the car appeared to be in good shape. I'd carry on. I put the thing in first gear, worked the revs up, let out the clutch — and I barely moved. My first thought was that the clutch was slipping, but in fact, I had one rear wheel in the dirt and it was spinning like mad while the car was getting nowhere.'

Then, suddenly, it gripped. The car shot forward at a fantastic rate, spun through 180 degrees there and then, leapt over the embankment at the side of the road and went crashing down to land on all fours. It all happened so quickly and so unexpectedly that I didn't know whether I was punchbored or countersunk. It was the most extraordinary thing because I just did not know what was going on. Anyway, I climbed out of the car, which was

51

not badly messed up, absolutely furious with myself. Very dejectedly indeed, I walked back to the pits.

The first thing I learned when I got there was that Chris Bristow was dead. This young driver had been having a tremendous battle with Willy Mairesse during the race and somehow had overcooked it on the same bend were Stirling had crashed. The poor fellow had gone off the road and hit houses, trees and heavens knows what. His car was completely and utterly destroyed and Bristow must have been killed instantly.

Then, very shortly after that, Alan Stacey went missing.

Oddly enough, I did not feel there was anything to worry about even if Alan was late in coming round. There were all sorts of conflicting reports about Stacey being all right, slightly hurt, a stretcher case and so on, but throughout, I did not feel too concerned. Alan, I had always felt, was indestructible. Even after all the appalling tragedy of Spa so far, I couldn't believe that anything could happen to him.

Eventually, Colin Chapman came across to me in the pits and said: 'I think you'd better go and find out exactly what has happened, Innes.'

'Oh, Alan will be all right,' I said, 'but he'll probably cadge a lift with the ambulance. I'll go over and find him.'

So I walked back down to the circuit hospital and saw an ambulance drive in and stop. The doors opened — and a priest got out, shaking his head; at the same instant, I saw Alan lying in the ambulance. He looked just as if he was asleep, the way I'd seen him a hundred times in countless hotel rooms.

I just couldn't believe my eyes. I was completely devastated. I don't think I had ever seen anyone dead before. I simply turned round in absolute horror and ran away. I don't remember where I ran to or what I did, but a little later I went back to the hospital and found they had laid Alan's body out with a winner's laurel wreath resting on him.

I just burst into uncontrollable tears.

I was so completely shattered by this experience that I wept for hours afterwards, unable to control myself properly. Later on that evening I had to get all Alan's kit packed up, and then the police wanted details from his driving licence and so on. I can't tell you how frightful that was.

The real tragedy of the whole thing was that the crash which killed Alan Stacey was one of those million-to-one chances that you would normally never think about. A bird hit him in the face while he was travelling at, I suppose, something like 140 miles an hour. Of course, Alan must have lost control, the car went in all directions and poor Alan was thrown out and killed — or maybe

52

he had been killed outright by the impact of the bird. I don't know. Whatever happened, it Was a terrible tragedy.

Alan Stacey had had to overcome the most difficult physical handicap to get into motor racing at all. He had a tin leg, yet he taught himself to use it and get along with it so well that only a handful of people at the time knew of his handicap.

His determination was such that, since he was unable to heel and toe with the brake and throttle while changing gear, he had a motor-cycle type twist-grip throttle built into the gear lever of all his cars so that he could operate the throttle manually when changing gear. I tried it and it was extremely difficult to do, but Alan mastered it;

He got a great deal of fun out of that leg. Many a chambermaid has run from his room at the sight of an apparently dismembered leg hanging over a chair, complete with shoe and sock.

One of his other favourite tricks was to take a pencil in his hand while talking, say, after dinner, and slowly and quite unconcernedly thrust it through one of the holes in his leg beneath his flannels. Anyone who did not know his leg was artificial would look aghast at the pencil boring into his leg. I remember once, too, when he lost a bolt out of his ankle and we spent hours searching for the damned thing. Eventually we had to get one out of the workshops.

Also, at some of the Continental meetings when we had to take a medical examination, there were all sorts of diversions created to prevent the doctors from realising that he did not have a proper leg. When they were testing for reflexes, the rest of us had to wait until he had his left leg done, then, as the doctor was about to hit Alan's tin knee with his little hammer somebody had to knock over a chair, or kick the pot under the bed, or fall down or trip up or something.

In the resulting confusion, Alan simply crossed his leg again and sat there waiting to be tapped. It never failed.

He had a marvellous family. I can remember going down to his home in Partridge Green, Essex, for a memorial service to him and meeting them all. Alan's girl friend was there, too, and I recall trying to comfort her with tears streaming down my own face, when Mrs Stacey came into the room. Her composure under what must have been a terrible strain, was marvellous to see. She just put her arms round us both and said very gently, 'Come on, Alan wouldn't want to see you crying.'

Just that. She did not make me feel stupid or embarrassed because I was crying; she was just understanding yet controlled and her bearing was altogether magnificent. I liked that family tremendously.

53

I still miss Alan, perhaps more than I care to admit. And I still retain the very best memories of a united family who were rightly proud of their son.

The effect of his death on myself was to knock some of the confidence out of me. After all, he was the first driver to be killed who was really close to me, and this did affect my view of life for a while. All motor racing drivers are, I think, fatalistic — always the bad accidents are going to happen to somebody else, not you — and being close to Alan I suppose I bracketed him along with myself. He was, to me, indestructible. When it was shown that he wasn't, I was badly shaken.

It was only a week after Alan's death that I was contracted to drive in the Le Mans 24-hour race — and I found that yet more disaster was to overtake me.

The awful thing about the circumstances of that Le Mans engagement were that I was to drive an experimental 2-litre Lotus Elite owned by Michael Taylor's father.

Michael himself was to be my co-driver. When he got badly injured in his crash at Spa, he asked Alan Stacey to take over his place and Alan agreed. Now Alan was dead.

A third co-driver stepped in — young Jonathan Sieff. And he never drove in the race either.

I wasn't too happy when I got to Le Mans, and even less happy when I first took the car out. This experimental Elite was not fully developed and consequently rather a handful to drive. Flat out on the straights it was rather like a ship at sea, and it had no brakes to speak of. In fact, one night on the way back to the hotel I went thundering down the Mulsanne straight and on to the circuit escape road which was in fact the road home. Too late, I discovered that the police had failed to take away the straw bales placed over the road when racing was in progress and, the brakes being what they were, I hit two rows of them. The funny thing was that I had come to rest and was sitting in silence when one of the bales which I must have sent flying straight up into the air landed on the roof of the car with a tremendous bang which made me nearly leap out of my shoes.

Apart from this, I didn't like the Elite at all. I had had one of my own which I used as my personal transport for some while, and I found the rear suspension always wearing badly and other strange things happening. So I was none too happy about things, and I began to think of what might happen to the car during 24 hours of racing.

When Jonathan came along to the circuit, we arranged for him to take an ordinary Lotus Elite around for the first day or so of practice so that he could get to learn the course while I tried to

54

iron out the tweaks in the 2-litre car we were to drive in the race. On the second night there, Sieffy decided to take his car out for a bit of night practice.

He was motoring along quite happily and must have been doing something in the region of 130 miles an hour when something went terribly wrong. The car slewed off the straight by the Hippodrome cafe, and caved in the side of a house after hitting a telegraph pole. The car was a complete and absolute wreck. Sieffy was shot out of the car and landed in an orchard some 80 yards away. It was about twenty or thirty minutes after this dreadful crash before they found him, terribly seriously injured.

I went along to the hospital afterwards with Roy Salvadori and, in the French manner, they took us right up outside the operating theatre. I'll never forget it. The noise he was making inside was indescribably horrifying.

Now I was in the depths of the most appalling depression.

Three men who were supposed to have been driving with me had met with terrible accidents. One was badly injured, one dead and one hanging between life and death. Sieffy's life was saved I am sure, only by the sheer weight of medical and surgical experience which was summoned from all over the world regardless of cost.

The fact that he can now walk about is, in my view, a miracle.

It was about midnight by the time I got back to the hotel, where I met Stan Chapman — Colin's father — who was in charge of the car I was due to drive.

He told me that a fourth co-driver, John Whitmore, was standing by — if I wanted to race.

I remember Stan Chapman in the hotel room, tense and worried-looking. He put the ball in my court right away.
'Do you want to go on with the race?' he asked. 'It's up to you no one will think any the worse of you if you don't want to. It's up to you.'

And it was up to me, I suppose, but I didn't feel any better about having to make the decision. All sorts of things flashed through my mind, as you might imagine. One factor was that I doubted if the 2-litre Lotus could stand up to 24 hours of continuous motoring.

I had the fear in the back of my mind that the car would break while I was driving it. Already, three drivers had met with accidents within a few days. In the end, I made up my mind.

'No,' I said. 'I'm not racing. For one thing, it wouldn't be fair to call in a fourth co-driver. For another, I just don't want to go out in that car.'

Everyone took the decision without comment, and suddenly I

55

was seized by the overwhelming desire to get away from Le Mans, from cars that went quickly — from racing itself.

I went to bed that night with my mind reeling. I tossed and turned and wrestled with the misery in my brain until at about three o'clock, I got up. I knew for sure that I had to get away from everything right there and then. I went along to Whitmore's room and asked if I could borrow his little Mini-van.

John, thank heaven, did not ask me any questions. He just threw me his ignition key. I ran back to my room, collected up my kit and threw it into the back of the Mini and took off. I drove like a maniac all the way to Le Touquet, caught the first air ferry across to Lydd and drove to my home in Wales.

During the whole journey, I was trying to sort out all the things that had happened in the last week or so. All I knew was that I couldn't get away from Le Mans quickly enough, and I couldn't get far enough away. In a funny sort of way, I was trying to leave motor racing behind me and escape from it because I was sick to my stomach of the whole thing. I'll never forget the feeling I had at that time. It was purely an urge to escape.

When I got home, I found my family had gone to stay with Brenda and Peter Davis, some friends on the West Wales coast, so I joined them there and that night we had a bit of a thrash. We all got a bit merry and that helped.

I felt that if I had not got away from Le Mans when I did, I should have gone mad or done something stupid. The odd thing was that I never, really seriously, thought of getting out of motor racing. I knew I would go on with it — I had to drive in the British Grand Prix at Silverstone within a few days.

However, the haunting effect of Alan's death and the other disasters did not leave me for a long time.

To add to my own personal problems at this time, I began to feel a little less happy about the cars I was driving, particularly with the background of the Moss crash, when the wheel virtually fell off, and remembering Michael Taylor's experience with the steering. I did not feel particularly confident.

During the British Grand Prix at Silverstone, for example, I found that my rear right-hand wheel began to behave in rather an independent manner, and I thought immediately of broken hubs! The wheel was not behaving particularly violently but it was quite obviously adrift somewhere; all the time I kept pressing on I would be taking hurried glances over my shoulder to see if the wheel was wobbling too much. The consequence was that I almost unthinkingly began to ease off — I suppose it was my built-in safety factor at work.

Clark and Surtees were both driving that day for Team Lotus

56

and after about 2/3 distance both passed me, first Surtees and then Clark. Clark in fact did not finish, but John took second place. I cruised in — very bad-tempered because the car had let me down —in third position.

I wasn't very thrilled when, after taking my car to the mechanics for them to check the rear wheel, I was told that my hub bearings had gone. By that time, in fact, the wheel was just about flapping in the wind.

I seem to remember that nobody thought much of my performance. It was at this time I began to read about myself in the press and note that I wasn't living up to the promise of earlier in the season. This made me extremely angry. Nobody seemed able to regard my driving in any other light but that of the Goodwood affair and took no account of my own personal feelings and the effect on them of the recent happenings. I resented this new attitude on the part of other people who seemed to be inferring that I was a flash in the pan of motor racing and that sort of thing. It sickened me.

I knew within myself that perhaps I did not have the fire in my driving that I had before Stacey's death, but I thought — indeed, I was sure — that this would be only a temporary thing and that I would get over it. I was not helped, however, by what I thought was a deterioration in the cars.

However, I got some of the lost confidence back in the Oulton Park Gold Cup later that year. I did not win the race — indeed, I didn't even finish — but I did have a very good race with Stirling Moss, back again after his Spa injury, and Jack Brabham, and was leading them both when the good old gearbox broke and I couldn't get any gears at all.

What put my tail up a bit in that race was that I took the lead fairly quickly after the start and held it until, approaching Cascades corner, I found one of my rear wheels all locked up and the car went tobogganing off the circuit and up the escape road.

However, I got going again and within three or four laps, I had re-passed both Moss and Brabham and was going well until the gears packed up.

I simply had to park the car on the edge of the circuit in the end and walk away and leave it. It so happened that in the crowd nearby stood Gregor Grant, of Autosport, and Dick Jeffrey, from Dunlop, who both commiserated with me in the most positive way, and I finished the race in the beer tent, which was tremendous because they were buying the drinks. By the time the flag dropped, I think I had had two gins too many but that, I always think, is far, far better than mooning around the pits!

There was just one other incident in the race which was to have

57

repercussions later. Jim Clark hung on to my tail like a leech during the time when I first led the race and in fact was lying second. On several occasions he tried very hard to pass me. Unfortunately he collided with a car driven by Brian Naylor, which we were both in the course of lapping. Now, I regard every car on the grid as being in the race to win and I was not about to complain if Clark thought he could overtake me and win the race. But whatever the circumstances, Clark's car was wrecked and we lost the possibility of Team Lotus finishing really well with two cars.

Chapman evidently saw the force of this, for in the final race of the season — and incidentally, the last of the 2½-litre Formula One Grandes Epreuves — which was the American Grand Prix at Riverside, California, he called myself, Clark and Surtees together in his hotel room to work out some sort of plan about the prize money for the race.

He mentioned Oulton Park and the fiasco in which one of the cars had been wrecked, and said. 'I suggest, that to avoid this sort of thing, you all agree to pool the prize money in tomorrow's race.'

Well, it was a pretty startling thing in a way. It had never happened before in Team Lotus, but I was perfectly prepared to see us share any prize money we won, but I made one provision.

'I don't mind in the least,' I told the others. 'But let me make it clear that as soon as the flag goes down I'm going out to have a go, whatever anyone else does.' I made this point since I had not put up so good a time in practice as either Clark or Surtees. I made it abundantly clear that I was not going to hang about and wait for the possibility of one of them getting a place simply because the money was being shared, and also because I was supposed to be the team leader.

So we all agreed that we would not scrap it out between us, but drive to bring as many of our three cars home as we could.

On the day of the race I lined up behind Clark and Surtees and in the early stages of the game I stayed that way.

But within two laps of the start, Clark and Surtees were out of the race altogether. They were haring around in close company when Surtees spun broadside across the track and Clark rammed him right up the middle. When I came round the corner a few seconds later, there was Clark neatly buried in the middle of Surtees car.

So much for team tactics.

It looked very soon afterwards that none of us were going to share anything in that race. Something went wrong with my brakes and every time I applied them the whole vehicle shook so severely

58

that I could barely focus properly on anything. Although I was lying third, behind Stirling. Moss and Jack Brabham, there was little I could do about catching them. But as luck had it, Brabham had to retire and I managed to keep going until the flag, taking second place.

Now, the prize money for second spot in this particular race was five thousand dollars — the biggest prize money I had ever won. And there I was, for the first time ever having to split it with the rest of the team! I must confess I was a little piqued at having to part with two-thirds of it to the other two, who had run into trouble before two laps had been completed, It galled me enormously.

I was perfectly friendly with Jim Clark who, on the death of Alan Stacey, had stepped up to the No. 2 spot with Team Lotus. We got along quite well and I was always very ready in those days, Clark's early days in Formula One, to give him any help I could when he asked about circuits that were new to him and so forth.

Chapman and I, at that time, had a good deal of fun together in various parts of the world. He had the 'gift of the gab' and was always able to make one feel most important to him and Team Lotus.

Indeed, Chapman and I were the best of friends and we remained so until the day we parted — even if we did have our differences. If ever I had anything to say about the cars or the way they were going, I said it without either of us crossing swords. Not that I threw my weight around — at that stage in my career, I didn't consider I had any weight to throw.

Racing in 1960 ended with the best party of the year, at Lance Reventlow's fabulous house in Beverly Hills shortly after the American Grand Prix. The theme of the thing was Hawaiian and I remember we were all garlanded with leis flown that day from Hawaii, which I thought was pretty good going.

I also remember — a good deal more vaguely — drinking those marvellous Hawaiian rum-based drinks which taste so sweet and innocuous, yet which carry a tremendous punch. I think I might have got a little out of hand that night, for I know I jumped into the swimming pool in my underpants. Lance had one of those terrific pools which are half in and half out of the house and you could jump into it in the garden and swim under the glass wall of the house and straight into the lounge or whatever it was. This I did and, of course, as soon as I swam into the room, people started to push one another in and we all ended up getting thoroughly soaked — inside and out.

It was a fine high note on which to end the 1960 World Championship season — a season in which I had done fairly well considering it was my first full year in Formula One.

At any rate, I was fourth in the World drivers' championship list at the end of it.

However, it was not the end of racing for me that year, for I was delighted to be asked to go with Team Lotus to Australia and New Zealand — what a wonderful country that is — for a series of races.

Nothing very spectacular happened, but it was while I was in Australia that I got bitten by the urge to fly aeroplanes. Ron Flockhart was out there at the time, planning a Sydney-London solo flight in an Air Force Mustang fighter. A year later, Ron was killed during his second attempt, but while I was staying in Sydney I went with him a number of times to the airfield where he kept the Mustang and, I suppose, showed great interest in the whole thing.

One morning, early in 1961, Flockhart suggested that I take lessons at the flying school which occupied part of the airfield he used. Since it seemed a damn good idea at the time, I decided to do it. However, I was only supposed to be staying in Australia for a further sixteen days and it was a toss-up whether I could learn the theory and practice of flying, navigation and — since the school airfield was radio-controlled — radio operation, in a little over a fortnight.

But I wanted to try. I contacted the school and talked fairly convincingly to the 'headmaster' and assured him that I could do the course provided he gave me the same instructor and the same plane throughout the sixteen days. He finally agreed, and I found myself under the instruction of a terrific fellow by the name of Warren Wilkes. This chap was only about 23, but he had already amassed some three thousand hours of flying and he was a first-class teacher as well as pilot.

I moved out of my hotel in Sydney and put up at the Aero Club on the airfield itself so that I could start lessons at six in the morning and fly hourly sessions throughout the day, which meant I was getting about four solid hours in the air every day.

Every evening, however, I had to study like mad at the theory of the thing, navigation, radio and so on because, to get my pilot's licence, I had to complete 22 exam papers on different aspects of flying. But I must say everyone was terribly helpful. They cut all sorts of corners for me to speed up the exam marking and that sort of thing. They really were very good about it.

To save time, they even allowed me to skip my solo cross-country flight, which is usually a compulsory thing. All that happened was that when I went for my accompanied cross-country

60

flight with Warren, the authorities assumed that during the second half of the flight, my instructor would be sleeping in the back seat - which he was!

Actually, I got my licence the day before I flew off from Sydney on my way home by airliner. I felt very pleased with myself indeed and could hardly wait to get back to England to get myself an aeroplane to fly.

So, when I came back to England some time in February, I set off looking for planes to buy with my shiny new licence in my hand. I eventually decided on a little Miles Messenger which I had been assured was a very good, safe aeroplane, which allowed me less chance to kill myself than most others. I always remember Warren Wilkes telling me: 'When you have got your licence, it's the next 50 hours that are critical. If you live through that, you'll do all right.' Pretty cryptic, but very true, as I was to find out for myself!

Anyway, I trotted off to an airfield in Northamptonshire and took a look at the plane. I loved it immediately. It was blue and white and looked absolutely superb. The only reservation I had at that moment was that I had never in my life flown a tail-down aeroplane — one with a wheel at the tail end. All my training had been on a tricycle undercarriage plane, which in fact is much more easy to land.

Another novelty to me was that this aeroplane, the Miles Messenger, had three tail fins which made it very sensitive to crosswinds when landing or taking off.

I signed the papers and did all the necessary things, after which I was ready to hop in and fly home to Radnorshire where I intended to land in what I thought was a fairly large field at the back of my house. Apparently, however, there was more to it than just writing a cheque and flying off.

'Have you got a Messenger on your licence?' they asked.

'No,' I said. 'I've only just qualified to fly.'

'Oh, well,' they said, 'you'll have to do a few circuits and bumps before we can hand it over to you.'

I protested that I did not have time. Already, it was getting on in the afternoon and I had to be home by tea-time or it would be dark and I'd sure as hell kill myself trying to land. However, they were adamant, so I charged off, climbed into the plane and we took off into the blue.

Maybe I did not line the Messenger up properly into the wind, but my take-off was a series of wild swerves across the airfield which must have put a tremendous strain on the undercarriage — I thought at one time that it would all fall off. Anyway, I got into the air, did a circuit and got back on the ground. The fellow who had come with me was not exactly impressed with my flying, but I pointed out that I had at least managed to get up and down in one piece and I would simply have to go.

In any case. I was not at all downhearted over my performance with the Messenger. In fact I was quite pleased with myself and I walked over to a friend of mine who had driven up to Northampton and was taking my car back home while I flew. He was an American, a highly amusing chap named Ed Ehlers.

'Well, Ed,' I asked, 'did you like the look of my flying. That wasn't too bad a landing, was it?'

Ed just looked at me. 'Landing?' he drawled. 'That wasn't a landing, that was a controlled crash.' That hurt my pride a little but was probably fairly accurate. Nonetheless, I set off on my first ever solo cross country flight and headed westward for Wales. I had drawn elaborate lines and reference points on my air map and I was pretty confident about the whole thing, estimating that the flight would take about an hour and five minutes and I would be home in time for tea.

Panic did not strike me until I got to a height of about two thousand feet and had been flying for a little while into a hazy sunset. I then found that I could not recognise anything on the ground at all.

It was one of those days when the haze prevents you seeing anything of the land ahead of you and you could only see the ground more or less straight beneath you. But that was a complete mystery to me, too!

The only thing I could think of doing was to hold my heading absolutely accurately and every time I found I could not recognise my check point, I simply pressed on hoping to locate the next one.

In fact, I never saw a bloody thing the whole way that I even remotely recognised or could co-relate to the map at all. After an hour of flying, I decided to make a determined effort to find out where I was and I searched the floor for some sign of the countryside near my home, since I knew I had to be somewhere in the region. At last, I saw a stone quarry on the side of a hill and I was certain that it was the quarry near my home. I put the plane into a screaming dive and went down into the valley and flew around for a bit. When I got down there, nothing looked in the least familiar. Panic had really set in by this time. I was all on my own, quite lost, and the sky seemed an awfully big place.

I was actually on the point of picking out somewhere to land and ask the way, when I came across the quarry again. This time I got my bearings right and found that it was indeed the one near home. So I took no further chances, but came' down low, found

62

the road to home and flew along it until I came to the house and the field I had chosen to land in.

Of course, when I had measured the field on the ground, it seemed perfectly adequate. But from the air it looked about as big as a threepenny stamp. The sight of it filled me with the fear of God. I had only landed this aircraft once before and Ed's description of a controlled crash seemed to take on an extra force in my mind.

I came down and made a pass at it, over-shot wildly and had to pull the plane back up again and come back for another try. By this time it was getting dark and I thought I had better do something pretty damned quick. So, on about my fourth attempt, I came staggering over the near hedge, cut off the power and crashed on to the ground more or less safely. And that was it. I had arrived.

However, as the year went on, I mastered that field until i[was able to plonk the plane down in any weather and even in the semidarkness. Even so, I managed to scare the pants off myself quite often. Once, when I was taking my wife and my little girl Christianne for a holiday in Scotland, and the plane was loaded with us and all our kit, I very nearly did not make it. The day was hot and I imagine the air must have been pretty thin, for I found myself rushing down the field without showing an inclination at all to leave the ground. The hedge at the far end of the field was coming towards me pretty quickly when I discovered that I had not put on any flap, so I hastily wound it on and eased the stick back. We just managed to stagger over the hedge at nought miles an hour -.- and then sank back down again into the next field! We touched down a couple of times there and eventually dragged ourselves into the air.

My very first take-off was a pretty alarming affair too, particularly as I had with me an old school friend called George Cannon who, at that time, was a test pilot working on the development of the Lightning jet fighter.

Quite how he managed to sit there so calmly with an idiot like myself in charge of his life, I'll never know. I remember that I made my usual slalom-type take-off run and found myself heading for a big tree. Fortunately, I got over the hedge all right and just as I did so, made a turn to avoid the tree which had fixed my attention. George hardly flinched as I made this manoeuvre but he didn't talk for a bit. However, when we got well airborne, he took a great big breath and remarked on the take-off.

'By Christ,' he muttered. 'We damned near hit that tree, didn't we?'

'Yes,' I said, 'but I got the wing over it when I turned.'

63

'Well, I wasn't actually thinking of the one on your side. It the one that brushed past me that had me worried.'

Of course, I hadn't even seen that one!

That year, I started flying to race meetings in the way that people like Colin Chapman and Jack Brabham always did. The first meeting I flew to was at Snetterton in Norfolk, which was a fairly long cross-country flight for me. When we got there, mainly thanks to the navigation of an old friend of mine named John Brisbane, I arrived with a flourish and a roar and a swish and a bang and I thought I was king of the air. Then I looked round for the windsock, to get an idea of the wind direction.

On the runway, I saw Chapman's plane parked, but could not see the windsock anywhere. I assumed, however, that this was the runway to land on.

Down I came and I was in fact committed to land on this runway when I practically flew right through the windsock which, until that moment, I simply had not seen. Worse still, it was indicating that I was landing in the wrong direction. It was too late, however, to do anything about this.

We hit the ground and then, of course, rose again in a gigantic hop. As we came back down again this second time, the plane did a sharp right-hand turn. Colin Chapman was actually standing at the far end of the runway at this time and he told me that it was the first time he had ever seen an aeroplane in a three-wheeled drift. Even the tyres, he said, were screaming as I skidded.

I shot straight through a hedge on the right-hand side of the runway. I can still see the showers of hedge flying up into the air as the propeller swathed through it. Eventually, we came to a ploughed field, by which time I had nearly got the thing stopped. The only thing I could possibly do then was to drive it back through the hole in the hedge and park on the runway again. This I did, with surprisingly little damage to the Messenger.

Having executed all these non-standard manoeuvres, I stepped from the plane — and came face to face with my insurance broker! Only a day or two previously, I had talked him into getting me insured for flying by telling him it was all perfectly safe and that I was quite competent. Now, he had seen the whole performance and I did not know how to look him in the eye.

I have parted with the Messenger now. It cost me quite a lot of money m the end, because some months after I bought it, I received a polite letter from a hire-purchase company informing me that the plane was owned by them and if I cared to write them out a cheque for £2,000, which was the amount of their 'interestedness', then I could keep it!

It turned out that the chap I had bought it from had re-financed

64

'I'd love you to get in, darling - but there isn't room!' Winning the American Grand Prix at Watkins Glen 1961.

Lifting a wheel with the F.I. Ferrari at Silverstone 1962.

(Photo: B.F.E.Clarke)

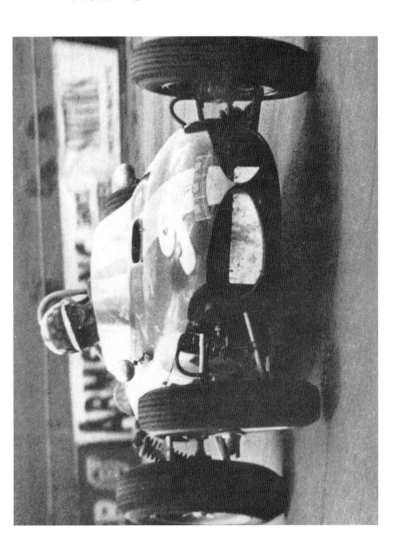

the plane half a dozen times or something, and it had never been his to sell.

Still, I got a lot of good flying out of it and when it went, I bought another aeroplane, a much more sophisticated American Beechcraft Bonanza.

I have done a lot of flying since those early days, but I have never forgotten the wisdom of Warren Wilkes' remark about the first fifty hours, for there were plenty of times when I thought I would not last another fifty seconds!

7

Nineteen-sixty-one was a poor year for British cars and their drivers. A new Formula One — 1500 cc — had been ordained for the following five years but thanks to a lot of behind-the-scenes wrangling among British constructors and engine builders, we found ourselves without a properly developed power unit, and we had to fall back on the old 1500 cc engine which had been used for Formula Two cars as far back as 1958. Although it was brushed up by the Coventry-Climax people it was hardly competitive with the developed Ferraris which appeared that season.

Actually, during 1961, I think I did as well as anybody by winning three Formula One races although only one counted towards the World Championship.

Yet even before I got to the grid for the first GP of the season, I had a monumental crash which put me out of racing for five weeks.

It happened in Monaco.

The cars we took to the meeting were new, lighter and cleaner-bodied. Also, Colin Chapman had abandoned his own design of gearbox and was experimenting with two types of ZF box, a four-speed and a five-speed.

They took a little getting used to. For one thing, instead of being on the left, as I had been accustomed to having it on my Formula One car, the gear lever was on the right. For another, the actual gear shift was back to front from the normal gear positions. That is, instead of having first gear on the forward left-hand side of the gate, it was on the right-hand side at the back — exactly opposite to what you might expect to find on an ordinary car. And the five-speed box was just a bit more complicated because you had this extra gear tucked in there somewhere.

Now, this was all right so long as you weren't trying to do anything

66

in a hurry. But at Monaco, you are always in a hurry to change gear. This circuit really was not the best place to try out the new boxes, but we had no alternative. It was fine as long as you were thinking what you were doing, but when you are racing or practising, you should not have to think about things like changing gear. It should be entirely automatic.

Having used the four-speed box most of the time I tried this five-speed box on the third and last day of practice and I set out to do a reasonably good time, since, at Monaco one has to qualify for the race on practice times. I took the Lotus around a time or two, still trying to sort out the gears, and then I thought I would try for a quicker lap. I suppose my mind was then more concentrated on getting round quickly than on the gear change positions, but everything went well until I came screaming round into the tunnel which is part of the Monaco circuit.

The entrance to the tunnel is on a curve and inside it is, by comparison, rather dim. The tunnel gives the impression of being lit only by a couple of Naafi-candle-type lights, and it is always a bit tricky rushing out of the bright sunshine into that kind of gloom. Pressing on, I found myself changing gear just as I was entering the tunnel.

I intended to snick the gear lever very, very quickly into fourth gear, but the habit of years with the old, conventional gate was my downfall. Instead of fourth gear, I selected second.

The odd thing was that just as I was letting the clutch in, and in the fraction of a second before it bit, I thought to myself:
'Christ, I'm in the wrong bloody gear!' But even as the thought flashed through my mind, the back wheels of the Lotus were locking up solid. Since the car was still set up to take the curve, it just flew off the road. For me, it was the most extraordinary experience because, being in almost pitch darkness, I had no idea which way the car was pointing.

Of course, in no time at all, I had hit the tunnel wall. And the noise! I can remember now the colossal crashing and banging that echoed through that enclosed space and beat on my eardrums.

I think the car was, in fact, going backwards when it hit the wall and I was thrown out of it.

By an absolute miracle, I was projected straight out of the tunnel at the far end, instead of being dashed up against the wall.

It was quite the strangest experience. I was thrown, I suppose, some fifty to eighty yards and to this day I can recall the impression I had of flying through the air. The roadway sped beneath me in a kind of blur, as it does when you are travelling fast in a car. I landed on the road with a pretty awful whack, but probably owe something to my Army parachute training for not hurting myself worse than I did. Of course. I scraped away my elbow down to the bone and stripped lumps off my back in landing, but it could have been worse. The other injuries I got -a fractured knee-cap and an inch or so off the front of my shinbone — happened, I think, as I was leaving the car.

I did not lose consciousness, for I remember thinking quite clearly that I really ought not to continue lying in the road with all the other chaps coming along, so I picked myself .up and walked across to the left-hand side of the road, hauled myself over the little kerbside safety barrier and lay down on the pavement. Something went through my mind about people walking around with broken ribs and doing themselves further injury, and I didn't know whether I had a broken rib or not. Anyway, I was not feeling very well and I thought it best to lie down until someone intelligent came along.

I had no idea while I was lying there, however, that fountains of blood were spurting from my left leg, which had been torn open by some projection or other, a bolt or something on the steering column I think it was. Anyway, my leg was in a mess, and by the time I was carted off, the pavement around me looked like a blood bank, with a hole in the bottom.

I know that subsequently, I had about 35 stitches sewn into the gash and since I had torn an artery in my leg, I was making a very nasty mess everywhere. Luckily there was a nurse posted at this point on the circuit and she came along and tied a rope round my leg to stop the blood flowing.

Actually, it wasn't until much later that I found out how lucky I was not to have been killed in that shunt. Apparently, Lucien Bianchi had been coming round the circuit fairly close behind me. Just as he was diving into the tunnel he either saw me lose it or had some instinct about it — he can't remember which — and slowed up considerably. As my car was destroying itself against the wall, it ripped the oil cooler off and flooded the road with oil, Bianchi hit the oil and had quite a time sorting his car out. He came Out of the tunnel just as I was hitting the road.

I take my hat off to Bianchi, for he told me that he had only just managed to miss me by a couple of inches. I don't, in fact, remember seeing his car go by — it must have been as I was bouncing along the road — but perhaps this was what subconsciously made me get up to go and lay on the pavement.

Anyway, I hadn't been lying there long before Stirling Moss came round and stopped. He was very good, I remember. He took charge, obtained a cigarette for me from one of the crowd and tried to make me comfortable.

By this time, a party of first-aid and stretcher people had arrived

68

and began simply drenching me in iodine. I can't tell you what stinging misery that was! They poured the stuff over me in bucketfuls.

Practice, of course, had been stopped by now, since my Lotus was strewn all over the road. Someone told me later that I and pieces of the car came out of the tunnel like a shot from a scattergun and I can well believe it; the car was completely destroyed and it lay all over the road like a Meccano set.

I was put on a stretcher and carried away. Now, I can only think that the ambulance people, or the police or someone wanted to practise one of their exercises, for, instead of being put in an ambulance and driven off, I found myself being carried down some steps to the seashore below the road where there was a launch waiting.

It was only an ordinary stretcher and as I felt myself being lowered rather awkwardly down the steps, I remember thinking to myself: 'They are going to drop me in the water. I know it. I'm going to have to swim!'

Fortunately they did not drop me in the drink and I was laid in the bottom of the boat which took off for the town harbour. Then I was humped up some steps and once again I was perfectly sure that I was going to slip off the stretcher and finish in the water. But somehow or other, they made it. Then they put me in the ambulance and I was whistled off.

Why they did not just bring the ambulance round to me, I can't think. Perhaps they wanted to practise things the way they would have to do it on race-day when, of course, the road would be shut to them. However, it was none too pleasant being used as their guinea pig, just so that they could find out whether or not they did drop people in the water!

Somehow or other, this sort of pantomime went on. I remember that I was left on the floor of a corridor in the hospital when I got there. Lots of priests, nuns and other people were floating about and they all looked about fifty feet tall to me, lying on the floor. There was one priest who came and stood by me lighting his pipe, bits of hot ash kept tumbling out of the bowl of this enormous thing and landing on me. The old chap was quite oblivious of what he was doing, even though I kept puffing and blowing to prevent the ashes falling on my face.

I can't imagine why I was left on the floor, but I was there some long time because I spent quite a bit of it cadging cigarettes from passers-by. All sorts of people kept coming along and asking how I was. It's quite extraordinary that when you are lying about on a stretcher, covered in blood and obviously looking like death, people always come along and ask you: 'How do you feel?'

69

The obvious answer is: 'I feel like — death'. However, that's hardly polite and one is forced to say, with a sweet smile, that one is fine, thank you.

Eventually, they worked on me a bit and I was moved into my room. When I came to, I found this was a most beautiful apartment with a balcony overlooking the Mediterranean. There was a beautifully equipped bathroom of my own, too! There was even a bidet — though heaven knows what they thought I was going to get up to in my condition! But I did appreciate the thought. The French think of everything.

Actually, when I first came to, I found the room absolutely full of people — Colin Chapman, Graham Hill, Jo Bonnier, Huschke von Hanstein from Porsche, Bernard Cahier, my very good French journalist friend, and all sorts of other people. Apparently, the minute I saw Chapman, I began to tell him that the whole thing had been my fault and that I had dropped a clanger by selecting the wrong gear. I didn't know I had said all this until the following day, when Chapman came in to see me once more and I began to say it all again.

For the first few days in hospital everything was fine. I had stacks of visitors, people from the motor race and so on, but of course, on the Tuesday after the race, they all went off to the next meeting and I was left behind. I can't tell you how utterly lonely and desperate I felt. It was an awful feeling. I have only been in hospital like that a couple of times as the results of motor accidents, but I always find I get terribly sorry for myself and frustrated to the point of tears. It's not that I'm sorry for myself because I have been hurt — just that I'm missing something. I hate being left out of things.

I am only grateful to all those people who came to visit me — total strangers most of them, like tourists who had read I was in hospital and just dropped in to say hello or see if I wanted anything. It was terribly nice of them all. All the same, I did get pretty miserable after four of five days, during which time I pestered the life out of the French doctors attending me to let me out of the place.

I had brought my own aeroplane with me to Monaco — the Miles Messenger — but since I still did not have much idea of how to get from one place to another by air navigation, I had again asked John Brisbane to navigate for me. He stayed in Monaco all the time I was there and was really a tremendous help. To alleviate the boredom we managed to have a fairly average uproarious time in my hospital room. Eventually, I did succeed in getting the French doctor to agree that I could leave the hospital on the Sunday, just a week after the crash.

70

Of course, I could not walk, and the Messenger was not big enough to accommodate me on a stretcher, so John tried to book six seats for us on a BEA plane to London that week-end. It so happened that it was Whitsun week-end in England and every plane to and from Europe appeared to be crammed full. We were unable even to get a booking for one, let alone six.

Naturally, I was pretty cheesed off with this, and I mentioned it in passing to some journalists who came to see me.

The next thing was that the London papers were full of headlines: 'Innes Ireland says "I'm stranded"'.

The net result of this was that I began to get overwhelmed with offers of private aeroplanes. I was quite flattered. Everyone with a private plane seemed to want to put it at my disposal at a moment's notice. One of the people who contacted me was Jack Bilmier, the late shipping owner, He turned up in my hospital room and began talking about my plight. Then he said: 'I've had a word with 'Arry, everything is fixed.'

'Who?' I asked politely, since it sounded as if he was dropping his 'H's.

'Arry', he said. 'Aristotle Onassis. He wants you to have the Comet.'

It was all rather splendid to have a Comet jet put at my service at the snap of a finger. Hughie Green was another who phoned to say that his plane was ready to fly out immediately. But, of course, having created such a furore over the BEA business, the airline had suddenly found six seats from somewhere and had booked me on a Britannia from Nice, so really I was unable to accept any of these quite splendid offers, grateful though I was.

It was quite a performance being carried up the steps of the plane, but anyway. I found I had these six seats between myself and Brisbane — actually, BEA only charged me for the two, which was nice of them — and I felt rather regal. Then another little drama developed. The call of nature became very urgent. I was quite unable to move, however, since I had been wrapped in plaster all down my left kg from my hip.

There was nothing for it but to ask the cabin staff on the aeroplane if they could help. I pressed the button for the steward. Of course as always happens in this kind of situation, the girl steward came along first of all and I had to ask her politely if she would send the male steward.

'Look, I'm in a bit of a spot,' I explained when the chap arrived. 'Have you anything I can use?'

'I'm afraid not, sir,' the steward said.

'Well, you'd better find something or your aeroplane is going to get all wet.' I really was most uncomfortable by this time.

the steward thought for a moment longer and then suggested using one of the plastic covers on the lifebelts. He fetched one and handed it to me, waited a minute or two while I performed, and took it back.

'I can't tell you how funny it was, for when this poor fellow started to carry the bag back along the gangway — he discovered it had a leak!

I shall never, never forget the sight of that steward, immaculately dressed in his smart blue uniform, hurrying along with the dripping bag held about two yards in front of him. I felt terribly sorry for the chap, but it was too hilarious for words. However, I think he must have dined out on that story a time or two for I met him again in America some two years later and he remembered the incident with great amusement.

I wanted to get back to London urgently, though, to go into St Thomas's Hospital for treatment by a surgeon who had previously treated Stirling Moss for similar injuries and had done wonders for him.

Back in London, I was whipped straight to St Thomas's, arriving there at eleven-thirty on Whit-Sunday. I was agreeably surprised to be woken next morning at eight-thirty to find Mr Urquhart the surgeon — a marvellous bone specialist — Waiting for me. I was particularly impressed that he did not waste a moment. He took away the great envelope full of photographs and notes which the French surgeon had handed me and came back half an hour later obviously quite certain what should be done.

'Right,' he said. 'Off with that plaster.' This surprised and delighted me, since the French doctor had said I would be in plaster for four or five weeks. Anyway, out came a great pair of things like bolt-cutters and the nurse cut the plaster off my leg.

Then Urquhart handed me a couple of little walking sticks and said: 'Right, let's see you walk up and down the room.'

I said: 'You're joking.'

'No, I'm not joking. You just get up and walk around the room.' For a moment I was quite nonplussed. One doctor was saying I would be in plaster for a month: now the other was asking me to get up and walk.

Urquhart persisted: 'Look, if you want to get better and get out of here quickly, you'll have to do it my way. Now, let's see you walk down the room.'

So I got out of bed, quite expecting to collapse in an unsavoury heap on the floor. But I didn't. I walked up to the door and back again. The surgeon really lived up to his reputation. Within about four days, he had me doing exercises to strengthen my leg, having got all the bits and pieces straight again. They have a wonderful

72

bit of apparatus in that hospital. I was wheeled along in a chair every morning to a room with a big tank of warm water in it. Then I sat in a kind of gantry affair, was hauled out to the middle of the tank and gently lowered into the water where they attached buoyancy floats to my ankles and made me drag them under. It was like lifting weights, only in reverse.

What's more, the nurses had to put on swimsuits and come in the water with me. What a marvellous way to recuperate!

It was a tremendous thing to see my leg getting better day by day. The doctors used to measure the angle at which I was able to bend the leg each day and I can't tell you how exciting it was to notice that I went a degree or two further every morning. I don't know whether the measurements were essential, clinically, but it was wonderful psychology for me.

The treatment I got at St Thomas's was really tremendous. Under Urquhart's direction, I was up and about within two weeks. In fact I left hospital just three weeks after the crash and was back in a racing car a fortnight after that.

I must confess, though, that while I was there, I had some terrific fun. There seemed to be a party every night in that room of mine. On the first day, Whit Monday, there was a race meeting at Crystal Palace which I watched on the goggle-box and after the meeting a whole bunch of people came to see me. Amongst them, I was delighted to see my old Army batman, a chap called Reid, who had read in the papers that I was in dock. I was quite taken aback, but highly delighted when he walked in. It was not long, either, before he was back in harness as it were, pouring drinks for everyone who came in.

Actually, I did extremely well for drinks all the time I was in St Thomas's most of my friends thought I would appreciate liquids rather more than flowers or fruit! I had a locker by my bed which was supposed to hold that nauseating bedpan thing which they have in hospitals. I had it thrown out and the locker filled with whisky and gin and so on — which horrified the matron and under the bed there was always a crate or two of beer and tonics and various other medicines, lit was all quite extraordinary. I remember that besides the late Reg Parnell, Roy Salvadori, John Coombs and a few other 'characters' who came into my room that first evening was one chap I did not recognise. I thought he was somebody's friend and he had a few drinks and then asked if he could take a photograph. Of course, I didn't mind a bit —he could have shot a whole feature film for all it worried me. I vaguely recall he was lying on top of the wardrobe when he eventually did take some pictures, but it seemed a perfectly normal thing to do at the time.

73

Anyway, he must have been from the Daily Express, for the next day, the William Hickey column carried this fabulous picture of my room full of people with the table over my bed just littered with bottles, glasses, ashtrays and all the paraphernalia of a first-rate thrash.

The day it appeared, though, the matron came round to my room and she gave me such a monumental rollicking.

'I don't care what you do in here, Mr Ireland,' she said. 'This is your own private room. But I would appreciate it very much if you would not get photographs in the newspapers. How on earth am I going to explain this to the Board of Governers?'

Probably the most spectacular thrash we had in hospital was on the day when Princess Margaret got married. We started at about two in the afternoon, finishing up at one-thirty the next morning! I remember that one chap who came along was a friend of mine called John Blake, press secretary of the Royal Aero Club. He was as always accompanied by his dog — a bloody great bull mastiff — which was perhaps as well, since by the time the party ended, only the dog knew the way home. But what the hound did not know was the way out of the hospital. When the pair of them left my room, they turned left instead of right. I saw them, but didn't feel too much like shouting out instructions at that hour, so I left them to it. Now, at the time, they were doing some redecoration in the hospital and a great heap of beds had been piled up in the corridor.

Sure enough, seconds after Blake and dog had left my room, there was the most appalling crash — it sounded like one of those old radio sound effects where the smash and tinkle of glass goes on for ten minutes. Only this was the clang of bedsteads being scattered around. It was Blake, of course. A few minutes later, having found out their mistake, I heard John staggering down the corridor, ricocheting from wall to wall with a heavy snorting noise from the dog just ahead of him.

Of course, when everyone else had gone, I had to face the night sister. She and the night nurses would swoop into my smoky, fume-filled room and throw open all the windows. At first, they used to open my door too, but since their desk was just outside and they nearly choked on the fumes, they eventually compromised with the window wide open and a tray of air fresheners dotted about the room.

One odd thing about being in that hospital was the speed with which one got used to hearing Big Ben. It was only just across the Thames and, of course, it strikes up every quarter of an hour. However, within a day it ceased to worry me.

By the time I left St Thomas's, I had things well organised. I

74

even found a way to keep the staff out of my room when I was busy with a party, or something. There was a small rectangular peephole in the door through which anyone could look in. So I got someone to make me a square pasteboard to fit in it.

On one side, it had written 'Go Away', and on the other it carried a marvellous picture of a half-closed, bloodshot eye, which became the universal sign to all the hospital staff that there was drinking in progress.

In all seriousness, I must say I take my hat off to the surgeon and the people in St Thomas's, not only for putting up with me, but for getting me on my feet so quickly.

It was just one day short of five weeks after the Monaco accident that I was back in the driving seat, practising for the Belgian Grand Prix at Spa.

8

I am lucky, I think, in as much as I never seem to suffer any twitches at getting back into a racing car after an accident. Monaco was the first really bad shunt I had had, but the idea of driving again at high speed did not worry me — only excited me. Anyway, as it turned out, my first drive after Monaco did not last very long, for at Spa the car did not behave itself at all and after a couple of laps, the engine blew up. Even in practice the engine had not been going very well, but I was disappointed to find that the only comment the Press could make on my return to racing was that I was still suffering from the aftermath of the accident.

After this, we all nipped off to Austria for the first Formula One race ever held at Zeltweg, and that was tremendous fun. They had a terrible circuit, but everyone was so friendly and the organisers so helpful that it was all worthwhile. I won the race, too. Actually, I surprised myself by winning because in practice I was making poor time.

The most memorable thing about that meeting, for me, was the curious situation I got myself into the day before the race.

I went deer-stalking.

I enjoy hunting, shooting and fishing. These are, I suppose my main recreations, hobbies, call them what you will. They appeal to me largely, I think, because of the sporting element in them — the man against the beast — and I have little time for people who decry these sports. They are sports. The deer I hunt, the fish I try to catch all have a sporting chance of leaving me empty-handed at the end of the day, and they have done that often enough.

When I am able to, I spend a lot of time in the real Highlands of Scotland, the parts of that lovely country, my homeland, which have not yet been twisted and changed by the all-engulfing tide of tourism.

76

Given the opportunity, I will indulge in the sport whenever and wherever I can. But this enthusiasm can lead one into some pretty odd situations, such as I found myself in Austria.

I had enquired at my hotel about the chance of going deer hunting, after noticing a magnificent set of antlers on the bar wall. The proprietor was immediately interested and the following day came back to me and said that he had fixed something up. In fact, he had contacted one of the local farmers and arranged for me to go out with him on a deer shoot. It was afternoon by the time I arrived at the farm, way up in the mountains. They lent me a gun and set up a target for me to practise on and seemed quite pleased, if not surprised, when I managed to hit it fairly convincingly.

After this, I was obviously intended to set off further up the mountains with one of the farmer's sons, and I must say I was looking forward to the whole thing tremendously. I was a little puzzled when the woman of the house kept shouting something about a 'mantel' and made it clear to me that I would be 'kalt' with the clothes I had on. After all, it seemed to me to be a tolerably warm afternoon. However, much though I protested, she produced the most massive overcoat I have ever seen and forced me to put it on. It was the most hideous bottle-green thing which reached to my ankles and flapped around my legs in the most cumbersome way.

However, I am a great believer in humouring the natives and abiding by their customs, so I kept it on and trudged up the hill in the wake of my guide. We could not say much, since he had no English and I had barely a word of German, so I simply followed where I was led and did as I was told in sign language.

Eventually, we came to a sort of clearing and before I could question my guide, he began climbing up a tree. There was nothing for it but to climb up with him, baffled as I was, and I found myself sharing a small platform about twice the size of an ordinary kitchen table.

Then this chap simply pulled his overcoat around him and settled down to sleep! It was all more than a little un-nerving, for this was certainly not the way I stalked deer. Furthermore, it became impossible to question the fellow since not only could I not converse, but he quickly fell into a deep sleep.

It must have been an hour and ten cigarettes later before anything happened at all in that silent forest. I then spotted a stag on the crest of an outcrop about a mile away. Excitedly, I nudged my companion, thinking we would nip down the tree and start stalking the thing. When he awoke, I made signs that we ought to make tracks. The reaction was nil. The fellow simply shrugged, grunted and pulled this coat around him again and fell asleep. To me, this was madness, for now the stag had come within rifle range and I was aching to have a shot at it.

So I did. When the stag meandered a little nearer, I raised my gun, touched the trigger and shot the animal through the heart. I knew I had hit it and was highly delighted with myself. The shot, of course, woke my guide with a tremendous start and the first thing he saw was the stag careering down the hill. Now, this nearly always happens with a heart-shot. After being hit, the animal's nervous system causes it to run for about fifty yards, after which it will drop dead. The Austrian fellow thought I 'had missed and began waving his arms and jumping up and down, but I persuaded him to come with me and take a look. Sure enough, we found the stag, suite dead, lying under a tree farther down the hill.

Now it was his turn to get excited and I gathered that the stag would provide enough meat for the local community for a week, hence I was treated like a hero, when I got back to the farmhouse.

It was dark by the time we got to the farm and the inside of the house was incredibly gloomy — so much so that I tripped over the chickens in the kitchen and bumped into the odd cow before I had gone more than a few steps. The stench in that house was indescribable and it was not surprising since the farm animals seemed to share the place with the family.

Anyhow, we sat down, wine was produced and I drank innumerable toasts to goodness knows what — and then we ate.

They produced some black bread and a plateful of the most hideous-looking mixture to spread on it. It looked like grey lard with white lumps in it — quite the most horrible stuff imaginable. Not wishing to offend, however, I tore off a great crust of bread, smothered it with the stuff and ate it with what must have appeared great gusto and enjoyment, for they quickly produced more for my pleasure.

I can't tell you how awful it tasted. It really was the most ghastly mixture and it was absolutely excruciating to eat. I was on the point of wishing that I had not shot the ruddy stag at all. Eventually I discovered the reason why we had climbed the tree and settled there. Apparently, the plan had been to perch there until dawn next morning, when the deer usually came to the clearing. No wonder the old lady had insisted on my borrowing the overcoat!

All in all, I regard that stag as being one of my most fortunate kills.

Had it not chanced along at that moment, I would have had to spend the pre-race night up a tree and what's more I would very likely have had to eat that ghastly meal for breakfast. But

78

in spite of the 'stuff', I enjoyed the warm hospitality of these humble, but happy people.

Further success — and considerable trouble — came to me at the next meeting, in Solitude, Germany. As its name implies, Solitude is indeed a beautiful place to race motor-cars. It is just outside Stuttgart and is like a miniature Nurburgring, with fast and slow corners, lots of ups and downs and all amid the loveliest wooded countryside.

It is also very near the Porsche works and it was not surprising to find that for the Solitude Grand Prix, Porsche had determined to win and three hundred thousand Germans turned up to see Porsche wipe the floor with everyone. The team turned out in full force with four cars driven by Jo Bonnier, Dan Gurney, Hans Hermann and Edgar Barth. They made most of the quick times in practice and they were confident of victory. I remember there was a race official in charge of the flagpole on the winning post rostrum whose job it was to hoist the national flag of the lap leader each lap. And I think he only bothered to get the German flag out of the locker on the day of the race.

Anyway, when the flag went down a great pack of us shot away from the grid. There was myself in my Lotus, Bruce McLaren in a Cooper, Jack Brabham, Bonnier, Gurney, Hermann — all trying very hard indeed.

As it happened I nosed into the lead and stayed there until the 19th lap — and I had time to notice that the gentleman on the flagpole did manage to find a Union Jack — then Jack Brabham squeezed past me. However, I returned the compliment and the Porsche pack followed suit.

At the end of the 24th lap, Bonnier, going absolutely balls to the wall, got in front of me — by this time there was only one lap to go — to the huge delight of the German crowd.

Up went the German flag at last, firmly knotted into position by our friend.

No doubt everyone present was satisfied Jo had run a crafty race — which he had — and, having taken the lead on the last lap, would be sure to take the flag. I was damned if I shared that view. So I hung on to Bonnier as closely as I could all the way round the last lap until we came to the straight at the back end of the circuit. Then, suddenly, Bonnier backed off a little and I found myself right up his tail end.

Now, the last section of the Solitude circuit is a series of about 18 's' bends and equally-matched cars cannot possibly overtake each other. At the end of the straight leading into the esses there is a very sharp right-hand corner, followed by a hairpin to the left and a short run down to another hairpin which is the start

79

of the esses. So whichever car got to the end of the straight first would almost certainly cross the finishing line first, since further overtaking was nearly impossible.

I knew full well that Bonnier's Porsche had the legs on me on the straight, and it occurred to me that Bonnier might want me to get ahead of him at the start of the straight, so that he could coast along in my slipstream until we got to the braking area when he could pull out and pass me for the last time.
But I stayed put, although I did make a show of passing him
— without any intention of doing so. We went on like this down the vital straight section. Now, I knew I could out-brake the Porsche — or at least, I thought I could, since braking had always been my strong point — so when we got to the end of the straight and into the braking area, I went to pass him on the right. However he moved over too, so far, in fact, that I finished up with all four wheels on the grass.

But I was in a pretty determined frame of mind — I was going to go past and that was it. I kept my foot hard in it until I Saw Bonnier braking. Then I had to pull the Lotus off the grass and start my own braking. I was never quite sure how I got it slowed down. I had everything locked up, crossed up and going sideways, but I made my point and I got in front of him. I stayed there all the way along the esses and I crossed the finishing line one tenth of a second ahead of him.

And Gurney was only three tenths behind me, so it was pretty tight at the end.

It had been a tremendous scrap, and the pace at which this last-lap dogfight had been carried on made Colin Chapman wince.

Apparently, as I went haring past the pits with Bonnier in front of me and Gurney up my exhaust pipe, he turned to the mechanics and said: 'Well, either we shall win this race or we shall never see Ireland again.

At the end of the race, of course, we all had to stagger up on to this rostrum thing, Dan, Jo, and myself, and Jo's face was absolutely as black as thunder. I knew jolly well what had caused it, As we had both dashed for the finishing line, Bonnier had pulled out behind me in a last desperate show of trying to get past me. I knew he didn't have a hope, but just to pay him back for our antics on the straight, I pulled over with him. Nothing serious, since he still had three-quarters of the road to play with. It evidently upset him, however, for he looked very glum indeed on the rostrum. Still, I felt the score was even after I had had all four wheels on the grass.

The funniest thing of all about the end of the race concerned our little friend in charge of the flags. He had been so sure of a

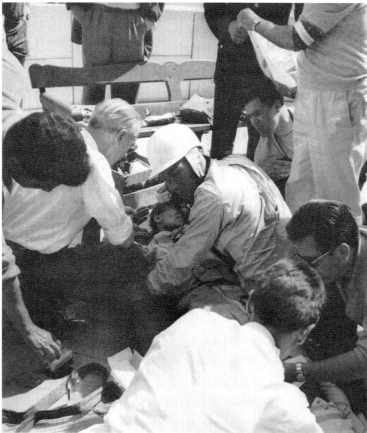

(Photo: *Phillipe Dreux*)

'It's all right Innes, ypu haven't lost anything vital,' says Stirling Moss after my 1961 Monaco crash.

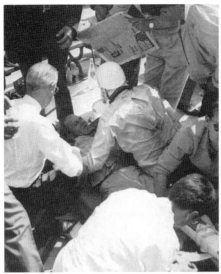

'Somebody's standing on my corns!' Making the most of a bad job at Monaco 1961.

(Photo: *Phillipe Dreux*)

(Photo: *Rene Maestri*)

What remained of the car after the crash.

'There are times when I just want to cry.' Dutch Grand Prix, Zandvoort 1962.

And Tony Robinson, my chief mechanics, wipes away a tear as he surveys the remains.

(Photo: *Flashpress-Informations, Paris*)

'I didn't quite know which way up this one went,' said William Luscombe, Editor of Pelham. Innes Ireland's steering failed during a practice run at Watkins Glen, New York, and he finished up slightly off course.

(Photo: *Associated Press*)

Porsche win when Bonnier roared past on the last lap, that he tied the German flag to the pole with a flourish and a very firm knot, apparently, and was quite unprepared for a British win. Consequently, and much to everyone else's embarrassments he couldn't get the German flag down.

In the circumstances it is significant that the first person to congratulate me was Huschke von Hanstein, the Porsche team manager.

Of course, I felt on top of the world. It had been a marvellous race and I felt particularly pleased with myself at having beaten Porsche on their own doorstep. So, for me anyway, the prize-giving dinner that night was tremendous fun. Much wine flowed, as they say, and I really was feeling rather good.

Then came the series of incidents, the mis-reporting of which echoed round the world, had me initially banned from the forth-coming German Grand Prix at Nurburgring and took a lot of explaining with the Royal Automobile Club.

The story was that I had got roaring drunk in a local hotel and ended up on the roof emptying a loaded pistol into the air and calling on the inhabitants of the town to surrender!
I have no doubt that would have been a marvellous story to dine out on, but it was well wide of the truth. This is actually what happened.

After the prize-giving, a friend and I decided to go back to the hotel where I was staying — I shan't name it because I wouldn't care to give the particular hostelry any more publicity. On the way, my companion, who was quite nicely affected by the spirit of the occasion, kept tossing thunderflashes out of the window of the Mercedes we were using. They made a tremendous noise, of course, and together with the fairly high speed at which we were travelling it must have sounded like something from Chicago in the '20's.

However, we arrived at the hotel without incident even if in fairly merry condition. When we went into the bar downstairs, there was a crowd of journalists there, together with a lot of the mechanics. So I bought a round of drinks, as befits a winner, and then I offered to buy another round. But the manager said the bar was closed. It wasn't late — about half past eleven, I think — and very good-humouredly I said he must have been joking and by this time, I was helping myself to a round of beers. I put the money on the counter, of course, but the manager grew very heated and was jumping up and down all the time we were seeing off that round.

Well, it was very pleasant company and not unnaturally, we wanted a few more beers. At this, the manager started calling for the police and I told him not to be so damned silly. However, he absolutely refused to bring out any more beer, so that was the end of that.

My friend and I then decided to go up to our rooms. I happened to have a bottle of wine in my coat and I suggested we go up for a drink and a flatter.

Now this hotel was not completely built. The two top floors, I think, were just Concrete structures without windows or proper floors and so on — but the lift did operate right to the top. So, when we got into the lift and I rather haphazardly pressed all the buttons, the thing shot to the top and we found ourselves in this bare concrete corridor.

Probably it was out of sheer desperation, but we began drinking the wine from my bottle since the lift had vanished anyway.

But sure enough, the manager appeared again, shouting Politzei, politzei and I was so bored with the whole business and this man — and since I dislike anyone who shouts 'Police' at me — that I grabbed him by the lapels and lifted him up the last two steps and pinned him against the wall. I took the chap's glasses off, I remember, and handed them to my friend and made it clear to the manager that if he didn't stop shouting for the police, I'd give him a thick ear — which may have been a mistake.

Let's face it, I was a tiny bit plastered, but I never hit the man other than picking him up by the lapels. In fact, I put him down, thinking it was time to call a truce, and tried to be friendly with him. I pointed out that we were simply having a good time, we were not breaking up his hotel, and would he join us in a drink. However, he slapped the drink from my hand, and I lost patience with him.

After this, it seemed to us that going to bed at this ridiculous time was out of the question and since the hotel bar was very firmly shut, we decided to go for a walk. Once more, my companion began throwing these little thunderflashes around and they were making the most monumental explosions in the relatively quiet streets.

Finally, we gave up and returned to the hotel and went to bed. That was all there was to it,

Unfortunately, some reporter or other from the German press thought up this sensational story.

When I read this extraordinary tale about firing pistol shots, hitting the manager, bursting open the hotel bar and all the rest of it, it rather made me wish I had done all these things, since I was getting the blame for them all anyway.

Of course, it made a great noise in the Press and on television and so much notice was taken of it — without hearing my side, naturally — that the organisers of the German Grand Prix which

82

was being run a fortnight later at Nurburgring said they were not prepared to let me compete. The RAC Competitions department, the people who licence me to race, also began to ask a lot of questions about my conduct.

Actually, I didn't hear about this story until some four or five days after the event. The first I heard came from my father who telephoned me in Wales and started giving me the biggest rocket of my life. However, I did manage to put people a little straight about the whole thing after meeting with Dean Delamont, the RAC Competitions manager, and holding a press conference about it all.

It was all a bit unfortunate, really, that this had been the second drama that had happened to me after the Solitude race. The previous year, Jim Clark and I had come close to being arrested in Stuttgart.

We had been to a nightclub in a whole bunch the night after the race. Colin Chapman had left the club to take somebody home and arranged to meet Clark and me at six o'clock in the morning to go back to our hotel.

As it happened, things went on a bit late at the club and it was some time around five when Clark and I left. We decided that since we had time to kill, we would go for a walk. It was a pleasant morning and we discovered there was a park at the bottom of the street and we strolled in there. Both of us, though, were pretty tired by this time and we sat on a park bench — or rather Jimmy sat, I laid flat out.

We had only been there about five minutes when a police car came up. Clark nudged me and said it looked as if trouble was coming our way, but i[couldn't think they were looking for us, since we had been behaving ourselves that night. However, they stopped in the road very near us with their big blue light flashing on top of the Mercedes and two policemen walked over to us and began saying something in German which sounded rather rude to me.

Having a perfectly clear conscience, I thought I might as well ignore them and I kept my eyes firmly closed and continued my slumbers. But it became impossible because the two policemen were growing very agitated indeed and started shouting at both Clark and me. When I opened my eyes again, I found them making sign language which obviously meant I should stand up. However, I was still rather tired and I stayed — and the next moment I was being yanked to my feet by one of the obviously very angry gendarmes. I grew very angry indeed at this and joined in the slanging match which was being carried on at the tops of our voices.

Finally, as always, they resorted to wanting to see our papers and we agreed to show them our passports and so on providing they would take us back to our hotel in the police car. However, as we walked nearer their car and they kept trying to hustle me forward into it, I began to wonder if they understood where I wanted to be taken.

I was quite relieved when Colin Chapman turned up at that moment in his car and, by dint of some loud shouting, made it clear that Clark and I were decent citizens and would cause no trouble if they would release us. Oddly enough, the policemen assented, and we shot off in Chapman's hired Volkswagen. Apparently, he had been looking for us for some little time and had eventually seen the little crowd gathered round a police car watching two men resisting arrest, and concluded it must be us!

Now, Chapman tends to worry about things like this, and it became clear that he was quite a bit worried when the police car started to follow us. He began to accelerate and we travelled at a fair rate of knots, screaming round corners and weaving down the highway until, inevitably, the police car stopped us again.

It transpired that in the course of two-and-a-half miles, Chapman had broken one or two traffic regulations, ranging from going the wrong way down one-way streets, speeding and jumping traffic lights, to going round roundabouts the wrong way and goodness knows what else.

Considering we spent the whole journey making signs at the policemen, the fact that we got away with it was really quite remarkable.

After the hotel affair had been sorted out, I was eventually given permission to drive at Nurburgring in the German Grand Prix a fortnight later.

Nurburgring is one of those circuits which is hardly worth my visiting. In the whole of my career, I don't think I have completed more than a couple of dozen laps at the most. In 1961, when I went, I had never actually raced there at all, and I had to work hard at learning it because it is a very, very exacting course.

On the grid, I had a fairly good position and from the start of the race I was keeping station at about sixth or seventh — reasonably within range of the leading bunch. The lap is very long at Nurburgring — going quickly, it takes something like 8 mins 50 secs to get round — so I must have been racing for about fifteen minutes when, quite suddenly I found myself on fire.

I was doing about 100 m.p.h. when the whole cockpit burst into flames.

I was literally sitting in the middle of a fire, so I stuck my hand up in the air to indicate to the other cars that I was going to pull

84

off to the side of the road. I spent a very hot and busy few seconds then, trying to switch the engine off, brake, get the car out of gear and steer it to the side of the road and by the time I did so, the cockpit was absolutely roaring with flames. Stopping only long enough to jam the Lotus in gear — I had stopped on a slight gradient and I didn't want the thing to run amok — I got out of it quicker than anyone has ever got out of a car. Boy, did I move!

Of course, I was on fire, too, by this time, but I ran down the road trailing flames, doing my damndest to get away from the car before the petrol tanks went up. The right arm of my overalls was burning merrily by the time I got about ten yards away, but then there was a hell of an explosion as the tanks blew up. Indeed, they went with such force that the trees by the edge of the road also caught fire. As this happened, I threw myself into a ditch, rolled about to put my own personal fire out and then crawled back again.

Before my eyes, as I sat there completely helpless, the car burned to an absolute cinder. It was about four minutes before anyone turned up with a fire extinguisher — and when they did arrive, they were only concerned with putting out the bushes.
It was utterly soul-destroying to have to sit there and watch the car burn itself to a smouldering ruin.

Every now and again, there'd be a bloody great bang and another puff of black smoke as a tyre burst. In the end, there was nothing left of the car at all. The steering wheel disappeared, the body burned to nothing, wheels, tyres, even part of the engine casing simply went up in smoke. The only thing left was the steel tubular framework, steel bolts and that sort of thing. I can't tell you how awful I felt just watching it burn. It was terrible.

Later on, when everything was analysed and sorted out, we figured out what had happened.

Since Nurburgring is such a long race, the petrol tanks had been filled to the very brim, right up to the filler cap which, in those days was inside the cockpit — another of the FIA's brilliant rules! It very often happened that petrol slopped out of the air vent in the filler cap and more often than not, one drove with one's right shoulder soaked in petrol for the first few laps. On top of that, one was sitting in the middle of a damned great petrol tank, for the tanks were situated each side of the cockpit and behind the seat. When petrol began to spill on to my shoulder, I took no notice. But this time, much more came out than usual and it slopped down into the bodywork of the car, which formed the floor of the cockpit. This would probably have been harmless, if it had not been for the fact that the oil pressure gauge pipe had broken, spewing oil out in the engine compartment behind the exhaust manifolds.

So I had been trailing round a nice mixture of explosive gases in the engine compartment until, after about a quarter of an hour, the engine and exhaust manifolds became so hot that they ignited the oil mist. Apparently, the car had been on fire for about a mile before it actually burst into flames around me. Roy Salvadori, I think it was, was behind me and he told me after the event that he had been trying desperately to catch me for the last mile to tell me I was on fire because it seemed to him to be going great guns.

I have worked it out that so long as I was going quickly, the fire was confined to the engine compartment. The moment I braked, however, all the petrol rushed down the front end of the car. Now, only petrol vapour catches fire, so when I came into the Carousel on the circuit and braked, the liquid petrol beneath me was still not alight. But as soon as I pulled away, sending the petrol rushing back to the back end of the car, the vapour left beneath me suddenly exploded, hence I found myself sitting in the fire.

Whatever the causes, that beautiful piece of machinery was destroyed within minutes. To this day, you can see the, patch on the road where the Lotus stood, burning itself out. There was not a thing on that car that was of the slightest use to anyone by the time the flames had finished with it with the help of about 30 gallons of petrol.

While this little drama was going on, Stirling Moss was winning the Grande Epreuve.

It was one of those times when, in an inferior car, he just drove the wheels off everyone else.

It's the Sort of thing, in my opinion, that nobody left in motor racing these days is capable of doing.

As a result of this win, Moss was in a very good position to take the World Championship and I think the thought that he might make it, even against the might of the Ferraris, was in all our minds when we went to Monza for the Italian Grand Prix.

In practice, it was obvious that my car — the third new one of the season — was in pretty good shape. It had a good engine and everything else appeared to work. In fact, I knew that mine must be a better car than the Lotus Which Moss was driving for Rob Walker's equipe. Mine was newer, lighter and had a better shape. Also, Monza is a very different proposition from Nurburgring. In Germany, it was possible for Stirling to win on sheer driving ability alone. At Monza, where they were using the combined road and banked circuit, the emphasis is on sheer speed. After all, anyone can get in a car and put their foot flat on the floor.

86

So, after all the practice was over, I went to Colin Chapman and put a proposition to him,

'Stirling is in a very good position to be World Champion this year,' I said. 'If he can win here, he's going to be in business. Why don't we give Stirling my car? After all, it will all be good for Lotus.'

Colin looked surprised: 'I'll think about it,' he said.

By dinner that night, he had thought about it and he came across to me in the hotel and took me aside.

'Were you serious about letting Stirling have your car?' he asked me. I said I was. So Chapman rushed off to see Rob Walker and Stirling. They accepted right away.

Of course it meant that Moss would have to go out and race with a car he had never actually driven before, but obviously he would get to know it within a lap or two. The following morning, I went with him to look at the car and I gave him my impressions of it, the clutch play, the braking characteristics and so on that he wanted to know about. The only other thing Stirling insisted on was to respray my green Lotus in the Rob Walker colours of Scottish racing blue, which he did in the circuit garage.

We had wonderfully high hopes and in fact during the race Stirling was going frightfully well — when a hub bearing collapsed on him and put him out. In retaliation, almost, the chassis of his car broke under me, making it handle so sloppily that I pulled into the pits and retired.

Actually, I wasn't sorry in a way. For shortly before I pulled out, I had seen the awful mess made by the Ferrari in which poor old Taffy Von Trips died. I was only about 100 yards behind him and Clark when they had this terrible accident and there were bits flying everywhere in a great cloud of smoke. It really was frightful.

Moss's misfortune with my car probably finished his chances of winning the World Championship that year and I really felt terribly sorry that it had let him down.

However, I hadn't heard the last of the affair. And really, this is, I think, a sad commentary on the state of motor racing.
There was a protest from the Esso petrol company, criticising me for lending my car to another driver — a BP driver.

It made me most angry. How unnecessary! If Stirling had won the race, they might have had a bit of a niggle, but in the circumstances, I strongly resented being rapped over the knuckles like that. They could easily have forgotten about it, but I presume it was one of the early indications that motor racing was becoming less and less a sport and more of a business of high finance.

However, the fact that Stirling's car had broken down, although it saddened me, did not particularly surprise me. Even in 1961, Lotuses were not noted for their reliability. It may have been, indeed probably was, that Chapman was too busy with plans for a new car for 1962, in which he aimed to fit the new, long-promised, V-8 Coventry Climax engine. Whatever the reasons; the fact was that the Lotus was still not a completely reliable racing car, although it was vastly improved when compared with those of 1959.

One of the last dramas I had with Team Lotus occurred shortly after this, when we went to the American Grand Prix at Watkins Glen, New York, in early October.

During practice, I was hurtling down the 145 m.p.h. straight bit and was about to enter the fast turn at the end, when one of the steering arms snapped.

I think it is one of the few times when I can honestly claim that it came apart in my hands! Of course, I never made the bend at all. Instead, I just kept straight on and took to the woods. I was pretty lucky to get out of it unharmed apart from the inevitable bruises, but the car was not so lucky. It was fairly well dented and although those heroic mechanics managed to iron out most of the kinks overnight, they were unable to do anything about a big dent in the petrol tank on one side. The result was that when they came to fill the car up on the day of the race, they found they couldn't get as much in as usual and I would be forced to carry a short measure of fuel. I don't know how much the tanks originally held, but I know that they held about two gallons less when dented.

The real contestants for the race were Stirling Moss and Jack Brabham and when we got under way, I was lying about third or fourth behind them in the early stages. But as luck would have it — their bad luck, my good fortune — both Stirling and Jack were forced to retire for some reason and I skipped into the lead.

I was motoring along quite happily without being badly pressed by anybody when, to my absolute horror, I found my fuel pressure gauge was reading less and less and less. At once, I began to back off a bit, so as to conserve my fuel without losing too much ground.

I felt absolutely frantic. Here I was leading quite comfortably and rapidly heading for my first-ever — and Lotuses first-ever — win in a World Championship Grande Epreuve. And I was running out of fuel.

In slowing down slightly, of course, my position became less and less secure. From my pit signals, I could see that Roy Salvadori was catching me by about a second a lap and from my

88

quick calculations I reckoned that I could just about keep ahead of him even at my reduced speeds provided the fuel held out.

My guardian angels were out in full force that day. A few laps from the end, poor old Roy's engine blew up. In his place, though, came Dan Gurney and he began to press me hard in a last all-out effort. By now, my fuel pressure gauge was registering a firm zero. I could only press on and hope and sweat.

The final five laps of the race were absolute misery. I became convinced that on the brink of success I was bound to run Out of fuel. Each lap seemed interminable and the suspense was agonising. All I could do was to pay attention to keeping on the road and to go on muttering prayers. Every time I came past the pits, I could see from the signals that Gurney was closing. Four laps... three.., two.., one.., still the Lotus was going, though Heaven knows where the fuel was coming from.

And then — victory.

I really did feel marvellous at winning that race. I had been lucky, certainly, but I reckoned Team Lotus were overdue for a bit of luck. And now we had won our first Championship Grand Prix.

Everyone in Lotus was beside himself with delight.

After the race, on a wave of enthusiasm and confidence, prospects for the 1962 season looked bright. I knew Chapman had a new car ready, the V-8 — Moss, in fact, had the first one which he used at Watkins Glen — and it seemed to me we could look forward at last to picking up the rewards of months and months of disappointment and perseverance.

How little I realised that the future held not a greater glory — but a rather nasty kick in the teeth.

Sixteen days after winning that race for Team Lotus, I was thrown out on my ear!

9

The end of my association with Team Lotus came suddenly.

I had absolutely no indication before it happened that I was to get the axe. On the contrary, after the Watkins Glen race, the talk was of big, new success in 1962.

I will not pretend that, at the time, being tossed out of Team Lotus — for whom, I think, I gave a great deal — was anything but a very unpleasant shock.

Let's examine the background to my racing career with Team Lotus.

When I signed for Colin Chapman to drive Lotus cars in 1959, I signed on a three-year contract. At the time, I was about ten thousand feet up in the air and riding on Cloud Seven, and I would have signed anything.

The basis on which I signed was this. In the first year, I would receive 25 per cent of the starting money, I think 331/3 per cent of bonus money and 50 per cent of prize money. (Actually, 45 per cent, since one traditionally gives the mechanics five per cent). In the second year, I was to get 331/3 per cent of the starting money and the third year, 50 per cent. So it was rather like serving an apprenticeship. I was perfectly happy with those conditions because, as I have said, the financial side of it was not what was governing my approach to the sport.

In 1959, my first year with Lotus, I was No. 2 to Graham Hill. Then, in 1960 I was, I suppose, promoted by the fact that Graham Hill decided he was not going to drive Lotus cars any longer. In his wisdom he decided it was time for him to get out of Team Lotus, which he did, and this then left me as No. 1.

In fact, I also had an offer to go to BRM with Graham Hill, but I felt that Chapman had tremendous ability and if we all stuck it out, he would make a good car in the end.

Anyway, in 1960, for one reason or another, I found myself No. 1 driver with Lotus and still I was mainly motoring for the fun of it — or the sport of the thing, as it still appeared to me.

I motored on. 1960 was not a particularly good year for me or Lotus, but I did my best with cars which had not yet been fully developed, and I won some five major international races.

And so we came to 1961 and I was again leading the team if only superficially on seniority with Jim Clark as the other driver. It had been made quite clear to me at the beginning of the season that there was to be no No. 1 and No. 2 and we were both equal in the team. That was fine with me. I think only once did I ever pull rank in that way and insist on a particular car.

Quite recently some American author wrote in glowing terms of Clark, and mentioned the time we were in the same team. He said that according to Chapman, although Clark was a faster driver than Ireland this was not entirely obvious since Ireland always had the faster car. Bearing in mind the team statute explained in the last paragraph I rather think the particular author got his facts wrong about the cars, although I think the records will show that in any race where my car was still in a healthy condition, I was in front of Jim.

1961, for British cars and drivers, was not particularly bright, because Ferraris had much more power and had begun to get their chassis working much better. We, however, were still stuck with the four-cylinder, 1½-litre engines which gave much less power than the Ferrari engine. In fact, Ferrari won the world constructor's championship and their leading driver, Phil Hill became World Champion. If one includes the points gained by Taffy von Trips I finished 6th in the Championship table with Clark 7th.

I did as well as any other British driver in a British car, I think, because I won three Formula One races, one in Austria, one in Germany — the Solitude GP — and the third being the only Grande Epreuve I have ever won, the United States Grand Prix at Watkins Glen. The strange thing was that this win was the first Grande Epreuve win Team Lotus ever notched up. Lotus cars had won before — Stirling Moss had won a couple earlier in the year at Monaco and Nurburgring — but in fact for Team Lotus, this was their first big win.

Naturally, I was on top of the world and even at that stage, three-quarters of the way through 1961, I was already talking to Chapman about our plans for 1962.

I did not know it, of course, but Chapman's plans for 1962 did not include me!

The axe fell during the 1961 Motor Show in London. I remember the occasion very clearly. It was October 24— 16 days after the American GP. I had been over to Paris and returned on the Wednesday before the Motor Show closed. I had been wandering about the place, looking at odd cars and things — I do not truly have much interest in going to the Motor Show, but it is the expected thing and you are supposed to go and talk to people about what is happening next year and so forth — and I met there the new competitions manager for Esso, a chap by the name of Geoff Murdoch.

Feeling in rather good spirits, I naturally talked to him and I think I said something like: 'Well, Geoff, what's the form for next year?'

I was a bit surprised to find that he looked very bashful, ill at ease and embarrassed as he said: 'Haven't you spoken to Colin?'

When I said I hadn't, he looked even more embarrassed and suggested I ought to go and have a word with him.

Still not smelling a rat, I trotted off and found Chapman. I told him I had been speaking to Murdoch and that Murdoch had advised me to see him. I then asked him what it was all about.

And Chapman, to my complete surprise, and looking down at his feet, said: 'Oh, I won't be requiring your services next year.'

That was it. That was the end of my association with Team Lotus.

Of course, I was absolutely shattered. I couldn't speak a word. I didn't even go back and speak to Murdoch. I simply left the Motor Show, got in my car and drove home to Wales.

The last time I had anything to do with Team Lotus was a couple of weeks later, when I drove to the Lotus factory in Cheshunt to ask about my travel tickets to South Africa for the Grand Prix there at the end of the year.

I had been told earlier in the season that I would be driving in the race and, in fact, there had been some publicity in the South African newspapers, about who was going to drive so there was no doubt in my mind that I was going.

Once more, however, I got the 'haven't you seen Colin?' bit.

Of course, I had not seen him, but it was quickly explained to me that I would not, in fact, be driving for Lotus in South Africa. To me, this was the final insult to add to the injury.

In all, my three years with Chapman and Lotus taught me a great deal. Not so much about motor racing as about the People in it. When I went in, I was prepared to give everything for the sake of the underdog, as it were — for Lotus was the underdog in those days, struggling to find a good car.

But when I left, I was much more realistic and not a little bitter about the treatment that I felt had been handed to me.

I think, in the circumstances. I can claim to have been quite devoted to the interests of Colin Chapman and Lotus. At that stage of my career, Chapman was being criticised by the Press for the poor state of preparation of his cars. But throughout, I had this 'we'll show 'em' attitude. We were the underdogs, but I was determined to get up and bite now and again. I always tried my best. Maybe my best was not good enough for Chapman — I just don't know.

So my racing year ended a little prematurely on a sour note.

Shortly after the Motor Show incident, I was approached by Ken Gregory, of what was then the United Dominions Trust — British Racing Partnership combine, and he asked how I felt about joining them in 1962. I think at the time I was so dejected by the Chapman affair that I said yes without really thinking about it. The following day, I had a call from BRM, asking if I felt like joining my old team-mate Graham Hill and driving with them.

Obviously, BRM would have been the wiser choice. I mean that in no way disrespectfully to BRP who, I found, were a very efficient, well-run and entirely professional team. But BRM was an established works team and it is obviously better to have the support of a factory like BRM behind you in motor sport. However, I had to tell them that I had verbally agreed to join BRP, and therefore could not accept their kind offer.

In any case, I was not thinking too clearly about the future.

Quite naturally, I think, I was smarting from the treatment I felt I had received at the hands of Team Lotus. When BRP came along with their offer, some of the faith in myself and in motor racing was restored.

Without wishing to sound pompous in any way, I think I was a pretty useful driver and I always felt I could hold my own with anyone — except perhaps Stirling Moss — provided I had as good a car.

It may be that Chapman felt that in his other driver, Jim Clark, he had someone who might be prepared to be more dedicated to motor racing than I was. If only he had said that, well, it would have been perfectly legitimate. Clark is much more dedicated than I am, or than I would be prepared to be.

From an impersonal point of view, Chapman had every right to do what he did.

In my view Lotuses, in the early days were not strong enough to cope with what they had to do. In one race, in Monza in 1959, the mechanics found fourteen major breaks in the chassis. I had breaks in the steering, wheels fell off, wishbones breaking — anything that could happen to a car.

I had the brakes fail four times in one season. Once I had finished up down the bottom of a ravine after a complete brake failure. And after another failure in that same year, also at Monza, I came into the pits for a check and found that the rear brakes had gone completely.

Subsequently, when I was trying hard, the front brakes were getting such a hammering that they caused terrific juddering of the chassis and the car started to handle frightfully badly, going down the straight in a series of weaves. Finally I thought it was time to call a halt. Next time round, I pulled into the pits and discovered that the whole of the front end of the chassis was about to fall off. The wheels juddering up and down so much, with the caning of the front brakes, just broke up the chassis, and the front end could have fallen off at any stage.

As I have said before, when I was driving in the same team as Jim Clark — who has since become a World Champion — I was usually ahead of him provided both our cars were running well. That had nothing to do with preference in cars or anything like that. So it could not have been on my driving ability that I was thrown out of the team. It may have been on the strength of future promise, but I should think that it was all governed by the fact that Chapman summed up the attitudes of Clark and myself, and decided that Clark was more likely to share his views on motor racing and take it all much more seriously than I.

However, by the start of 1962, I had signed to drive for BRP. Everything looked pretty rosy at the time. For one thing the BRP team was efficient, well-managed, well turned out and thoroughly professional in every way.

We had been promised the very latest Lotus cars in time for the start of the season.

Chapman had made this promise in writing to BRP and assured us that we would get the best possible service and consideration from him. In fact, our cars were to be basically the same as those raced by Team Lotus.

I did have the occasional success, but during 1962, we were plagued with gearbox troubles and so on, and successes were few. In addition, my temper was not improved when I went to the Belgian Grand Prix at Spa that year and I found my BRP Lotus did not handle at all well. During the race, I found that on the straight, the car started weaving about and it got worse and worse until I was forced to make a pit stop. I knew there

94

was something wrong with the car, but couldn't pinpoint it. The mechanics had a quick look round, pulled at the wheels and so on and said they could find nothing wrong, so off I went again.

Yet very soon, the weaving about got worse still. Going through the Kink, down the very fast straight section of the track, I very nearly lost it and hit the house which stands on the right-hand side. This really put me off, and I thought there really must be something seriously amiss with the car, so I cruised round to the pits and stopped again. I told the chief mechanic Tony Robinson that even if he couldn't find anything wrong with the car, I knew damned well there was something very wrong and I wouldn't drive it another yard. So they had a closer look round and found that the inside wishbone pick-up on both sides had cracked three-quarters of the way round. If I had kept racing, I could — and very likely would — have found myself doing 140 m.p.h. with the rear suspension falling off. It was so bad, in fact, that nothing could be done about it on the spot and the car was wheeled away, put in the transporter and driven back to London.

When the transporter was opened up back at the works in London the following day, the mechanics found the rear end of the car lying flat on the floor. The bottom wishbone had fallen off under the swaying of the ride back to England.

I reckon that if I had motored another half a lap with that particular Lotus, I would have found myself in a very nasty situation indeed.

And this was largely the type of situation we found ourselves in, at BRP, throughout 1962.

However, it was not all gloom. Joining BRP meant, for one thing, that I was driving with Stirling Moss, at least in non-championship events, and I could see that this would do me no harm at all. Moss did not, in fact, take a terribly active part in the BRP affairs except that he was a director of the company and continued to drive for Rob Walker in Formula One championship events. However, in most other races, I was to be No. 2 to him and in GT races and that sort of thing, his co-driver.

I had not long been a BRP driver when I found I was to go to America to drive with Stirling in races at Daytona and Sebring.

It proved to be the introduction to a way of life which only American cattle and oil millionaires can afford.

Ken Gregory and I flew out ahead of Stirling, via New York and Miami, where Gregory had arranged for us to be picked up and flown to Daytona. The man who was to meet us was a character named Don Miles whom I had never previously met.

At Miami airport, there was no sign of anyone meeting us, so Gregory went off to telephone leaving me standing looking hopeful by the enquiry desk. A few minutes later, a huge, fellow came bounding over and greeted me enthusiastically.

'Say, you must be Innes Ireland,' he roared, squashing my right hand in a tremendous handshake. I agreed, and he introduced himself. This was Don Miles, former Brooklyn Dodgers baseball player, now the extremely wealthy son-in-law of a Texas cattle and oil millionaire — but it was hard to believe it at first, for he was dressed in a shirt with the top buttons undone, a pair of jeans and sneakers, the last man one would expect to own an expensive private aeroplane. I was to learn that everything about Don Miles was very expensive but entirely casual.

It was typical of him that he never had any money with him. I remember that later in the year, I was flying with him from Texas to New York for the Grand Prix at Watkins Glen and we were delayed by bad weather at Nashville, Tennessee. Miles, as always, did not have a cent on him, so he walked into the airport bank and asked the teller for some money.

'I don't have a cheque book,' Miles drawled, 'but I guess you can fix that.'

'Er... yes,' said the teller, eyeing Miles none to happily. 'How much did you require?'

'Oh, a thousand bucks will do.'

The teller coughed and then, in the way of suspicious bank clerks the world over, slipped away and went to see the manager. When the manager returned and asked Miles for some form of identity, Miles had none to produce, but he gave the manager the name of a vice-president of a bank in Victoria, Texas and asked him to telephone there.

Within a few minutes, the manager was back. This time he was all smiles. Apparently the bank official in Texas had assured the Nashville man that Miles was 22-carat, and had said: 'If he wants to buy the airport — sell it to him!'

However, on this first meeting, we flew in Miles' fabulous twin-engine aeroplane to Daytona where we were met by a fleet of four massive Cadillacs. He gave me a beautiful white drop-head to drive and insisted I kept it all the time I was at the meeting.

In the Daytona race itself, I was driving a Berlinetta Ferrari, a most marvellous motor-car which handled like an absolute dream. Stirling drove another, newer Ferrari. However, I had not been going long in the race itself when, in taking a fairly quick corner, something happened in the back of the car and there was the most alarming bang, clatter, crunch, graunch, and I left the

96

(Photo: *Patrick Benjafield*)

Above: The B.R.P. GTO Ferrari at Goodwood the year the author won the Tourist Trophy - 1962.

Below: 'I'm glad Fangio got the least attractive one,' says the author. With the B.M.C in America 1962.

(Photo: *B.M.C.*)

'Please may I have another drink?' Tourist Trophy, Goodwood
1962, with B.R.P. Ferrari.

road sideways, finishing up a few feet short of dropping into a pedestrian tunnel. When I got out. I found that one of the rear wheels was a complete shambles with all the spokes chewed out. What had happened was that the brake disc had broken and a lump of it had flown off and wrecked the wheel. End of the race for Ireland. It was a bit depressing — even if I had the best car in the world it seemed, something had to fall off.

I remember there was one amusing thing happened on the night before the race. I had turned in early, for a change —I think I was trying to impress Gregory on my first trip abroad with BRP! — and, quite unexpectedly, a cousin of mine from Edinburgh now living in the States, turned up to see me.

Cousin Edith was an attractive girl who married an American working at the space base in Cape Canaveral — now Cape Kennedy — and she had read somewhere that I was racing at Daytona so she came over to look me up. By the time she arrived, I was, as I say, in bed. She apparently asked at the reception desk for me and was directed into the bar where Ken Gregory and some of the mechanics and people had congregated.

She went across to Ken and asked: 'Is Innes around? I'd like to see him.'

Ken took one look at this attractive creature and obviously leapt to the wrong conclusion. 'I'm afraid you can't see him,' he said. 'He's asleep and anyway, he's racing tomorrow. I can't let you see him tonight.'

'Oh, but I'm his cousin,' said Edith.

'Yes...' replied Gregory doubtfully. 'But he needs the sleep. You'll have to wait until tomorrow.'

The net result was that poor Edith had to check in at the hotel and wait until breakfast to say hello to her long-lost relation. Just beforehand, though, Gregory told me that a pretty girl had turned up the night before looking for me and I had all sorts of fits until I found it was Edith!

The night after the race, Don Miles and I, with a bunch of others, had a tremendous thrash. Actually, during the course of it, I agreed to buy his second aeroplane, a beautiful single-engined Beech Bonanza which he had been letting me fly.

He had been contemplating buying a superb Beech Baron which he had on trial, and some time during the middle of the night's proceedings, he came to a decision. And since I had fallen in love with the Bonanza, I made a decision too.

'Hell,' roared Don. 'I'll buy the Baron.'

'Hell, I'll buy the Bonanza from you,' I cried — and we had another drink to settle the deal. We were both a little in our cups by this time and he quoted a price to me which I knew to

97

be extremely reasonable. Although in the cold light of the following morning I offered to let him retract it, he stuck to the figure. That, I thought, was the attitude of a gentleman.

Anyway, this was quite a thrash. I seem to remember dancing about on top of the bar at this hotel and generally getting quite out of hand. About the last thing I recall was tottering up to some fairly attractive girl, with my trousers neatly folded over my arm, asking her if she would care to dance. I don't think she did care to dance, actually...

By about 4.30 in the morning, Don's personal pilot, a splendid fellow named Slim Fury decided that he had had enough and staggered off up to bed. An hour later, Don had the wild idea of sending Slim up something to eat, so he ordered a full scale dinner with hors d'oeuvres and an enormous great T-bone steak and he had it sent up to Slim's room. As he told us next day, Slim was furious at being woken up, but was also determined not to waste the food, so he ate the lot and then went back to sleep.

All in all, we made a lot of noise and probably did get quite out of hand. After such things, I always feel quite contrite and wake up the next day with the feeling that I shall have to pay for something — either in cash or with a sore head. However, although I felt a little weak, I was surprised at the attitude of the bar manager.

'Who was that guy who was dancing on the bar?' he asked Miles 'Do you think he'll take a job with us? He's the best entertainment we've had here in years.' And, according to Don, the fellow was quite sincere. So, far from being presented with a breakages bill, I was offered employment. However, I don't think I could have stood the pace!

One thing I had noticed during this early friendship with Miles was that every evening, he used to excuse himself and go off to telephone someone he referred to as 'The Chief'. The day after the race, when Ken Gregory and I were thinking of moving on, Don said that 'The Chief' would like to meet us. He, apparently, was staying in New Orleans and if I cared to fly the Bonanza down there, Don would bring Ken and Stirling down in his plane. This was too big a carrot for me to refuse. Flying the plane I was about to buy was too much to resist — so off we went to New Orleans.

There, I met Tom O'Connor Jnr. Cattle rancher, oilman, millionaire and one of 'nature's real gentlemen'. He was, in fact, Don Miles's father-in-law.

We got on like a house on fire right from the very start.

Actually, I don't think I looked too impressive when I first met

98

him. I knocked on the door of his very elegant hotel room wearing slacks, sweater, and, I think, 1 had my deerstalker on, but he took it all very well and we hit it off from the word go. Tom had a great interest in motor racing since he owned the Rosebud Racing team for whom I later drove in several races in North America.

Eventually Don turned up with Ken and Stirling and that night we went out on the town in a big way. During the evening Stirling danced with one of Tom's daughters and she was fabulous at the Twist. Stirling is a pretty good dancer, I think, but she had the heels off him that evening and pretty soon after that, when we got back to London, I remember seeing in the papers that Stirling Moss was taking Twist lessons! Nothing if not thorough, was Stirling. During the course of that evening, too, we very nearly got thrown out of the New Orleans Playboy Club.

I just got fascinated by the tail of one of the Bunny hostesses and quickly learned that it is one of the golden rules in these places that you never, ever touch a Bunny, and they have a squad of very large bouncers to enforce it.

Being with Tom O'Connor meant 'travelling first-class', to coin a phrase. When we went out to his ranch in Victoria, Texas, for example, we all piled into Cadillacs and drove to the airport, but instead of going to the ticket office as I had expected, we drove straight on to the tarmac and stopped beside a huge orange and white Convair airliner. Tom's personal transport! Inside, it was like a luxury fiat on wings with a galley, bedroom, bathroom and lounge all beautifully and tastefully furnished.

Of course, he had his own crew for the Convair, plus pilots for his helicopters which we and his guests used as casually as bicycles to supervise or visit the far corners of his 300,000-acre ranch. When we got to Victoria we were met by a fleet of Lincoln Continentals and driven to his home. Which was the last word in quiet, luxurious comfort. As a friend once said to him. 'You ain't exactly camping here, Tom.'

I was quite overwhelmed, in a way, at the casual manner of this millionaire life. I remember Gregory and I dined with Tom the night before we were due to fly back to England — a flight which involved going from Victoria to Houston, catching a plane from there to New York and thence to London. During dinner, Tom just picked up the phone and called his crew captain at Victoria airport and arranged to have the Convair fly us to Houston. It must have cost as much to warm up that aeroplane and get it to the holding position at the end of the runway as it did for us to fly the rest of the way to London!

Not surprisingly, I found that I had a taste for this kind of life, and I was to be Tom O'Connor's guest on many occasions there-after.

A month or so later, Stirling and I were due to drive in the Sebring 12-hour race with a Testa Rossa Ferrari entered by the North American Racing Team.

That race proved to be a drama all on its own, and ended in a headline-hitting hoo-hah between the race authorities and us over their interpretation of the rules.

Practising for the race, everything was fine and I found I had put up times within a second or two of Stirling's. That, for me, was highly satisfying. It was a marvellous car. You could throw it into corners, put opposite lock on and it would react perfectly; what's more, it sounded like a car; the engine made a sound like tearing calico, like a real beefy engine ought to sound. Also, the engine was in the front, where I firmly believe engines ought to be, if one wants to have sheer fun out of driving.

For some reason which I have never fathomed, Stirling elected me to start the race. It was a Le Mans-type start, and Moss is famed for his quick getaways in those circumstances, but anyway, he handed the start to me. I made a good start and did not hit anybody as I got away and in the first half-lap I passed the rest of the field with the exception of an American chap called George Constantine, a delightful character and a great one for having a go in a race. He was driving another but larger Ferrari. I slipstreamed him down the straight and pulled, out to pass him going into the braking area, but I could see that he was just going to press on until I put the brakes on. So I put them on a little early, and when I did so, he followed suit. Just as he slowed, I accelerated like mad past him until I was right in the corner, when I stood on the brakes and hauled the Ferrari round on its very limit. As I accelerated, George accelerated too but he was in no position to take the corner and the last I saw of him, in my mirror, he was going straight on, through the track markers, rubber cones, straw bales and all, followed by several other cars doing the same thing! We often laughed together about that incident, later.

By the end of the first lap, I was in the lead and held it for some time until I was passed by one of the Rodriguez Brothers. I kept second station until it was time for my pit stop and change of drivers, when Stirling roared off. By the time he next came in to hand over to me he had again recovered the lead. Halfway through my second session, however, the brakes started to fail. I hung on until they became really diabolical and I was unable to stop the car properly, then I made a pit stop. I came tearing into the pits, shouting to the Ferrari mechanics to change the front brake pads.

100

Luigi Cinetti — Ferrari concessionaire in the United States and manager of the North American Racing team quickly got the car jacked up and whipped in new brake pads. While he did so, one of the Italian mechanics opened the petrol filler cap and topped the car up with petrol. As all this was going on, I noticed a pit marshal hanging about, but took no special notice of him.

We had had a bit of a contretemps earlier when I came into the pits for the first driver change. You know, one wants to waste as little time as possible on change-overs and I had come into the pits fairly rapidly, with lights on and horn blowing. I was going quickly, but I certainly wasn't being stupid and there were no dramas. This same marshal had then come rushing up to me shouting: 'I'm going to disqualify you.'

I said: 'What the hell for?'

'Because you came into the pits too fast,' he said.

I told him not to be so bloody silly, adding that I knew a damned sight more about coming into pits than he did and it was up to him and everyone else to keep out of the way. Perhaps this was all unnecessary, but he tackled me just as I got out of the car and in a state of excitement and tension I let fly at him. I possibly made several unfortunate suggestions in the heat of the moment and the whole incident ended with us getting penalised by five minutes.

That was the first drama. Then came the incident where the mechanic put the petrol in. It happened at about two o'clock.

By five-thirty or so in the afternoon, we were well in the lead — in fact, by over a lap, since the Rodriguez car had blown up somewhere. It was around this time that I came into the pits again to hand over to Stirling.

I found everyone in the pits standing about with long faces. I leapt out of the Ferrari, but was puzzled to find Moss making no attempt to get in my place. Then he told me why.

'We've been disqualified,' he said.

I could hardly believe it for a moment, but it was true. The officials had disqualified us because when the mechanic — who, incidentally neither spoke nor understood English — had filled the car with petrol, we had infringed the race rules by taking on fuel earlier than was allowed.

But, as I have said, this incident happened at about two. It was now just after five-thirty.

So we had been driving the car quite unnecessarily for over three hours and this burned up both Moss and myself. I can't tell you how furious I was. My language, I know, was quite unbelievably bad, and I told everyone in sight just what I thought of them and their lousy race.

It was very hard luck that the mechanic put petrol on board during that stop, but he obviously didn't understand the rules and since it was his job to fill the car with fuel, he just did so. The real fault lay with the team manager, who ought to have bad all the rules at his fingertips and seen to it that no fuel was put on at that time — it was, in fact, about six or seven laps before we were officially allowed to refuel. The galling thing was that, at the time, we had masses of fuel in the tank and had no need to take on more.

Anyway, all right, we had committed this breach of the rules and disqualification was to be expected. But one would have expected it to happen within a couple of minutes at the outside, not three and a half hours later!

The organisers allowed Stirling and I to motor on with that car for all that time, during which we could have broken our necks, or anything could have happened. That, I feel, was not only grossly unfair, but damned dangerous. One is left with the impression that the organisers did not want to disqualify Moss, the main attraction of the race, too early and while the customers were still coming in.

There is no question that because of the inefficiency of our pit work, we broke the rules and should have been disqualified. No argument about that at all. It should, however, have happened by 2.15 at the latest, and not three hours later. There is absolutely no justification for allowing a car to run for all that time before acting on an infringement of the regulations.

Anyway, after Sebring, Stirling and I buzzed off to Washington where we were doing some publicity thing with the British Motor Corporation to promote the Mini in America. It was after this that we were interviewed by a large number of pressmen to try and square away this Sebring thing. I suppose, naturally enough, this was not nearly so disastrous to Stirling as it was to me, since Moss had won lots of important races before but I hadn't. I still felt very sore about it, and I was probably a great deal more outspoken than Moss, with the result that there were a great many comments and letters in the American press criticising us for our attitude.

We came back to England shortly after that — to Goodwood where Stirling ended his racing career in a terrible shunt. I don't think I can say anything about that awful accident. Except to say again that it robbed motor racing of its finest exponent. Moss was quite incomparable — certainly the greatest racing driver 1 ever saw in action in any branch of the sport.

102

A fortnight after that, I got back into the European circuit again with the Dutch Grand Prix at Zandvoort.

It was here that Lotus introduced their monocoque car, and Chapman told me that this was not for BRP because it was Lotus's 1963 car— pretty extraordinary, since it was only May, 1962.

Actually, Chapman and I never spoke about my demise with Team Lotus. I still seethed when I thought about it but he was always perfectly affable when I spoke to him. If he ever felt anything about his actions, he never showed it.

However, we soldiered on with the Lotuses we did have and, in fact, until the closing stages of this race, I was lying third. However, in the second half of the Grand Prix, I had been having some trouble with the brakes locking on now and again. And having regard to all the troubles I had known with Lotus cars, I was a little apprehensive. Still, it was my first Grande Epreuve with British Racing Partnership and I badly wanted to keep going. Actually, I did keep going — right through a bloody great fence a couple of laps further on. I was approaching the corner at the end of the pits straight and just touched the brakes and found them locking up the back wheels. I took my foot off the pedal pretty damned quick, but nothing happened and by this time the car was swerving violently. As I tried hard to bring it back under control, I noticed a group of people near the fence further down into the corner and I knew that if I tried to bring the car back to the track, I would, in all probability, collect these people. So I chose the fence.

I took the fence at about 125 miles an hour and climbed up it and over, landing on the other side in a great sand dune. Bits of the car flew in all directions and it came to rest in a great cloud of sand, minus a couple of wheels and in a pretty sad state altogether. Apparently, it was a fairly impressive spectacle. Especially since it was all on television.

I got away with only a couple of cuts and bruises, but it was pretty irritating to have the Lotus still playing its old tricks. Especially as neither Tony Robinson, BRP's chief mechanic, nor the Girling engineers who inspected the car afterwards, could find anything wrong with the brakes. I felt that it might look as if one was making excuses for having wrecked a car. But I assure you, I wasn't.

Monaco was next on the schedule and I went there reflecting on the thought that it would be nice, at last, actually to race there again since I had not got that far the previous year! And this time, I did get on the starting grid. In fact, I even started the race — but I had not gone more than a couple of hundred yards before

103

I found myself sitting on top of a roadside wall, complete with car.

It happened during the mad scramble for the gasworks hairpin immediately after the start. This was the last year they used this starting point, because it always produced a mad shunting match. Never a year went by without somebody getting their front or back end stuffed in, and if you got round the first corner at Monaco you were doing well.

I got away to a pretty good start, but as I approached the corner, I became aware of Willy Mairesse in a Ferrari screeching through on the inside. I saw his rear wheel hit the wall as he took the hairpin. He started a kind of chain reaction and everyone, myself included, had to move left a little before turning right into the corner. Just as I was making this move I felt the most almighty thump up the rear, the car shot round and went careering backwards up on to the wall on the outside of the bend.

I found out later that Ritchie Ginther in a BRM somewhere behind me had a jammed throttle. He had come haring into the bend flat out, collected someone and then had shunted me. In addition, Maurice Trintignant had been badly thumped — so badly in fact, that one of his wheels was torn off and it careered away and hit one of the track marshals, fatally injuring him.

When I found myself sitting in the car on top of the wall, I remember I felt fairly alarmed for some reason and I leaped out in a great hurry. I think it occurred to me that the car might catch fire. Anyway, I was all for getting out of the way. Then, on closer inspection, I discovered that the Lotus was not, in fact, so badly damaged. I managed to heave it off the wall and back on to the road. Starting again, I drove the few hundred yards to the pits for a quick check.

I was later told that this whole crazy incident was on television since one of the cameras had been positioned on the bend.

Back at home, my little daughter Christianne had been watching the race with my wife and when she saw me coming backwards towards the wall, she called out excitely: 'Oh, look Mummy, here comes Daddy!' I imagine she thought I was going to come crashing through the television screen!

Anyway, the mechanics found nothing desperately wrong with the car, so I hopped in and took off. I was well out of the race really, because by the time I got going again. I was lapped by the leader, Graham Hill, and we kept close company for a number of laps. It was, if nothing else, good practice for me because I found -that I was still able to keep up with Graham and I was quite enjoying myself for a while. Then I began to grow aware of a terrible smell of petrol. I could feel it on my legs, nipping my thighs and shins. However, I pressed on regardless until I realised that I was behaving quite oddly.

First, I noticed that I was losing ground to Hill, and then that my braking was getting terribly woolly and my driving quite erratic. The funny thing is that I knew I was driving sloppily and that I wasn't all that safe, but somehow, I wanted to keep going. I suppose it is like driving after a few drinks. The longer I went on, however, the worse I became.

It was the petrol fumes which were making me dizzy. Finally, I stopped at the pits and was violently sick. I got washed down with water, the mechanics again checked the car and found it in good running order, so I hopped in again and carried on.

From then on, the race became a succession of pits stops between periods of asphyxiation and perhaps it was just as well that eventually, the engine began to misfire badly and I had to retire. We then found that the original shunt had popped a rivet in the fuel tank over my legs and the petrol had been dripping out of there fairly consistently.

So far, then, two Grandes Epreuves, two retirements. Not surprising that I looked forward to something slightly more relaxed.

Stirling and I had been engaged to drive a pair of 1,000 cc Fiat-Abarth cars in a race in Italy at Lake Garda, but since Stirling was still in hospital, I went alone to drive for the Abarth team in this three-hour race. It really was quite a lot of fun, since the circuit wound through the town, by the lake, up a mountain and was generally most interesting. What's more, I would almost certainly have won the race — if my command of Italian and French had been better than they were.

The Abarth team was rigorously controlled by Snr. Abarth himself, a big, imposing and rather fierce gentleman who put the fear of God into everyone in the team. He had rules for everything —even down to the exact number of revs you could warm up your car at and for exactly how many minutes and so on. And, of course, he laid down race tactics. As I understood it we were to race as hard as we could until the last couple of laps, when upon a signal from Abarth, we were to hold station in the position we had then attained; That's what I thought.

I led almost from the start, and was certainly in the lead in the closing stages, with another team car, driven by the Italian Scarfiotti, lying a handy second. We had been having a tremendous ding-dong battle the whole time, with him pressing me very hard. Several times, I broke the circuit record, which finally stood to my credit. In these closing stages, I watched out for Abarth's signal to relax and hold station and sure enough, it came as I motored past the pits, on, I believe, the last-but-one lap. Abarth simply

105

came out and stood in the middle of road with both arms high above his head. Actually, I narrowly missed him but I got what I thought was the message. I eased off a little and sat back to enjoy the rest of the ride.

On an uphill section shortly after receiving the pit signal, I went quickly into top gear and cruised gently up the hill at about 80 or 90 miles an hour — when suddenly, Scarfiotti roared by me in a cloud of dust, going like the clappers. At first, I thought he was just fooling about or showing off — but no, he kept going and it was quite apparent that he was going to press on to win. It took me a few seconds to sort myself out. I changed down a gear, put my foot right in it and set about chasing Scarfiotti, for I was damned if I was going to be robbed of a certain win by these tactics.

I drove like a maniac, pressing on harder than ever, even though during the race I had broken the lap record consistently. However, there was one bit of the circuit where one came to a very fast downhill right-hand bend followed by a left-hander.

When I had been feeling really courageous during the race, I had been taking them at about 6,400 revs in top gear which was scratching a bit. 7,000 revs in top on this very speedy little car gave you about 130 miles an hour, so you can imagine it was a fairly fast old corner. On this occasion I tried taking the corner damned nearly flat out and, naturally, the back end would not have it. The car careered down the road, spinning round and round and round so that I didn't have any idea whether I was coming or going. I was missing concrete telegraph poles and walls and all sorts of things. Eventually the car finished up pointing the right way and I managed to collect it at about 60 miles an hour and thrashed on after Scarfiotti. I don't think I lost much time with this manoeuvre, but I sweated blood.

It all proved to be a waste of effort. I did not have much hope of catching the Italian and in fact he won the race with me a furious second. I was hopping mad when the race ended and I had a little moan about Scarfiotti's tactics, but all I got was a shrug of the shoulder. So I shut up.

Actually, everyone else was mighty pleased with the result. I remember the crowd on the last lap giving me a tremendous cheer as I went by and I imagine they thought I had let Scarfiotti go by so that he could win the race on his native soil. If only they had known,..

I have often wondered whether or not this race had any bearing on the rather extraordinary event that happened a couple of weeks later when I got back to England.

I became, I think, the only person to be given a fully-prepared works Ferrari Formula One car to drive while not a member of the Ferrari works team.

This was a total surprise and quite inexplicable. Indeed, I still don't know why it happened since there was no suggestion, as far as I ever knew, of my being put on trial as a possible Ferrari works driver. It happened at the May meeting at Silverstone in 1962. First, I heard that Ferrari were not going to enter a works team, and then I got a call from Enzo Ferrari, asking if I would care to drive a works car for him in the race. Naturally, I was delighted. The next thing I knew, I was on my way to the Modena works in Italy for a 'fitting' of the car in company with Ken Gregory, and Ronnie Hoare, the Ferrari concessionaire in England. We were received quite royally. I was shown the car and climbed in while the Ferrari technicians measured me for a new seat, altered the pedals to exactly the right position, adjusted the steering wheel to suit me, and asked if there was anything else I required. With all the attendance being danced around I felt I ought to suggest something. I had to rack my brains to think of anything but I remember finding something for them to do. It was all most impressive.

Immediately afterwards we lunched with Enzo Ferrari, although I found that lunch with the world's best car-maker was no fabulous affair. No, lunch with him meant eating in a workmen's café across the road from the factory gates — which was something that endeared me to him no end. The only difference between his table and the rest of the workers' was that his had a white table-cloth on it. I thought that was quite something.

Another little courtesy which Ferrari arranged for us was the drive from Milan airport out to Modena and back. Each time we had the same chauffeur. Each time he used a different Two-plus-Two Ferrari — and on both occasions it was absolutely hair-raising. He knew only one way to drive. Flat out all the way. What's more, he kept a cigarette in his mouth throughout the journeys and half-closed his eyes against the smoke as he drove. This, coupled with the fact that he held the steering wheel low down with the fingertips of one hand whilst averaging 120 m.p.h. down the Auto-strada did not enthrall me one bit.

I know I am a terrible passenger in a car! I usually feel scared to death when I'm in the wrong seat, but this time I felt I was justified in being terror-stricken. Still, I suppose one must hand it to the fellow, He did get us there and back in one piece.

Speaking of being a terror-stricken passenger reminds me of the time, some little while later, when I went for a ride with Enzo Ferrari himself in a little baby Ferrari which he was considering putting into production but never did, It was an extremely fast

little machine with something like a 1,500 cc engine. Anyway.
Ferrari decided to take me for a run in it.

We left the factory with a tremendous flourish, no suggestion
here of stopping at the factory gate and taking a quick look up the
main road that runs by — just a blare on the horn for the gateman
to open up as we sped towards him, and out on to the road with
the tyres screeching madly.

The road past the factory winds through endless little cobble-
stoned villages and the speed at which we travelled was quite
alarming. I knew that Enzo Ferrari had been a racing driver once.
What puzzled me was why be didn't still go on racing. I can only
imagine that the local villagers must have got used to Signor Ferrari
screaming sideways round the corners of their streets. Everything
on that drive was at maximum. On the way back, he made no
attempt to stop at the factory gates but went bounding on down
the road with the horns blaring. I noticed that the factory gates
were firmly closed as we fairly rocketed past at about 125 miles
an hour. But we had only passed the factory by a matter of three
hundred yards, when he just stood on the brakes. I mean, he really
leapt on the brake pedal and we came to a grinding, screaming
halt. He looked at me with a great grin on his face and said: 'Hey,
freno bene, Si?' — or whatever the Italian is for 'Aren't these
brakes good?'

It was impossible to answer. My stomach was way out
somewhere on the front of the bonnet. Much as I love Mr Ferrari's
motor cars, I can't say I am too anxious to go for another ride
with him.

In May of 1962, I drove a works Formula One Ferrari for the
first and last time. As I say, I never discovered why I was invited
to do so, except that I was asked to make a report on the machine.
I certainly was not being considered as a works driver.

Whatever the reasons, they certainly did it in style.

They turned up at Silverstone with the car in a works transporter
with a team of mechanics and six technicians, and I must say I felt
wildly important while all this was going on. They had done
everything perfectly. The seat was just right, the pedals were just
right, the steering column was just right — everything was perfect,
except that the car handled like a bowl of soup. We worked for
hours and hours but all the mechanics and all the technicians were
unable to get it to handle properly. It either understeered like mad,
or oversteered like hell, and in the end the best we could get was
an odd combination of both, so that whenever I took a corner the
handling characteristics changed halfway through. However, it was
tremendous fun and in the race itself I managed to finish fourth
which appeared to please everybody.

108

What impressed me more than anything was the feeling of taking a car out to race in the wet — it poured with rain at Silverstone for the first part of that meeting — and feeling safe about it. No other Formula One car I had ever driven felt as sure in the wet as the Ferrari. Somehow, I never felt that it was going to get the better of me. It was always controllable despite the wet condition of the track, and this was a great comfort. I wrote my report and sent it back to Modena and that was the end of the affair.

10

It was at the Reims Grand Prix in France that year that I got myself a little bit sorted out with regard to my attitude to Team Lotus and the people in it. Up until then I must admit I had let some of the bitterness in me spill over on to Trevor Taylor, the man who had replaced me in the Lotus team which went to South Africa at the end of the previous year. Quite ridiculously, I had allowed myself to get my relationship with him completely out of proportion.

I never, of course, went out of my way to be unpleasant to Trevor, but equally I never bothered to be too friendly. I knew for a long time that I was being stupid and that my attitude puzzled him, since beforehand, we had been perfectly friendly. In the end, he gave up being friendly with me. It was absolutely childish of me, I know.

A couple of days before the race, I went out on the town, found myself in a dim and dark little club somewhere, and came across Trevor. He had been having quite a good time and called me over. Before long we began to get things sorted out.

Trevor is extremely blunt and called me all kinds of strange Yorkshire names when he found out what was bugging me. I was in a mood to be honest with myself and once I got that cleared off my chest, it did me a power of good.

We had quite a lot of drinks to celebrate the fact that we had unscrambled the problem. I remember that by the time we left the club, the sun was well up in the sky and we were behaving like two long-lost blood brothers. It was very satisfying to have ironed the whole affair out like that and since then, Trevor and I have been the best of friends again.

If I got my personal affairs sorted out a bit that year, I was less successful in other directions. As far as World Championship

Formula One races went, I was never in the hunt. The whole season, really, was a succession of disasters through broken gearboxes, cracked chassis, wheels coming off and so forth.

In 1962, I think I picked up one championship point.

There were, however, a number of brighter spots. I won practically all the races I entered with the BRP Lotus 19 sports car, and notched up a few lap records. I also won a race or two with the new GTO Ferrari. The biggest disappointment with that car was in the Le Mans 24-hour race. We were leading the GT category when, the electrics packed up in the middle of the night, the lights went out and the plugs ceased to spark. So we had to call it a day.

I also raced for Tom O'Connor's Rosebud racing team in sports car races in America.

I went out to America for my first race under Tom's colours shortly before the American Grand Prix which was again being held at Watkins Glen, New York. It must have been about a week or two before the Grande Epreuve that I went with Rosebud to Mosport Park, near Toronto, to drive their ex-BRP Lotus 19.

I had been to Mosport only once before, earlier in the year, when I drove a rear-engined Ferrari sports car and had had the alarming experience of finding the throttle stuck wide open at one point. This meant I had to motor round the rest of the lap switching the engine off every time I had to change gear or wanted to slow down. I remember this particular meeting well, because immediately afterwards, I flew back to England for the Whit Monday meeting at Crystal Palace, arriving in London only the night before the race. I started from the back of the grid since I had done no official practice and I recall thinking that driving in two races four thousand miles apart in three days was cutting things a bit fine. Anyway, I must have been so dozy after the flight that I won the race.

The first time out with Rosebud, I was determined to do well, for it was obvious that O'Connor intended to spare no expense or trouble to do well with his hobby of running a racing team.

First, he asked me to go to Coventry and get the Coventry-Climax people to build him a brand-new 2½-litre engine — that set him back two thousand pounds for a start.

However, we did not get away to the most brilliant of starts. I had the engine sent from Coventry to Toronto, where Jock Ross, Rosebud's chief mechanic, fitted it into the Lotus. When I arrived, it was all ready and I set off to do a few quiet laps to run the engine in, bed it down properly and so on. My fortune was holding true to form and I was just about working the engine up to 5,000-odd revs after a considerable number of slower laps — when it blew up!

Brand-new and straight from the Climax factory, it threw a con-rod and wrecked just about everything in 'the engine compartment. Still, that's motor racing.' We immediately shipped the engine back to Coventry and fitted an old 2-litre motor into the Lotus for the race.

Mosport is a fairly tweaky old drivers' circuit and even though it was raining, I got going pretty well. I was trying very hard to do well for Rosebud — maybe a bit too hard, though, for after dicing with Pedro Rodriguez and passing him in his big Testa Rossa Ferrari, I came to a reasonably fast bend and lost the Car. I spun round a couple of times, bumped the nose against the banking, then regained control and went whistling on.

I went screaming up the straight, just about getting into fifth gear, when the whole of the front part of the car came off! Everything, from the headlamps to the windscreen inclusive, just flew over my head and went sailing up the banking, leaving me driving a framework.

I had absolutely no warning of what was going to happen. The front part didn't start quivering or anything; it just suddenly got draughty and there was no front on the car. The effect of losing the front was that the doors were left flapping around in the wind with nothing to catch on to, so I had to go screaming into the pits to have them wired shut.

Tom O'Connor, although I didn't know it then, evidently nearly died laughing when I came to rest by the pit counter, because, looking serious, I shouted to Jock Ross: 'The front's come off.' As Tom said, nothing more obvious could be imagined. However, they very quickly tied the doors down and I shot off once more. It was rather an odd sensation, actually, for not only was I getting very wet, but I had the experience of watching my feet at work on the pedals, which was something I had never witnessed before. It was quite fascinating.

Unfortunately, the oil tank was also at the front of the car. This had sprung a leak, with the result that oil kept being ejected from the top of the tank. I was not only wet and cold, but now I began to get sprayed with a film of hot oil. About every lap, I had to try to wipe my goggles clear of the stuff; before long I could taste oil in my mouth and it was all rather unpleasant.

Eventually I retired. I can't quite remember why — probably I was frozen!

After the meeting, I flew with Tom and Don Miles in the family Convair to spend a week or so with them in Victoria, Texas, before

112

flying back to Watkins Glen for the American Grand Prix, where I rejoined Ken Gregory and the BRP team.

I arrived in the nick of time for practice, since I had travelled with Don Miles in his new Beech Baron and he simply refused to fly if the weather was bad, even though the plane has as much electronic and radar equipment on board as a Boeing 707. We got as far as Nashville, Tennessee, where we were told the weather forecast for New York was bad, so he simply stopped where he was and I had to dash around and get a commercial flight. By the time I got to the Circuit, Tony Robinson, chief mechanic, and the rest of the BRP crew were hopping up and down wondering where the hell I had got to.

Travel with Don Miles always appeared to be 'organised' in the most disorganised way known to man — yet it nearly always worked m the end. It was just a question of incorporating every conceivable form of transport. When Tom O'Connor and his family arrived in Watkins Glen for the race — he brought his daughters Louise and Katherine with their husbands Don Miles and Ralph Gilster — the transport at our disposal consisted of a Convair, three hired cars and a chartered helicopter. This last item was Miles' idea. He remembered that the previous meeting had been a series of traffic jams all the way to the circuit and this worried him.

He therefore telephoned all over the State of New York to find a helicopter, finally traced one in Buffalo, about 160 miles away, had it sent down on the day of the race. To cut out the traffic jams, we used it to ferry us from the hotel to the circuit, and then Don went up in to watch the race from above. Needless to say, it was grossly expensive. I think it worked out at 90 dollars an hour and we had it for a complete day.

I can't recall what happened in that race, except that I retired.

The day after driving in the Grand Prix, I got arrested for driving at five miles an hour over the limit.

Being arrested by an American policeman is probably one of the most unpleasant experiences I have had. It has happened to me a number of times for speeding in various parts of America, but take this time as a typical example of the way they carry on.

For a start, the patrol officer who stopped me as we reached the airfield near Watkins Glen was intolerably rude. All gun and swagger, he leapt out of the police car which had forced me to stop and came bounding over to me with a face like thunder.

'OK, fella, what's the hurry?' he began.

I started to explain, quietly, that I had not noticed the needle creep over the speed limit, and that I was intent on catching the Convair — which we could both see on the other side of the road —

113

since the pilots had filed a flight plan for take off in about 15 minutes time.

'Gimme the car papers,' he interrupted.

I handed him the hire car documents and he flipped through them.

'These ain't the papers for this car, buddy,' he said accusingly. 'This ain't a Victoria, it's a Cadillac.'

I pointed out that Victoria was my address in the United States and that a description of the car was on another part of the document and this made him really angry.

'Where's your driver's licence?'

'I'm afraid it is with my baggage on the plane,' I said, indicating the Convair on the other side of the airfield fence.

'Oh, yeah? Well, we'll go and get it. Get in the car.' Don and Ralph, who were in the car with me, began to protest that we could just as easily drive ourselves into the airfield without my having to travel in the police car, but the patrolman told them to mind their own business and he opened the door of my car and walked me across to the police vehicle.

I felt like a real criminal in the back of the police car, since it had a steel mesh between me and the driver and the officer got in with me and kept a close eye on me throughout. Anyway, we reached the Convair and after a lot of digging about in my suitcases and kit, I found my licence.

'OK,' said the policeman. 'Now, we'll go and see Judge Some-body-or-other.' And once again, I was driven off.

Don Miles and Ralph Glister followed in the hire car to the Judges' home. In the Judge's office, the policeman gave his evidence while I sat down and said absolutely nothing.

In the end, I was given a 25-dollar suspended fine, which meant I didn't have to pay anything after all, I was only five miles an hour over the limit.

After the hearing, Ralph and Miles told me to go and wait in the car. They went back to see the judge and told him, apparently, that the behaviour of the patrolman had been absolutely abominable and was the worst kind of advertisement for America that one could imagine. I think the judge must have given the officer a rocket, for he came out looking slightly red-faced a little later. I must say, though, that his co-driver or whatever, was highly embarrassed all the time at his partner's aggressive attitude.

The irritating thing, to me, about policemen who treat ordinary people like criminals is that it is so totally unnecessary — and also bad for the blood pressure. When I get someone starting to talk to me in that manner, I personally get very hot round the collar. Maybe that is why some policemen act that way — just to see how

114

far they can provoke one. However, on this occasion, I did manage to stay perfectly calm.

From one aspect of the American treatment of strangers I found another at a race meeting at Seattle.

I suppose the meeting at Seattle, tucked away in the North-West corner of the United States, is regarded as being of minor importance in the motor racing calendar, but it is the kind of meeting I like to go to.

As in Austria, the meeting is organised and run by enthusiasts, people who do it for the sport of the thing. They really make you feel that as a driver taking part in the races, you are important to the success of the whole event. One is treated with courtesy and consideration and the whole meeting conducted in an atmosphere of cordiality and sportsmanship. I like it. How different it is to some of the bigger events, where officials can be quite capable of making one feel an intruder amongst all their nicely-laid plans. I fervently hope that the people who stage these friendly little races will always manage to carry on, despite the face that the greed and avarice which has crept into motor racing is making everything more and more expensive for promoters of their type.

Rosebud Racing had a tolerable meeting there and I think I won the 2-litre class with the Lotus 19. We stayed out on the West Coast for two more meetings, at Riverside and Laguna Seca, both in California.

At Riverside, Don Miles and I became friendly with Richard Boone, who at the time was starring in the TV series, 'Have Gun, Will Travel', a programme I used to enjoy, and we got along very well. He was interested in motor racing and spent a lot of time with us.

I think the last time I saw him was the night the police were called to a club we were in near Riverside.

It was all very unfortunate. Some other inmate of this place who had had far too much to drink started annoying Boone by being rude to him and jibing at him. Boone, I must say, kept his temper extraordinarily well and tried to ignore the drunk, even though the fellow was saying things like: 'Hey, you ain't so goddamned tough. I seen you cardboard cowboys before. 'And that sort of thing.

Eventually, Don went over to the drunk and told him to shut up or he'd be in trouble. Now, you would have thought the chap might have taken note of that, for Don is a huge man built like an ox — I must say I always feel very brave when he is around —but after staggering away for a minute or two, he came back. For some reason or other, he wanted to have a punch-up with Boone.

115

The latter naturally didn't want to get mixed up in a night-club brawl and continued to ignore the insults.

There came a point when this chap hit Don, who instinctively hit him back. Miles just hit him. Such a thump, and the chap Went careering across the bar in a tangle of tables and chairs — real Wild West stuff. Don, who was really mad, went after the fellow. I thought he was going to beat him to death. Both Tom O'Connor and myself actually leapt on Miles' back to try and haul him off but it took a good half-minute to make any impression at all on such a massive character.

Eventually, the blue suited gentlemen made an appearance — and Richard Boone quietly vanished.

For once, I found myself on the peacemaking side of the fence. I went out to see the police, calmed them down and managed to square away the whole thing while the mess inside was being cleared up. Finally they marched the drunk off and that was the end of the affair. I must say it rather amused me to play the truce-maker instead of my more usual role opposite the police!

At Laguna Seca, a very lovely part of the world near Monterey, there was another amusing drama after the race meeting. At the big motel where we were all staying, some discussion arose about whether the headlights of a car would work under water. I remember somebody bet a fellow called Augie that the light on his car would not function under water.

Now, it happened that this hotel had a huge swimming pool set amid the most glorious gardens at the back of the building — and the next thing was that Augie came charging across the lawns in his Hertz rented car and drove straight into the pool. It hovered on the surface for a little while and then gradually went glug, glug, glug to the bottom, at which time Augie got out. As we crowded round the pool to watch this performance, there was a terrible yell from Walt Hansgen, the American racing driver who was killed whilst practising the 1965 Le Mans trials. He remembered that he had left his brief case, cameras and all sorts of kit in the boot of Augie's car. So he had to jump in and get the key out of the ignition, then swim round to the boot and rescue his gear.

Actually, the lights on the car did stay on for about an hour after that.

It was an even more hilarious performance when Augie telephoned the Hertz people to tell them what had happened to their lovely motor-car. The Hertz people had a slogan which is something like 'You leave it, we'll collect it' which is, of course, good advertising for the renting business.

116

When Augie got on the phone that night, he put Hertz to their biggest test.

'Hello,' he said. 'I have your car, number...', what ever it was — 'and I'd like you to collect it.'

After a pause, he went on: 'Well, actually, it's at the bottom of the swimming pool at my hotel ... yes, that's right.., at the bottom.'

To begin with, the hire people were very, very tarty about it, but then they saw the publicity value of the situation. Next day, they indeed turned up to collect the car where Augie had left it and the photographs and stories in the press that day must have been worth a million dollars in advertising for them.

There was a delightful tail-piece to the story. The next year, when I went back to the hotel at Monteroy, they had, anchored in the middle of the pool a neat little sign — 'No Parking'.

After Laguna Seca, I had about a month to spare before my next commitment either with BRP or Rosebud, so I spent it playing cowboys on Tom's ranch.

I think, in many ways, the times I spent out on that vast Texas ranch were some of the happiest days of my life. When I went back home with Tom O'Connor on this occasion, it was the season of the year when the older calves are sold to be fattened and the herds are being rounded up for the best beef to be cut out and driven to the stock pens for shipment.

This cutting out process involves some of the hardest and most saddle-sore work in the world. I used to get up at about six in the morning and drive into town with Tom to have breakfast at a little cafe near his heliport. After the meal, a helicopter flew us across miles and miles of rangeland to the area where the herd of the day was being worked. On landing, Tom's ranch manager Denny Williams got a saddled horse for each of us — and then Ireland became a cowboy for the day. It was tremendous, exhausting, exciting work even though, in truth, I did more watching than working at first.

Most of the ranch hands were Mexicans and all of them were wonderful horsemen; it was poetry in rhythm to see them ride.

The whole operation of cutting out the beef was a marvel of organisation. First, they rounded up the whole herd and kept them milling round and round in circles. Then, into the bunch, rode Tom and Denny Williams and they began to pick out the best beef, gradually edging the selected animals to the outside of the circle.

Meanwhile, the cowhands were riding round the perimeter of the herd to keep the cattle where they were. When one of the selected cows with her calf was edged to the outside of the ring.

117

they were escorted some way across the prairie to join a fresh herd of selected animals. This was where I helped out. Whenever Tom raised his riding whip to indicate he had an animal coming out of the pack, the nearest hand — and sometimes it was me— took over and drove the animal to the selected herd.

They use special horses for this cutting Out work. They are magnificently intelligent animals, these cutting horses. Once Tom showed his horse a steer that he Wanted out from the herd, the horse took over and began edging it towards the outside of the ring. Of course, the cattle hate being isolated from the herd and they try dodging back, but the horse anticipates everything the other animal does — it was absolutely fascinating to watch.

Although they have mechanised ranging to a certain extent — they drive cattle over rough country with helicopters, for example — most of the work and the way it is done is exactly what we have all seen in Western films. Even branding. They still use a hot branding iron heated in an open fire and sear the skin of the young cattle. On Tom's ranch, they used either 'TC' for O'Connor's own cattle, or 'OC' for the ranch herd — all Herefords, by the way.

The first couple of days in the saddle made me ache in places I didn't even know I possessed.

You have to be terribly quick to keep a young steer going in the right direction, for they twist and dodge about, trying all the time to get back into the main herd, so you are constantly changing pace and direction. Although I have been riding horses since I was about six, I was perfectly seized up at the end of the first day.

One thing I did learn though, was that cowboys do not wear spurs just for the effect of the thing. During the first morning's work, when I rode without spurs, I found it terribly difficult to get my horse, good and strong though he was, to accelerate rapidly enough to keep on the right side of the young cattle I was trying to drive, while the cowhands' horses would leap into top gear almost immediately they were called on. So in the afternoon, Tom fixed me up with a pair of spurs.

I went back to the horse with the spurs clinking at my heels, and as soon as I got within earshot of the horse, it suddenly whipped its head round and looked at me as if to say 'Man, you've got wise.' After that, boy, it just jumped into action automatically at the lightest touch of the spurs.

The whole thing was absolutely thrilling. It was exactly what we all imagine cattle droving to be — the dust, the noise of the cattle and the whooping and hollering of the cowboys shouting at them. Those Mexicans really enjoy what they are doing and appear to get tremendous fun out of the life they lead. Most of them have

118

been with Tom for years and they obviously do not want to know any other way of life.

Among the hands was one marvellous old Mexican — the only man in the world, I should think, with a credit account at all the local jails!

This old chap had first come to work on the ranch with Tom's father. He never ever left the ranch except perhaps eight times a year. When the mood takes him, he gathers up all his pay and takes off for two or three days on the most fantastic bender. Maybe he'll take with him three hundred or more dollars and he always ends up absolutely paralytic without a bean in his pocket. Of course, eventually he gets arrested, for being drunk, vagrant or some such thing and every single time he ends up in the 'nick'. Of course, by the time he has got to jail and is hauled in front of the judge, he never has a penny piece to his name.

The police never mind. They just send him back home to the ranch and wait for the next bender. This has been going on so long that they know the old fellow's system. Next time out, he hops into his bent old Ford and drives straight to the last jail — and pays his fine first. Then, and only then, he goes off on the next blinding session. And wherever he ends up, in whichever jail he finally comes to, the sheriff knows that he can perfectly well let the old Mexican go without paying his fine because next time out, he'll be back to settle up.

After about a month of this kind of he-man, open-air life on the range, it was with some regret that I turned back again to motor racing. Towards the end of the summer of 1962, I went to Mexico city for the first Mexican Grand Prix.

Incidentally, it was while we were on the way there, Don Miles and myself, that I learned a thing or two about the use of the 'long hogs' — or money as it is sometimes known, to smooth out troubled waters of officialdom.

The journey with Don Miles was the usual disorganised shambles. I had told him when I needed to be in Mexico City for practice and accordingly arranged to get up at the crack of dawn that day. Don and I staggered out of our beds at some unearthly hour and I asked him: 'What time is Slim coming down with the plane?'

'Goddam, I forgot to tell him,' said Miles. So a small drama ensued in which we got the pilot to grab some maps and so on and hurry down to the ranch to pick us up. From there on, things were fine until we landed at the Mexican border. Miles, in his usual fashion, had simply got up, put on a shirt and slacks and started travelling. Consequently, when we got to the border and the Mexican police wanted to see his passport, papers and what have you, he couldn't produce them. Naturally, he didn't have any money with him. So he borrowed twenty-five dollars from Slim and slipped it to the customs officer, and we got through with the aid of the magic greenback.

The same thing happened again when we got to Mexico City.

The customs people there were going to make life very difficult for us, even though we had all the aircraft documents and a chit for Miles which the border guards had scribbled out for him. In fact, all these people wanted was a back-hander.

In the middle of all the argument, Don sighed and turned to Slim. 'Give me another twenty-five bucks', he said. And he handed it to the customs man. The effect was magical. Immediately it was yes sir, no sir, three bags full and we were waved through all other formalities and out of the airport. I was absolutely furious at this open extortion, but Don shut me up.

'When in Mexico, do as the Mexicans do,' he said. 'It's the only way to get by in this country.'

At the Hotel Isabella — Mexico City's newest and best — Don did his usual performance of wandering up to-the desk and asking for the very best suite in the place and getting the usual sidelong look from the desk clerk. However, we got it, and a splendid place it was. We had two huge bedrooms, three bathrooms, two dressing-rooms and a very elaborate drawing-room.

My introduction to motor racing in Mexico was rather unfortunate. During practice, I was whistling around the circuit when the left rear-wheel flew off and I stopped in my usual cloud of dust. The wheel casting had collapsed. The central hub was intact, but the casting failure left the rim and tyre to go flying into the air. The wheel very narrowly missed a young girl and a little boy who were standing on the perimeter watching practice. Literally two feet from them, the wheel completely snapped a concrete post.

After a good deal of arms and elbows with the steering, I managed to park myself alongside a massive bit of banking which had loomed up terrifyingly while I was going round and round in circles.

Once again, this sort of thing had never, ever happened to a Lotus before. Everyone was puzzled about it, but even then, at the end of 1962, the unexpected was still happening to me.

Actually, the practice session for the Mexican Grand Prix was a tragedy. Ricardo Rodriguez, the very good and fast Mexican driver, was killed in practice, also in a Lotus 24. There was a great deal of discussion later about whether Ricardo had simply 'lost it on the banked bend, or whether' the car had broken, but it was never satisfactorily resolved. Of course, this accident put a

120

tremendous damper on the whole thing, for Ricardo was an awfully nice fellow. One becomes very depressed when something happens to a chap one knew, talked to, and discussed motor racing with so often. It cast a particular shadow over the racing, because Rodriguez himself came from Mexico City and was therefore the local hero.

For myself, I could hardly wait to get away from the place. However, the gloom which hung over Mexico City was dispelled by the brilliant sunshine of Nassau, where I went to race for Rosebud Racing in the Nassau Gold Cup.

Apart from the racing, I'm afraid things got rather out of hand again on that beautiful island.

11

The Nassau event consists of eight days of pretty high-spirited activity. The races themselves appear rather secondary to the festivities, since the whole operation is mounted to boost the tourist trade on the island during the slack season.

In great style, as always, I flew with Tom O'Connor and the family, and found myself ensconced in a massive suite at the Emerald Beach Hotel in absolutely luxurious surroundings. The first night, we fell foul of the management over some trivial matter — not being allowed to drink coffee in the bar or something — but this caused a certain amount of drama and rather set the pattern for our whole stay.

There was something of a riot the following night. I had been out deep-sea fishing for the day and had been lucky enough to land a big barracuda. This, I thought, could provide us with a little amusement that night. We decided to slip it under Ralph Gilster's pillow and scare the pants off him when he turned m, particularly as his wife Kathie was in on the joke and had in fact told us that Ralph always slept with his arms stretched out under his bead.

The fearsome-looking fish was duly placed in his bed and the rest of the family and myself gathered quietly in the ante-room of the Gilster's suite to hear what happened.

We heard Gillie say good-night to Kathie. He yawned, then slid between the sheets. Don Miles nearly bust a rib trying to keep quiet during the next half-minute of silence which was then broken by a howl from the other side of the door.

'Jesus Christ!' came Gillie's voice. 'Kathy! What the hell...' By this time he was out of bed and the lights went on in the room. Gillie was last seen rushing out of the other bedroom door yelling.

'Chief, Chief,' he hollered. 'Where are you, you..

122

The sight of him dashing down the hotel corridor, where we presently found him, was worth a million dollars. Gillie, we noticed, wore a red flannel nightshirt down to his ankles and with this thing flapping about and a damned great fish in his arms he looked like an escapee from a nut house. We even got the house detective on the phone, telling him that there was a madman on the penthouse floor rushing about in a red nightshirt with a barracuda in his hand. Poor Gilster was practically locked up — and he didn't think it too hilariously funny at the time, either!

The following evening many of the drivers over for the races went out on a bit of a thrash during which we found ourselves in a nightclub called the Confidential. Things were going along quite nicely until the band began to play the theme tune from the film *Never on Sunday.*

I saw this film and had been terribly impressed by the scene in which the hero gets rather tipsy, and begins to dance and throw his empty glasses about. Whenever I hear the tune, I get the urge to start doing likewise. It crossed my mind then, when I heard it in the club, but I did nothing. A few drinks later, they played it again, and this time I felt myself getting a bit out of hand. I started whirling round and threw the brandy glass on the floor in great style. Oddly enough, the manager of the club thought this was great stuff and he was applauding wildly. From there, the idea became contagious. The band struck up the tune again and this started other people throwing their brandy glasses about and in the end, the place was ankle deep in broken glass. By the end of the evening, the bill for the drinks was 109 dollars — but the bill for broken glasses was more than 200 dollars.

Of course, everyone was in great form by the end of the proceedings and we left the club still dancing about like mad. 'Quite how it happened, I am not sure, but I clearly remember dancing on the root of the Ford Cortina I had hired for the week and leaping up and down on the boot with gay abandon.

Finally, we sorted ourselves out and Don Miles, one of Tom's Convair pilots Leon Foules, and myself decided to head back for the hotel. However, it was quite clear that none of us were capable of driving a car, and in any case, my Cortina was a bit of a mess. Just then, a young coloured chap came by and I collared him and asked if he could drive a car.

He said he could, so I asked him to drive us to the Emerald Beach Hotel. This he did, but when he dumped us in the forecourt, he confessed he had a bit of a problem.

'How's I gonna get home Massa?'

'Oh, that's no problem,' I said gaily. 'Take the car and bring it back in the morning.'

'Sure thing,' he grinned, leapt into the Cortina and drove off at high speed.

That was the last anyone ever saw of that car.

I had expected, of course, that he would bring it back in the morning and pick up a tip for his trouble, but in fact he never came back at all!

This was not the last of the night's dramas. When we went into the hotel, we tried very hard indeed to make a good impression and not look affected by any outside influences such as alcohol. This was because one of the under-managers was eyeing us very warily from the reception desk and, in fact, watched the three of us very closely as we navigated across the lobby.

Facing us were the lifts, which we needed to take us up to the suites. The call button for the elevators was situated right in the middle of a large mirror between the two lift shafts. It was a very large mirror, I might say, stretching from floor to ceiling and I concentrated on taking aim at the button because I did not want the under-manager to see me fumbling about trying to locate it.

Unfortunately, I just missed the button.

Maybe I pressed too hard or something, but suddenly the whole mirror disintegrated into a thousand pieces. It seemed like slow motion, for first the mirror cracked, then slowly sagged and finally cascaded all over the floor carpet. While all this was going on, I did manage to press the button and the lift appeared almost immediately.

There was a terrible silence for a moment as I stood looking rather stupidly, I imagine — at the wall where the mirror had been, whilst the under-manager gaped in absolute horror.

Then Don shoved me into the lift, calmly followed me, and said over his shoulder: 'OK. Put it on the bill.'

I have only the haziest recollections of what happened after that. I know that we got everyone else out of bed and started the most tremendous chase through the suites and along the corridors. Somewhere along the line, the fire hose came out and I can't tell you what a horrible mess the place was in before I was finally overpowered by Don and dumped into bed.

It certainly was an amusing interlude. I can more clearly remember the next morning — I felt like death.

We had a number of other fairly hefty thrashes in that hotel and by the time we had done, the management had evacuated the entire top floor because other guests would not stay there.

Actually, about halfway through our stay, I did get a twinge of conscience and in a quieter moment, I talked to Tom O'Connor about it.

124

'Perhaps we had better take it a bit easy,' I suggested, 'You know, we might get thrown out.'

'Aw, no,' Tom drawled. 'I don't reckon they'll throw us out of here.'

I was a little surprised and relieved at Tom's confidence, but on making a few further anxious enquiries, I found out the reason why he was so sure the hotel would put up with us.

He'd put up the money for the place to be built.

As it happened, when he got the bill, he must have thought he was paying for the place all over again. The accommodation bill for out eight or nine days' stay was 4,500 dollars, plus 1,500 dollars there and then, and a little later a further bill for damages of 500 dollars. On top of that, came the cost of a lost hire car, the damage to the other one, and two scooters which, between them, Don Miles and Ralph Gilster had mislaid.

There was also motor racing. A number of minor races, which nobody seemed to know much about took place during the week, but the big race was the Nassau Gold Cup, which was run on the Sunday.

This was a race for big sports cars, with a Le Mans-type start, in which I drove the Rosebud Racing Lotus 19. It had been raining very heavily before the race and the whole thing took place in the wet. Oddly enough, I managed to stay on the road throughout the 250 miles and I won the race.

At this stage I was forced to think about the Formula One circus again, because the South African season was starting immediately after the Nassau races. In fact, I had to leave Nassau on the night of the Gold Cup race in order to get to Johannesburg for the first of the Grand Prix meetings.

This put me in a bit of a fix, for the prizegiving for the Nassau races was being held on the Monday, by which time I should be on my way to South Africa via London. I had explained this to the organisers before the Nassau races began,

The point was that if a prize winner did not attend the prize giving, he would forfeit half the prize money of 5,000 dollars.

When I happened to win the big race of the week, I took the matter up again with the organisers and explained that I had a contract with BRP to fulfil and much though I would like to have stayed for the prize giving, I simply could not do so because I did not have the time. All in vain. The organisers stuck to their rule and insisted they would keep back half the prize money and give it to some charity or other,

I later discovered that when Tom O'Connor had asked the organisers' head man if he could be allowed to explain at the dinner why I was not there, he was refused.

However, Masten Gregory who had to make a speech on accepting one of the other prizes very sportingly made my apologies for me the moment he rose to speak. I was very grateful to him, for I certainly did not want anyone to think that I had just won the race and then cleared off.

I don't think many people had too high a regard for the organisers for taking the implacable attitude which they did. Furthermore, Torn O'Connor capped the whole thing by contributing the remaining half of his prize money also to charity —provided that the whole lot went to an organisation of his own choosing.

Meanwhile I had left to start the long haul to Johannesburg. I flew to Miami, on to New York, across to London, drove home to Wales for a night, dashed back to catch a plane from London to Johannesburg and arrived in South Africa in time for practice on the Thursday morning. It all seemed to take forever because being flown in other people's aeroplanes bores me. Actually this was only the first leg of a fantastic travel saga, for, after the first of the two races in South Africa, I had to nip back home to look after some of my own business interests, then return to South Africa for the Grand Prix at East London. After that event it was on to Australia and New Zealand for more races, and finally back to Texas. I think I did 25,000 miles in about a fortnight, which sounds nice, but is really rather tiresome. I checked on the air mileage I had done around about that time and found that as a passenger, I covered some 180,000 miles in five months.

The South African Grand Prix was right at the end of the year — and was the race which Graham Hill won to become World Champion.

I was going on from South Africa to New Zealand to drive with Graham in the experimental Ferguson four-wheel-drive car which proved to be tremendous fun.

To get to New Zealand from South Africa was a terrible trip. First, I flew to Nairobi, waited for a connection and then continued on to Karachi in Pakistan. BOAC had very kindly arranged to divert one of their normal Boeing 707 flights to stop there and pick up the pack of us. Unfortunately, the day we landed in Karachi was New Year's Eve and, being a true son of Scotland, I could not really resist the temptation to celebrate Hogmanay in the traditional style.

Somewhere along the line we fell foul of the immigration police and a few of us saw in the New Year in a rather nasty sort of jail house.

It was only natural, of course, that since we had to wait overnight, another chap and myself should make a bit of whoopee.

126

I have no idea why we were 'put away', but I do remember being hustled into jail. They have a funny habit in Pakistan, I found, of spraying one with a kind of DDT or something before they actually put you in the lock-up. I was quite taken aback when a policeman gave us both a smart spraying with the contents of an aerosol can.

But not my companion. For some reason — and again I can't think why — he had in his pocket a can of push-button shaving soap. Quick as a flash, he drew it out and returned a volley of shaving soap which covered the astonished gendarme from fez to belt. I don't think I have ever seen anyone look quite so surprised.

However, being inside did not mean the end of Hogmanay for us. Despite the shaving soap incident, we prevailed on our captors to let us telephone the local BOAC public relations man to explain our predicament. This chap could do nothing to get us out, but, God bless him, he did his best to make our stay a pleasant one. Within twenty minutes, he was at the police station and handed us a bottle of brandy to help things along. We demolished that in the cell before we both keeled over and slept like babes until 1963 dawned on us.

Breakfast, which consisted of a very hard and tiny fried egg on an enormous cold plate, was pretty difficult to face but we managed it. Then, to our surprise, we were simply taken out, put in a car with a police escort and driven to our waiting 707.

The officer who accompanied us seemed a decent sort of fellow but, just as we stood at the bottom of the steps to the airliner, he did make one plea in that terribly attractive Peter Sellars' type accent. 'Please, not to come back again to Karachi.'

I assured him that, for my part, nothing would make me set foot in his parish again, and he departed.

Actually, I stuck rigidly to my word. As it happened, the Boeing sprung a hydraulic leak before we took off and all the passengers were invited back to the airport lounge while the mechanics worked on the fault. Not me, however. I sat where I was, nursing a throbbing head, and waiting for the trouble to be fixed.

That flight seemed endless. We stopped at Delhi, Rangoon, Singapore and all sorts of odd places like that, before reaching Darwin, where the plane finally packed up and had to have spares flown up to it from Sydney. We were stuck there, in the most appalling heat. BOAC put us up at an hotel, but it was a waste of money, for it was so hot that it was quite impossible to sleep and we all felt like merry death in the morning. In fact, having left South Africa in the Sunday morning, we reached Auckland, New Zealand, on the following Friday morning — at 1.30 a.m. Practice for the race was at 10 o'clock that day!

127

In this series of races, I was more or less second-string to Graham Hill in driving the Ferguson. Those races which Graham did not want to take part in, I took. I felt a bit like the tea boy, but I did manage to get a few drives in this very exciting motorcar.

The first race in which I piloted the Ferguson was at a place called Levin, in North Island, and I found that driving the car was a very unusual experience. We had a 2½-litre engine running on petrol, whereas all the other chaps had 2.7 engines running on methanol. However, the power of the Ferguson was tremendous, as was its road-holding in the wet, and although practice took place in the rain, I was on the front of the grid.

Jack Brabham had pole position, I think, but I was about third fastest. In practice, I found that the most difficult thing to do in the Ferguson was taking your foot off the throttle. The torque reversal set up when taking your foot off, and transmitted to all four wheels, was such that if you were not careful, you found the car spinning in much the same way as it might if you trod on the brakes.

However, I got the hang of it in time for the race, by just taking my foot off gently. When accelerating from the apex to a corner, especially in the wet, it was possible just to stuff your foot in it and drive out at high speed, because the power went on to all four wheels.

Even so, I was not quite prepared for the kind of start you could get with the car. In the race, Brabham did one of his immaculate starts. I had about 4,000 revs running as the starter dropped the flag and when I let the clutch in the car gave a sort of leap on all four wheels and then the engine very nearly died on me. With the four-wheel drive I had insufficient power on. However, I managed to snatch it back, rev up, let in the clutch again and then I put my foot right down to the floorboards.

And the car just took off like a rocket. It was all go — no wheelspin or anything, all four wheels gripped and I passed Brabham way before we got to the first bend, even after his immaculate start.

I remember after the race, Jack talked to me about it and said: 'You came past me so fast, I thought I had broken a half-shaft.'

I motored on happily in the lead and found that on that rather twisty circuit, the Ferguson was just marvellous, although Brabham was just about able to close on me on the straights with his superior engine.

I had a spot of trouble on the bumpy bits, though — and there were many of them. On one particular corner the car leaped about like a grasshopper, although I was thoroughly enjoying hurling the

128

'This motor racing is thirsty work,' says the author.

'But Dick, I didn't think you'd miss one or two!' Silverstone 1962.

car around. It was only after the race that the other chaps told me that they grew positively alarmed at the sight of my car skipping about, and refused to come near me on that bit of the track. Bruce McLaren said afterwards that he had closed up on me at the point, but wouldn't try to overtake because he couldn't tell which way I was going to bounce!

I was going along merrily in the lead until right near the end, when the car jammed in fourth gear. However, I had made so much time on the others that I still managed to finish third.

The next race was at Christchurch and in practice I had a rather alarming experience with the Ferguson. I went screaming round a corner of the circuit, which was on a military airfield, and lifted off the throttle to prepare for a slow chicane, when something drastic happened. The car suddenly went shooting off towards a line of bloody great hangars at the edge of the track. I managed to get myself pointing away from the hangars, but I went down the road in a series of the wildest slides you can imagine.

I was trying to steer it, of course, but whatever I did seemed to have no effect. Every time I wound the wheel on nothing would happen for a second, and then the wheels would grip and I'd shoot off in the opposite direction.

Eventually, I managed to stop the car with its nose almost touching the chicane wall, to find that the rear right-hand hub structure had broken away and the wheel was waving about in the breeze. It took quite a bit of time to repair, with the result that I did not get any practice for the race and ended up on the back of the grid.

Most of the other chaps had cottoned on to the idea that the machine I was driving was pretty lethal in getting away from a standing start, so I had a word with them as we waited on the grid.

'Look,' I told them. 'When I let this thing loose, it goes like a bat out of hell. So leave me some room.' They all agreed to keep clear of me. From the back of the grid, it was probably no more than 200 yards to the first corner and right from the back, behind fourteen or fifteen cars, I found myself fourth as I went into the corner. The way I was passing cars was just ridiculous. After about a couple of laps, though, I noticed the engine temperature was leaping up, so I went into the pits and found the engine was pretty well cooked. We topped it up with water, but then found it wouldn't start. So we dragged it round to the back of the pits, hitched it behind a private car and towed it until the engine caught.

Then, they topped up the water again. It must have been squirting out from somewhere all the time as I pressed on, because we really cooked the engine. By the time I brought it in to retire all

E   129 the rubber had melted off the plug leads and the whole thing was sizzling like bacon in a pan. In fact the engine was completely ruined.

It was an extremely exhilarating car to drive and I couldn't have enjoyed myself more. The four-wheeled drive certainly got the power on to the road, no question of that.

I came back to England through Hawaii, Los Angeles, Texas and New York, arriving home in the middle of a blizzard! At this time, I had bought my first Snow-Trac, a Swedish designed vehicle with tracked propulsion, built to operate on steep gradients in the snow. So I went up to Scotland with it and spent a couple of weeks playing with the thing, rescuing sheep and shepherds from snowdrifts, and towing cars Out of ditches.

While I was there, the British Racing Partnership asked if I would race for them again in 1963 and I agreed to do so, although I never bothered to sign a contract, being perfectly happy to settle the thing on the shake of the hand.

1962, for sure, had not been a brilliant season. However, BRP were to build their own cars for the coming season, and I looked forward to driving for this team and also for the American Rosebud team once again.

12

Before the 1963 European season opened. I was asked by Torn O'Connor to go over to the United States and drive a GTO Ferrari for Rosebud in the Sebring 12-hour race, with Ritchie Ginther as co-driver. Naturally, I agreed. After the rigours of the Scottish winter, it was pleasant to go across to Florida and find warm sunshine again.

When I arrived I met up with Tom, Don Miles and the other members of the family and we had an extremely happy get-together. As to the racing, I can't remember quite what happened but I don't think Ritchie and I did anything spectacular, other than change brake pads with monotonous regularity and have a puncture. What I remember most clearly about that week-end was that we again fell into the expensive habit of losing a motor-car.

It was a fairly new Ford Galaxie which we had hired in rather unusual circumstances. Everything is a bit off-season in Florida at that time of the year and it was not easy to hire cars and things like that. Even the hotels had to import staff from other parts of the States during this boom week-end of motor racing.

It was decided that we needed another hire car, but, search though we did, we could not trace one. However, one of the maids in the hotel at which we stayed had this Galaxie, so, through the management, we arranged to hire it from her for a few days.

Everything went well until the Sunday after the race when it was time to leave and, of course, to hand the car back to the girl. It was nowhere to be found.

None of us could quite remember who had used it last. My own recollection had been of seeing it in the paddock area behind the pits at the circuit. Later, I had noticed it missing, but presumed

131

somebody connected with Rosebud had taken it back to the hotel. However, the girl we had hired it from needed the car that day to get back home, which presented something of a problem.

When I saw Tom O'Connor later in the day, he was wandering around the hotel with a worried frown on his face, asking: 'Anybody know where I can buy a Ford Galaxie drophead on a Sunday?'

He managed it somehow and that night the hotel maid set off for her home at the wheel of a new Galaxie. It was a different colour to her original one, but after a minor quibble about that, she drove off happily enough. I kept thinking that really we ought to be a little less careless about leaving cars around. I can't imagine what happened to it, whether it was stolen or what. For all I know it might be at Sebring yet.

Back at home, the season started reasonably well. In the earlier meetings at Goodwood and Aintree, I was first and second respectively in the then two-year-old Lotus 24 with a BRM engine.

During the Aintree race, I was pressing Graham Hill very hard and going well when I found the car becoming literally too hot to handle.

At first, it just got very hot in the driving compartment. Then the pedals actually began to burn the soles of my feet and I singed my leg on the petrol tank above my knees — even my wrist watch got so hot that it burned my wrist! Before long, it grew so uncomfortable that I lost ground to Graham simply because I was unable to brake properly — every time I pressed my foot on the anchor pedal, the heat hurt my foot abominably. At the end of the race, I had to be more or less lifted out of the car because I was quite exhausted and in considerable pain.

The cause of it all was that the BRM engine, which we had decided to use in the Lotus, ran very much hotter than the Climax engine we had previously used. The heat of the engine is dispelled by the radiator situated in the front end of the car. This caused a flow of high-temperature air to blast back through the cockpit until it heated all the metal parts to the point where they became too hot to touch. I did not stifle though, because my face was in the outside windstream — but the rest of me practically cooked. All in all, I was quite pleased with my performance in coming second under such circumstances.

I was not, however, quite so pleased with my next outing. This was at Silverstone, where I got into a monumental spin, in the pits area right in front of the grandstand crowd and in full view of the TV cameras relaying every embarrassing gyration to a vast number of viewers.

I became quite famous for a while as a result of this tremendous

132

gilhooley, and gained a reputation as being a masterly driver of cars going sideways and backwards.

In fact, what happened was that I hit a patch of oil which had been dropping out of John Surtees' car; my machine simply took charge of itself and went round and round and round. It was just fortunate that I did not hit anything. Unhappily, I lost the engine in the middle of it all and must have sat with my nose up against the pit counter for some ten seconds before I got the car started again and roared off. From then on, things went wonderfully well, for I really tried hard to retrieve myself and in the last five laps put up successive lap records. Indeed, my record on the last lap with that two-year-old Lotus withstood the British Grand Prix held at Silverstone later in the year and was the fastest lap of the year for the circuit.

By this time, BRP had reached the final stages in the design and construction of their own cars. Tony Robinson and his men had designed a beautiful monocoque machine with a BRM engine which was ready in time for the first of the World Championship events, Monaco. However, they did not consider it worth entering the new car on such a tricky circuit — where my record, to put it mildly, was dubious! — so we went down there with a sawn-off version of the old Lotus, with a shorter nose. Their judgement proved to be a wise one, for once again, my trip to Monaco did not prove to be the happiest of outings.

I had the distinction of being the only driver to have an accident that year. It happened just after the Station Hairpin bend as I was approaching the seafront, where there is a first-gear downhill right-hand corner. I had got up to about 11,000 revs in first gear coming up to the corner but as I put the brakes on, the car jumped out of gear.

Of course, one depends on the engine a good deal to slow up with, so by the time I had wrestled with the gear lever, played with the brakes and blipped the throttle, I was well into the bend and going too fast. I slid off and clobbered the wall, knocking a front wheel off in the process.

The first appearance of the BRP monocoque was in the Belgium Grand Prix at Spa. At first it performed quite well, although, unfortunately, the gear change mechanism went haywire and started to select gears for itself, regardless of what slot I put it into. I knew that the gears were not quite right before we ever got to the circuit, because we had been in difficulties about where to locate the gear lever. Eventually it was placed on the left-hand side of the cockpit above the fuel tank. The gear lever itself stuck out horizontally and was not too easy to get used to. During the race, the linkages got terribly sloppy and I never knew which gear I was going to get. After my experiences in the tunnel at Monaco, this just wasn't on for me and I retired.

After that, it took a long while to iron out the kinks in the car. We finished fourth in the Dutch Grand Prix at Zandvoort, but at Silverstone, for the British Grand Prix, we had fuel feed trouble and the engine kept misfiring.

No one was ever able to discover what was wrong there, even though we called in all the experts from the petrol, fuel injection and electrical companies. It remained a mystery, although it magically cured itself in the end.

The next race was at Nurburgring for the German Grand Prix. Very conscious of the fact that I had never completed more than a dozen laps on this particular circuit, I was motoring round quite sedately in my first practice lap when, coming into a corner where somebody had let out a lot of oil, the car just floated gracefully across the track into a hedge, made a sharp left turn and ploughed through it. I finished up with the back wheels up on the hedge and the rest of the car hanging down a steep bank at an angle of about 60 degrees.

This, unfortunately, bent the car beyond the point where it could be repaired for the race, so I went back to using one of the old Lotus 24's. There was no question of my taking over the car of my team-mate Jim Hall. For one thing, this long Texan was so big that I could never have reached the pedals on his car!

I very nearly completed a lap in the race itself.

I was plodding along fairly nicely behind the leading pack and intent only on finishing for the first time. As I came to take a bend just before the Carousel, Lorenzo Bandini in the Centro-Sud BRM came screaming up at a rate of knots on my right-hand side with everything locked solid and clouds of smoke coming from his tyres.

I immediately backed off because I was absolutely certain he would never get round the corner. Sure enough, he spun it right in front of me. He was going all over the place, and, as fast as I tried to get round the left of him, so he slid to the left; when I switched to the right, he appeared on the right. I had very nearly got past him, when he slid back and clouted my rear wheel.

It was a fairly severe bang — enough, anyway, to bend up the suspension and shunt me into the ditch, from where I bounced back on to the road. I motored slowly along to the pits with the rear wheel sounding like an old mangle. Once more I retired — and once more, I didn't race at Nurburgring.

I wasn't having too lucky a season, in fact, and in one race at least, my terrible luck was acknowledged. This was in the race at Zeltweg, Austria, where I was driving in a non-championship

134

Formula One race for BRP. Once again, I was at the wheel of the old Lotus 24 but managed to put up a good show, clinging tightly to Jim Clark — in the, Works Lotus 25 or whatever it was called then — and Jack Brabham. I was second to Clark when something on his car blew up and I went into the lead. I managed to keep ahead of Jack for some time until my engine started playing tricks and he overtook me. Then, quite inexplicably, the engine came back 'on song' again, and I took over once more at the front. This was the way things went on until a couple of laps from the end — and then the engine really went sick and I had to pull into the pits. It really was too ill to press on and I had to retire from the race altogether. I could have wept.

However, it was rather pleasant at the prize-giving that night. After the prizes had been handed out, my own name was called — I could not think why, since I had won nothing. It appeared that the newspaper people in the area had awarded a sort of 'Hard Luck Trophy', and I had been singled out for this honour!

The trophy was a large metal plate with a broken bolt embossed on it in gold. Rather symbolic, I thought. It really is one of my more treasured trophies.

Anyway, the prize-giving was a somewhat hilarious affair, and the *joie de vivre* of the occasion led to a rather unhappy accident on the way back to the hotel where I and most of the other people were staying, When I left the prize-giving in the Volkswagen I had hired, I noticed that I was being very closely followed by another car which continued to sit right up my bumper bar. I knew it was one of the lads and so I started to fool about, weaving all over the road and up on to the grass bank and that sort of thing. Sure enough, the other car followed me inch for inch.

The entrance to our hotel was just a gap in the wall which ran down the length of this particular road, and was a rather narrow gap at that. I knew the VW could only just get through the archway driven slowly and cold stone sober, and for some reason I thought the car behind must know where I was going and that I would be turning into the hotel entrance. So, without giving much warning of what I was doing, I stamped on the brakes at the last moment and swung towards the hole in the wall.

Unfortunately, the driver of the car behind did not appreciate what was going on. Instead of going to my right to miss me, he came to the left and, of course, hit the Volkswagen right up the backside. Maybe it was just as well he did, for on reflection I don't think I would have got through the hole in the wall. As it was, I piled into a line of cars parked on the kerb,

It was most unfortunate that the nearest car to me was a brand new Jaguar E-Type, which had only done 800 kilometres. One of

135

his front wings was slightly bent and it ran back into a Porsche which was parked behind. The car which hit me also collected a Mini Minor, making a total of five cars involved. My poor Volkswagen had all four corners poked in. As I climbed out of the wreckage, the Street became filled with everyone from the hotel who had heard the appalling clatter, bang and tinkle which followed the collision.

I remember someone let out the yell: 'Ireland's arrived!' Regrettably this was true — he had, in the middle of a great heap of debris which we had to shovel up pretty quickly, in order to keep the local gendarmes happy!

Anyway, we squared up the police by pretending, when straightening out the bent wing of the car behind, that we were changing a wheel. In fact, people were standing around all the bent parts and doing their best to kick the broken glass into the gutter.

The Austrian races were the beginning of a fairly hectic time, for after leaving Zeltweg, I flew my own Bonanza to London, then hopped on a Pan Am 707 to New York and on to Texas, where I picked up Don Miles. We returned the next day to Europe via Dallas, New York and Milan for the Italian Grand Prix at Monza. Don had decided that he wanted to spend a week or two in London, looking around and visiting one or two of the finer gentlemen's outfitters. It was a long way to come for a couple of suits, but that was Miles' way of life...

I thought we ought to do the whole thing in style, so I hired for myself a Silver Cloud Rolls-Royce complete with chauffeur, the admirable Steer. After all, it would have cost us pounds in parking fines to have driven round London ourselves — and it is rather pleasant to be driven around instead of fighting the traffic oneself. I remember we were staying at the Hilton and the bill at the end of our stay was more like the national debt. Anyway, Don got his suits — I remember my tailor being absolutely staggered at the sheer size of Miles and looking repeatedly in disbelief at his tape measure when taking the American's chest and shoulder measurements.

I was next due to drive for Rosebud Racing in the North-West Pacific Grand Prix at Seattle, so Miles and I arranged to fly over to San Francisco to join Tom O'Connor. Incidentally, Miles had taken such a liking to Steer, who had proved a very resourceful and useful chap to have around, that he suggested taking him over to the States with us, and he jumped at the chance.

We caught the plane to New York and on to 'Frisco and it was during this second leg of the journey that I began to be afflicted with the curious premonition that something was to happen to me.

136

It was the only time I ever had that feeling but the message came through loud and clear. I knew something was going to go wrong. What went wrong, you will have read in the first chapter of this book.

It wasn't until I knew I had lost it on the crest of the hill, saw the earth banking behind me and that Mercedes parked there that, for a second, I recalled my earlier fears.

The first person to get to me, as I remember it, was a medic. He came bounding over, obviously saw that I was in pain and began to brandish a hypodermic syringe. Now, I had discovered at the Monaco accident that I was allergic to all pain-killing drugs. I had nearly died from morphia in the South of France and ever since then I have constantly worn a gold medallion around my neck proclaiming the fact that I have this allergy.

Yet ever since then, I have lived with the fear that someone would not see the medallion and inject me with morphia. It therefore seemed to me a fair bet that morphia was in the syringe that this chap was about to jab into my arm.

Fortunately, I had not lost consciousness, and saw the medic bearing down on me with his needle, delighted to have found a customer at last. He was going to give me morphia whether I liked it or not.

Quite calmly, I asked him: 'Is that morphia?' And he said it was

'Well, I'm allergic to it.' I said. But he obviously thought I was drivelling.

'Oh, it's all right, it won't hurt,' he said and began pulling up the sleeve of my overalls. I got worried at this.

'Look.., off,' I said, 'I can't have morphia. See, it says so here.' And I showed him the medallion. Still he ignored it and I can only assume that the fellow did not speak or read English. Luckily. Don Miles and our chief mechanic Jock Ross had arrived by this time and Don just quietly lifted the medical man out of the way!

It was none too comfortable lying there in the wreck of the Lotus. My feet were trapped and all the time I was being cut out — for, by now there were squads of people around — I was worrying about the risk of the car catching fire with me firmly anchored to it.

During the whole twenty-five minutes or so which it took to extricate me from the mess, Don Miles was standing over me holding on to my shoulders. He told me afterwards that if the car had caught fire, he was going to yank me bodily out of the driver's seat. I shudder to think what would have happened if he had.

When they eventually lifted me out of the car, it was only by

137

exercising maximum self control that I managed to keep my composure, since the pain I was facing was quite severe.

I was carted off to the nearest hospital where the doctor seemed very overwrought. When he got me on to his table, he was apparently going to operate there and then, for he had all the knives ready and so on. However, Tom O'Connor and the rest of the family were at the hospital and Tom told the doctor that he wanted to get me transferred to the Swedish hospital in Seattle where a bone specialist had been summoned to treat me.

The ambulance which transferred me to the Swedish hospital was an enormous Cadillac with, springing as soft as a cradle, but even so I felt my hip was on fire every time it took a right-hand bend.

My hip-bone had been completely dislocated and in fact my right leg was eight inches shorter than the left because the leg-bone had disappeared eight inches up my rear end. Since I could not have pain-killing drugs, it felt like merry hell. Halfway through the journey. I had to ask Tom O'Connor to tell the driver not to be so enthusiastic since I could feel every bump in the road.

At the Swedish hospital, there, was the agony of X-rays. Naturally they wanted to get as many pictures as they could and kept rolling me around to photograph my hip-bone from different angles. This was all rather difficult to endure and in the end, I reached the screaming stage. I tried very hard not to make a fuss, but when somebody moved my leg just a little roughly I simply howled. This had the desired effect and they cut short their photography session.

The doctors had been rather puzzled when my leg had not broken under the tremendous blow needed to dislocate the hip joint, and during the X-rays they found that I had an extra thick bone structure which accounted for this.

They said later that getting my hip-bone back into place was a tough job even for a team of three doctors, and before they finally succeeded, they even thought of sending for Don Miles to help them wrench the thing into position.

After giving me a dose of Pentathol, they operated on me and I awoke to find myself in bed, with a damned great bottle of white liquid dripping, via two tubes, into my arm. This horrified me, for they had tied my arm to the bed and I did not intend to be tied to the bed at all. So I called the nurse and we had a squabble about that. Eventually Tom came in and persuaded me it was a good thing because the drip was glucose, and was feeding me to keep up my strength.

Finally, in the middle of the night, I couldn't stand it any more and I persuaded the nurse to take the thing away. It made me feel

138

awful having a couple of tubes stuffed into my arm. And anyway, I wasn't hungry!

For the next six days, we turned the Swedish Hospital, Seattle, completely upside down. The whole O'Connor family stayed there with me, taking it in turns to go out and eat. Half the time there was somebody lying on a blanket on the floor fast asleep. I began moaning at the doctors to let me out after a couple of days because I loathe being trapped in a hospital bed at the best of times, but on this occasion I was also in traction. This meant that my right leg was up in the air suspended on pulleys with weights on the end, and it was absolute misery.

I was in hospital for six days, in all, at the end of which time I had to organise our departure from my hospital bed. It so happened that Tom O'Connor had to get back to Texas to attend the funeral of a very dear old friend of the family, and he had tried without success to get a seat on a commercial airline, leaving the Convair and the rest of the family behind. I thought this was taking his incredible kindness just too far and I said that I would leave hospital the day he wanted to travel and to hell with the doctors. Actually, the doctor let me out only on condition that I would stay in bed when I got to Texas, and I reluctantly agreed. Then, by 'phone, I rounded up the O'Connor family and got them ready to travel.

Tom was quite staggered at the way the family moved themselves at a couple of hours notice, for he always said that, with their mountains of luggage and so on, it always took him three days to organise them for any trip.

It took me as long as anyone to get sorted out, for my room in the hospital was a complete shambles. There were bottles and papers and letters and clothes and all sorts of bits and pieces lying around, and we had to arrange for an ambulance to take me to the airport.

But finally, we all made it. I was loaded into the big double bed at the back end of the Convair and we all settled in comfortably, but a little breathlessly, for the flight back to Texas.

13

The flight back to my convalescence in Texas was pretty hilarious. I remember that Tom had even organised a bed pan for me in case I felt the need for the thing, but by the time we were halfway this particular implement was being used for things not even remotely connected with hygiene. Don Miles was serving hot-dogs out of it at one stage and a bottle which had also been provided for a similar use was filled with rye whisky.

Hub, the pilot, had decided that although we could have made it all the way to Victoria, Texas, we did not have enough fuel to play with in case the weather was bad so he landed at San Antonio. I must say that by the time we arrived there we were all in pretty good condition. We landed only for Hub to discover that one of the propellers would not come out of reverse thrust when he tried to take off again; accordingly we parked on the airport while mechanics sorted the thing out. At two o'clock in the morning, we were all still grogging it up very nicely — I remember my chauffeur, Steer, doing a Highland fling up and down the Convair's gangway — and the party ended with huge plates of ham and eggs fetched from the airport restaurant.

I should imagine that the mechanics swarming over the plane probably had their doubts about our future in the air, for the plane must have seemed loaded with an out of hand concert party.

It was a hell of a way to get better!

When we reached the ranch, I found that Tom had converted one of the rooms of his home into a pukka hospital room for me, which I greatly appreciated. He had put an extra bed in the room so that Steer could sleep there as well, which was a great help to me, just having someone always around, The next day, Tom had a consultant bone specialist flown in from Houston to have a look at me. He decided that I still needed my leg in traction, so Tom

140

and the specialist went rushing off to Victoria County hospital and came back with a great Meccano set of tubes, pulleys, ropes, weights and all manner of things. Actually I nearly fell out of bed and undid all the doctors' work because it was so funny to see them trying to rig up this contraption. It was rather marvellous the way this very eminent bone man got down to the work of putting this thing together. Watching them both was like seeing a troop of Boy Scouts trying to put up a tent in a gale, but they got it together somehow and I submitted to having my leg strung up.

Then the specialist said that I would have to be taken into Victoria hospital every day for treatment in a Hubbard tank. This was a big stainless steel tank filled with hot water circulated by an electric pump in which I did exercises. It was similar to the treatment I had had in St Thomas's after the Monaco affair.

However, Tom thought it was too much of a performance getting up to the hospital each day so he simply had the whole contraption brought down and set up in the house! For the next three weeks I was put into this tank each morning, always with a fresh load of a thousand gallons of water at 102 degrees for my benefit.

It is only one of the many things for which I am indebted to Tom O'Connor. It is still amazing that he did all this for me. 'Grateful' is a much-used and often-debased word, but I shall always be grateful to him for everything he has done for me these past three years or so. I know I couldn't even begin to repay him for his kindness, his consideration, and his wise counsel.

Tom allotted two chaps to look after me, both house-servants. These two were Negroes of incredible strength and yet they moved me with tremendous gentleness and sympathy. They were absolutely marvellous to me.

In fact, the whole lot of them were marvellous to me. I only once had a moment of discomfort, and that was when Don Miles brought his three boys to see me. I was chatting to Miles while they were playing about the room, when suddenly I felt myself being dragged towards the end of the bed and in fact I had half disappeared under the sheets when Don discovered that one of his sons was swinging on the lead weights holding my leg up!

It was a month before I got out of bed and by that time, my hip was in good shape again. With a pair of crutches, I could get around in fine style.

Even today, however, there is still a final examination to be made on my leg. Apparently, there is a five-to-one chance that the blood vessels in my hip may not do their work properly and this might affect the bone. Happily, it feels all right most of the time.

141

It took a little time, of course, to get used to my crutches but I mastered them fairly quickly and started getting around the ranch again by helicopter. I spent lots of time cruising around, shooting timber wolves which always threatened the cattle, and so on.

Rufus, Tom's helicopter pilot, and I became good friends since we were out together nearly every day, but a couple of weeks after I got to my feet again, I landed both of us in a considerable drama.

It happened that Steve McQueen, whom I had met a number of times at Sebring and other places, was making a film on location in Texas at a town about 80 miles away from the ranch. He invited me over to see him on the set, and for a few drinks afterwards.

So Rufus and I set off in the chopper for the town of Wharton where the film was being shot.

When we arrived at the location, I looked down and saw all the arc lamps, cameras, wires and other equipment all over the road, and squads of people milling about. It was all pretty congested, since the shooting was taking place right in the middle of the town, with the Houston Highway running close by.

We started to come down slowly and I could see people point-up to us and so forth. I commented to Rufus: 'Oh, look, they're waving to us.' It was very encouraging to be given such an enthusiastic welcome, so I decided we ought to get down as quickly as possible. I pointed out to Rufus a tiny postage stamp of a lawn in front of somebody's house and suggested we put the chopper down there. And we did.

Immediately we got out of the machine, we were involved in a most tremendous row. The director of the film was absolutely doing his nut, for they had been in the middle of filming some scene or other. We had come along, making a tremendous racket which completely drowned everything, and had thrown up gales of dust which ruined the whole thing.

No wonder they were waving at us!

Anyway, Steve came bounding up in his usual enthusiastic manner and we stood laughing and chatting for a minute or two. Then I noticed that poor old Rufus was surrounded by policemen who were, in fact, in the process of marching him off.

Of course, I hobbled across as fast as my little crutches would carry me, and asked what on earth was happening. From out of the melee came the Chief of Police or someone equally imposing, and he glared at me.

'Is this your helicopter?'

'Why.., yes,' I said.

142

'Well, you're gonna have to take it Out of here on a truck, mister,' he said.

Naturally, I knew that one is not normally supposed to land helicopters in the middle of town, but I genuinely thought Steve had cleared permission with the police and I explained this to the Chief. He retorted that nobody had done any such goddamned thing — and he very nearly marched me off as well.

We eventually calmed the police down and contacted the Mayor of the town who intervened on our behalf. No doubt he didn't want trouble because he was having a big movie shot in his town. The whole thing was therefore forgotten, and they allowed Rufus to fly the chopper out to a field on the edge of town, where Steve and I later joined him.

Purely by chance Tom was driving his car home that evening with the radio switched on, and he almost left the road when he heard on the news bulletin that the British race driver Innes Ireland had almost been arrested, along with his pilot and a helicopter!

He was quite calm about it when I got home that night, though.

'Well, Ireland,' he drawled. 'Do I still own a helicopter? And is Rufus still in jail?'

In all, it was quite a day, for when Steve and I rejoined the chopper and flew back to Steve's motel some miles from Wharton, McQueen had put the fear of a third world war into all the residents by seizing the microphone of the loud-hailer fixed to the machine and bawling into it!

'This is an atomic warning! Go immediately to the blast shelters!

Needless to say the confusion below was quite considerable. There were people running out of the rooms in their underwear, springing up in alarm from the edge of the swimming pool, and others leaping about all over the place.

I had another rather amusing experience with the police a few days later. I was on my way to one of the ranches in Don's Buick Riviera and, since I was a bit late, I put my little trotter down the minute I got out on to the open highway. In America, in common with our new legislation, they have lots of these ridiculous speed limits even on the highways, with a maximum of something like seventy.

However, I was motoring along as fast as this Buick would go, which I imagine was about 120 miles an hour. I had gone about twenty miles out of town when I happened to overshoot the side turning off the highway, so I jumped on the brakes and reversed back to the turning.

Just as I stopped a police car came roaring up with tyres

143

screeching and steam coming from everything as he pulled in behind me. The driver came rushing over yanked the door open and roared! 'Get out!'

In my best cultured English voice, I said: 'I beg your pardon officer?'

'Get out of there,' he repeated.

'What's wrong?' I asked innocently.

'Don't argue, just get out,' policeman thundered. By this time he had his hand on the butt of his pistol and obviously meant me to get out!

I reached back inside the car for my crutches and hobbled out, not knowing what to expect. The officer was obviously staggered to see me totter out on crutches and plainly surprised to find me sober. Anyway, we chatted for a little while, and he explained: 'Anybody who drives at that speed has either just committed a crime or they're roaring drunk.' I was happy to point out that neither was the case.

'In any case,' I added. 'I didn't think I was going that quickly.'

'Well,' he drawled, 'I've been trying to catch you ever since you left Victoria. Matter of fact, I was so sure you were a drunk I radioed ahead for roadblocks further down the highway.'

Then I looked at his car. Boy, was it in a mess! When he switched off the engine, it ran on for about five minutes, thumping and crashing, with steam hissing from the radiator and the whole car practically on fire.

When he asked me whose car I was driving and I told him, his attitude softened.

'Say, you must be the English race driver,' he said. 'And I guess you ain't got your driver's licence this time either?'

It turned out that the same man had stopped me some time the previous year and I had not been able to produce my licence. I couldn't do so this time either, but it did not seem to matter too much. However, since he had gone to the trouble of setting up road blocks by radio he had to take some kind of action, so he gave me a speeding ticket. He also had to write some kind of speed on it — something not too terrifying — so he put my rate of knots at 100 m.p.h. which was pretty hot stuff for that part of the world.

What was very funny to me was that while all this was going on I had the intercom radio in the car switched on. This connects with all the other O'Connor ranch cars and the helicopter. Tom, flying from the River Ranch back to town — passed close by overhead, and as I was trying desperately to pacify the policeman, I heard his voice chuckling at the other end of my receiver. His delightful Texas accent came through: 'In trouble with the cops again, Ireland?'

144

'I see no ships...' Le Mans 1964.

(Photo: *Rene Maestri*)

Above: 'Roll me over...' Mosport 1962.

Below: '...lay me down...' Monaco 1964.

(Photo: *B.M.C.*)

'...I've done it again!'
Brands Hatch 1959.

(Photo: *Peter Elinskas*)

(Photo: *Rene Maestri)*

'They only told me where reverse was!' Monaco 1964.

Up at my duck pool with 'Seal', Christianne, Pauline Jobeson and Joan Cahier.

(Photo: *Bernard Cahier)*

I had a ball one way and another while I was recovering deep in the heart of Texas, but it meant that I did not do any motor racing. I missed the Mexican and American Grands Prix with BRP and since the Rosebud Lotus 19 was now a complete and utter wreck, I did no more racing in 1963.

I came back to England just before Christmas that year, still on crutches but mending fast.

I arrived back just in time for the British Racing Drivers' Club dinner dance at the Dorchester and, anxious to meet all the chaps again, I went along to it. I stayed with Graham and Bette Hill for a couple of days and we went to the dinner together. I did, in fact, collect a trophy while I was there, for the fastest lap of the year at Silverstone. This particularly pleased me because I had earned it with an out-dated Lotus 24 earlier in the season.

After the dinner, I fortified myself with about four Drambuies for the speechmaking, and after that all my friends were offering me drinks at each table I went to. Of course, with such a marvellous mixture of hooch, I got into a pretty hilarious condition — I even managed the Twist on my crutches, I'm told.

I somehow arrived home with Graham and Bette, but the next morning Graham asked me: 'How's your leg?' I said it was fine, thinking this was just a routine enquiry.

'Oh,' he said, 'I thought you had gone and broken it again last night.' I looked a bit puzzled, and he went on: 'Don't you remember falling down the steps of the Dorchester?' Apparently I had gone base over apex while tottering out of the hotel, had tumbled, with crutches flying in all directions, and hit the steps pretty hard. Fortunately, I couldn't remember a thing about it, nor, as far as I could discover, had I hurt myself.

I threw away my crutches on New Year's Eve, 1963, just three months after the accident.

Five days after that, I was, learning to ski while taking a short holiday in Switzerland. I fell over a great many times and in fact managed to graunch another lump out of my leg with a ski, which did not help matters much, The great thing was that my leg stood up to it all and by the time racing began again in England, I was fit, well and raring to go after a six-month lay-off.

The first race of the year for me was at Snetterton in March — and Snetterton in March is just about the bleakest place in the world! It was blowing a gale and pouring with rain. Conditions were really disgusting and I was of the opinion that we should all have retired quietly to the bar and forgotten the whole thing. However, racing did take place. I was driving the old prototype Formula One BRP car, for Tony Robinson and the rest of the

145

mechanics were still working on a brand-new machine for the Grand Prix season.

By this time, Trevor Taylor had joined BRP, since he had left Team Lotus at the end of 1963. I was delighted to have him alongside me in the BRP team.

We both got off to a good start in blinding rain and I settled down to enjoy myself, motoring quite sedately and trying very hard to stay on the road. All sorts of dramas were taking place in the rain. People were spinning off and disappearing from the pit signal boards, and I began moving comfortably up the field.

I remember Jack Brabham thundering past me and staying there for a couple of laps, until I saw him pointing out of a hedge somewhere with all his exhaust pipes bent. At this stage I found myself in second place behind Jo Bonnier. Receiving pit signals to this effect, I started to press on a little harder. I remember I followed him closely in a dense cloud of spray for quite a while, and, of course, I could not see a thing. There was a huge puddle lying on the track near the S-bends, and throughout the race I had steered clear of it rather nicely. Now, however, motoring practically blind, I hit it and spun around a bit, before getting the car pointed in the right direction and haring off again after Jo. I did catch and pass him in front of the pits as we both hit a great stream of water. I pulled out quite a lead on him and after a while I was going so nicely that I began to think that everybody else had got bored with the whole thing and gone home, for I simply could not see anyone else on the track.

Eventually, the chequered flag waved for me and 1 had won. Really I think I just happened to be the chap who stayed on the road longest, for the race was run in the most appalling conditions I ever experienced. Nonetheless, it was pleasant to have won my first race of the season, and I felt good about having done it in the wet since I was not usually too happy or convincing in the rain.

Things did not go quite so marvellously at Goodwood, where I drove in my next race on Easter Monday. I got involved in a bit of a drama on a corner when I had to brake very sharply to avoid Peter Arundel, and I spun like a top. Unluckily Bruce McLaren was sitting on my tail and as I spun we collected each other and ended up in a heap on the banking with rather dented cars.

A little later, I endured a week of incidents which made me believe for a while that I was incapable of getting into any sort of motor-car without becoming involved in a crash.

It started at Silverstone where, in a Formula One race, I was handed the first of the BRP 1964 cars to drive. This was a

146

beautiful machine which had been personally tailored for me. In fact, they took my measurements and built the car around them. The seat in the cockpit was just twelve inches wide - which happens to be the width of my behind — and the cockpit tapered down to a mere nine inches where the pedals were clustered. It was so tight, in fact, that I was only able to drive the car in one particular pair of shoes — any others wouldn't fit the car!

The BRP had been fairly well sorted out. We had a new six-speed gear box from BRM to match the BRM engine we were using and a better gear-shift position with improved linkages and' so forth — but somehow or other, the car did not go too well in that first outing.

Well enough, though, to hold sixth or seventh position for most' of the race. Then, very near the end, as I came through Abbey Curve, the car suddenly took charge of itself. For absolutely no reason, it flicked round and went crashing into a bloody great earth banking. I can't think why it happened since I was almost out of the corner. I hit the banking about three times as I was spinning along rattling around inside, with bits and pieces flying off all around me.

This, unfortunately, wrecked our brand-new car — which pleased' the mechanics no end.

This happened on a Saturday. The following Wednesday I was in Monaco prior to the first of the season's Grands Prix, living on a yacht in the harbour with Ken Gregory. Tony Robinson was due to arrive in nearby Nice that day, so I elected to drive over to the airport and pick him up. A friend of ours, a chap named Leslie Singer, lent me his hired Renault Floride and, with him and Trevor Taylor, I drove to Nice. I remember I was dressed in just a pair of short shorts, without socks or shoes or anything since we had been living on the yacht, the weather was warm and we anticipated no trouble on the journey.

We came barrelling down the big dual carriageway road from Nice and, on nearing the airport, took a slip road which curved round under the main road and into the airport. There was absolutely nothing on this little road, as far as I could see, to say that it developed into a two-way road, so I just went screaming down it.

As I got to the bend under the main road and was driving on the left — which is apparently not the side they drive on in France! — I met another car coming straight for me. I tried to dive back to my own side of the road, but I had only got about halfway when there was a hell of a great crash. It all reminded me of a Jacques Tati film really, for when all the banging and crashing and tinkle-tinkle had subsided, the horn on the other car started blowing

147

continuously and would not cease. I decided I would have to stop the noise or it would have driven me crazy, so I leapt out of my car and disconnected the battery of the other vehicle. This was in full view since the bonnet had flown off completely.

Just as I got that fixed, the horn on my own car began blaring, so I had to rush around and find the battery in the Renault and undo that.

Next I went across to help a lady who had unfortunately cut her head on the driving mirror of the other ear. I intended to assist her to the side of the road and sit her under a tree in the shade. I had her supported on my arm and was helping her across the road when, quite suddenly, her companion, a young Frenchman, marched up and bit me a fourpenny one on the chin.

I thought this was bloody marvellous! There we were in the middle of an accident and this stupid fellow starts a punchup! Anyway, I didn't feel like hitting him back because that would really have started things off, so I ignored it as best I could and went on helping the lady.

As the drama went on, I saw that Leslie Singer was still sitting in our car, holding his sides and not breathing too well. I assumed he had been laughing at the antics of myself and the Frenchman and got a stitch or something. Every time I said something to him it seemed to make him Worse. I didn't see what was so damned funny myself, so I left him to it. It wasn't until ten minutes later that I found out he had cracked a rib in the pile-up and he had to go to hospital.

Pretty soon, the police arrived. They said I would have to get the wreckage of my car removed, so I toddled off into Nice airport to phone the hire car company. Only when I got there did I see what a horrible mess I was. I had blood running down my leg, my bare feet were filthy dirty from the dust in the road and I was wearing only a pair of shorts anyway — and then I found I didn't have a penny on me and had to cadge the price of a phone call from someone.

Anyway, I did it and hurried back to the scene of the drama.

The next thing I knew, I had been arrested!

It was all a bit crazy from the first. On the way to the police station in a black maria thing, a very pretty girl in an open car passed us and immediately the police driver began blowing his hooter and waving at her as Frenchmen will. In the end, the lot of us, prisoner and policemen, were wolf-whistling at this creature like a lorryload of lunatics.

I thought it was all going to be a good giggle, but, by heavens, the moment we got to the police station, it was a different matter. I got a tremendous grilling from hosts of gendarmes who couldn't

148

understand who I was or what I was doing wandering around in just a pair of shorts without a passport, driving licence, money or anything else. It was then I realised I was in trouble.

Fortunately, bad news travels fast, and after some six or seven hours, Bernard Cahier, the French motoring journalist, spoke to the Chief of Police or whatever, and sorted it out.

When they turned me out of the police station it was dark and very cold and there I was standing on the sidewalk in a pair of shorts, all grime and goosepimples. Fortunately, Trevor Taylor had stayed behind for me and he called a taxi and hurried me back to the yacht. I can't think I was desperately popular at that stage, having written off a brand new racing car and now a hire car.

However, there was worse to come!

The following day, during practice for the Grand Prix, I found that the brakes on the old Lotus 24 I was using — the new BRP was still in bits after Silverstone — were not working properly. As I came downhill towards the chicane on the harbour waterfront, my right rear wheel locked solid and I went careering across the road and took a dive into a concrete wall.

There was the old familiar crash and bang, as wheels and bits flew off. After crashing through straw bales and so forth, I finished up about fifty yards along the escape road, sitting in another fairly well wrecked car.

Actually, I think it was just as well that I didn't manage to get the car through the chicane in its condition, for I am quite certain that had I done so I would have taken a header into the harbour itself.

As I climbed wearily from the remains of the Lotus, I looked up to see our yacht and all the people on board only thirty yards away!

I was so depressed at having destroyed two-thirds of the team cars that I just persuaded someone to run me out to the yacht in a motor boat, went straight down below decks and disappeared for the rest of the week.

Tony Robinson was not, in fact, too worried about the Lotus. For weeks, he had been trying unsuccessfully to sell it, and was wondering what to do with the thing when I solved the problem for him.

This thought, however, didn't do anything for the depression which settled on me for the next few days.

14

I began to believe there was a jinx on me. It seemed impossible for me to get into a car without something going very wrong and me ending up sitting in a heap of wreckage. In five days I had written off two-thirds of the BRP team plus a hire car and I can't tell you how depressed it all made me. Of course, I took no part in the Monaco race since I had seen off my own cars and nobody was about to suggest that I took over Trevor's! Least of all me. I think I read a book during the actual hours of racing, because I was so upset I couldn't bear to watch the contest, although I was in the pits.

If there was a jinx on me, it persisted, for a piece of very cruel luck was, I am sure, all that prevented Graham Hill and myself from winning the classic Nurburgring 1,000 Kilometre race in Germany shortly afterwards.

Graham and myself were co-drivers in a Ferrari 330P GT car entered in the race by Maranello Concessionaires, the British Ferrari agents. We were up against two works Ferraris driven by Surtees and Bandini and Scarfiotti and Vacarella. It was all very exciting for me, for the 330P was indeed a magnificent car and I was looking forward to getting a real race in at Nurburgring after all the miserable memories I had of the place.

We had arranged that Graham would drive the first leg of fifteen laps, I would take the middle fifteen and leave Hill for the finishing fifteen. It worked very well — as far as it went.

Graham got off to a fairly good start, but by the time the pit stops were due, Surtees had a 64-second lead over him. Further-more, by the time I got into the car and took off, we had been further delayed by some fumble or other in the pits, with the result that both Bandini and Vacarella were well ahead of me. However, all thoughts of jinxes and that sort of thing were behind me when I eventually roared off, I was determined to try and do well and I found the Ferrari a joy to handle, so that by the end of my first lap, I had closed the gap between myself and Bandini to 37 seconds and was only 12 seconds behind Vacarella. I was really in my element and, for the first time, picking up confidence about driving at Nurburgring.

Halfway through my driving stint, I passed Vacarella and a lap after that, I squeezed past Bandini too. Thoroughly enjoying myself, I pressed on and soon had a lead of about 12 seconds over Bandini. I felt, for a change, that everything was going to go along nicely.

Then the car started to handle badly, slipping about and so on. I put it down at first to some oil on the circuit, so I motored on although the car was sliding about in quite alarming fashion at times.

Bandini began to close on me little by little and to add to my troubles, I got terribly baulked by a car which was obviously very sick and not motoring at competitive speed at all. This held me up for about half to three-quarters of a mile.

Bandini, of course, was roaring up behind me and by the time I had got this chap sorted out and passed him, Lorenzo came thundering up and overtook me. I was absolutely furious because I had probably had a ten-second lead and I lost the whole lot because of this goon in a sick motor car.

However, I carried on behind Bandini until I had done thirteen laps — leaving two to go — when the engine started misfiring. It felt to me as if the car was running out of petrol but I could hardly believe this since enough fuel had been put into the car for eighteen or nineteen laps. Sure enough, however, we were short of the stuff, so I switched on to the reserve tank when I was about halfway round the circuit from the pits. I knew now that I had to be very careful, for the Ferrari reserve tank held only enough petrol for half a lap at Nurburgring — God knows why Ferraris put in such a meagre reserve tank. I therefore kept the car in top gear whenever I could and cruised round gently. When I got to a straight bit, I worked up the speed, then took the car out of gear and coasted along to conserve petrol. In this fashion I got to within about 500 yards of the pits — and then the engine quit dead.

The car stopped pretty smartly too, for this was on an uphill section.

My first thought was to try and push the car to the pits, but I didn't take into account the weight of the Ferrari. Not only could I not push it, but it began to push me back down the incline.

Pretty soon, I was in a very unsavoury position. I had kept a bit of right-hand lock on the car and it rolled back and trapped me against a sapling tree at the side of the road; there I was caught with my legs wrapped round the tree with this bloody great Ferrari holding me very firmly in position. However, I did finally manage to extricate myself and I ran up the hill to the pits. By the time I arrived, I was absolutely clapped out and I could just about manage to gasp: 'Petrol!' before I fell into a heap.

Graham immediately grabbed a can of petrol and dashed down the road with it, but since you are not allowed to refuel between scheduled pit stops anyway, that was the end of our race.

We then discovered what had happened. The wretched fuel tank had split! This accounted not only for the fact that I ran out of petrol, but also for the sloppy way in which the car had been handling, for the fuel was running out of the main tank straight on to the rear tyres.

I was dreadfully disappointed about the whole thing. I would dearly have loved to have won that race, for it is a classic in the motor racing calendar. What's more, I am sure we could have done. Had I been able to keep going properly, I think I could have handed over to Graham with a fair lead in hand and I am certain he would have been first across the line.

For the rest of the Formula One season in 1964, we at BRP were hardly in it.

The engines we were getting from BRM just did not seem to go as well as they had the previous year. I can't explain it, although there probably are explanations. All I know is that in 1963 I had given Graham Hill, the BRM Works driver, a good run for his money on a couple of occasions and had beaten his second string. Now, we were just not quick enough to be competitive. I remember at Aintree, Graham passed me on the straight as if I had been tied to a tree. It was absurd that in 1964, with the latest specification BRM engine, we were going slower than we had the previous year. I think the directors of BRP in fact had a few strong words with their counterparts at BRM, but they countered with the argument that my engine was, in fact, quicker than Graham's. I know this to be untrue, though, for whenever I came out of a corner behind Graham, he would take off away from me and yet I can put my foot on the floor just as well as anyone else. Whatever the reasons, I certainly wasn't getting enough out of my car often enough to win many races.

152

Of course, it did occasionally run well. At Rouen for the French Grand Prix, for example, the engine went extremely well and I thought it was at least better than Ritchie Ginther's engine in the number two BRM. Unfortunately, at Rouen, I performed another of my familiar gyrations. Exactly the same as at Silverstone, the car suddenly twitched on a corner and refused to go into the appex of the bend. I finished up doing a wall of death act along a high banking on the left-hand side of the road at over 125 m.p.h.

I eventually came down off the banking into a ditch at the bottom, and went crunching and graunching along that until I once more came to a halt with bent metal and loose ends all around me.

These two events — Silverstone and Rouen — did set Tony Robinson doing some pretty serious thinking about the car. In both cases, I had not the slightest idea what was happening to the machine and I was quite unable to give him any clue as to the cause. Normally, a driver can always tell why he had an accident — he has either fallen asleep at the wheel or made some other kind of driver error — in which case he will — or ought to — have the intelligence to tell the mechanics so. Another reason is that something breaks on the car and a driver can always tell roughly what happened to him before he flies off the road. A third alternative might be oil or something on the road and once again, a driver knows about it. I was, however, quite unable to give Tony any reason why the accidents had occurred.

Tony is a pretty brilliant motor engineer and he came up with a modification to the rear suspension which, in fact, made the world of difference to the control of the vehicle and I was much happier with it. Before I had always felt on a knife-edge with the car, always expecting something to go wrong. Unfortunately, I think we cured that part of the trouble too late to make much difference to the result we got with the car in the season's races.

I found generally in 1964 that there was much more fun to be had out of GT races and sports car racing.

I did the Targa Florio race in Sicily that year for the first time, racing AC Cobras for Carroll Shelby, with Masten Gregory, Dan Gurney and Phil Hill. We really had a good time there. It was a tremendously difficult course through the mountains, with each lap 44 miles long, so there wasn't too much of learning the circuit intimately beforehand. I remember we had a Ford Cortina handed to us in which to get to know the road and each of us regularly wore out two sets of tyres and a set of brake pads every day. Actually, nothing good happened in the race, for my co-pilot

Masten Gregory disappeared over a wall complete with the car. Nonetheless, I enjoyed myself.

I also went to Zeltweg, in Austria, for the first Formula One world championship race to be held there in which I did reasonably well, except that the engine went a bit sick at the end, firing on only six cylinders, and I scrambled home fifth — I think!

There was a terrible drama after the race. Jo Bonnier had been, at one stage a lap ahead of me but I had caught him up again when his car got a bit ill and passed him into fifth place. Bonnier then claimed that he had, in fact, been two laps ahead of me when I began chasing him and he put in a protest to the organisers. Everyone got into a great state of confusion and half a dozen different race results were put out over the loud-speakers.

My own pit were quite sure that Jo had been only a lap ahead of me and that when I passed him I had gone ahead of him in the race result.

After the race, though, when everyone had quietened down, we all went to the prize giving where Austrian hospitality overcame most of us. After that we drifted on to a party which was being thrown by someone or other at a motel just out of town.

We were joined during the early hours, I remember, by a couple of young chaps, holidaymakers I think, who happened to be wearing kilts. So Clark and I, both Scots, of course, took these two chaps outside, did a quick deal with them and came back in borrowed kilts! I did the traditional Scottish thing in not wearing anything underneath the tartan and when Jim and I did a couple of Highland Flings or whatever, it all got a bit bawdy and in fact we had great fun.

Until someone did a most grievous mischief...

I only wish I had seen him coming, but in fact he crept up on me with a cactus which he had taken out of a pot — and rammed it up my kilt!

Of course, he got me in a very vital spot, but at the time I didn't feel anything in particular except a little bit of discomfort, but by the time I got back to my hotel, I was in absolute agony, because, of course, cactus plants are covered with millions of tiny prickles. On a close examination of the afflicted area, I found that most of them had come off on me. All the way up the inside of my leg had come up in a bright scarlet rash — and I was painfully affected in other parts too!

Actually, I spent a very interesting couple of hours that night with a magnifying glass and a pair of tweezers...

154

I was only glad to hear, after that, at least my attacker had felt some effect for his dastardly deed for his hand was similarly covered with the wretched prickles.

I managed, however, to get myself in good order again in time for the next World Championship event. This was at Monza and proved to be the first of another pair of very disappointing races for me. At Monza, I had a new BRP car, this time fitted with long-range fuel tanks, which meant mounting an additional tank over my knees. It added extra weight to the car, but I soon found that it somehow helped the roadholding of the machine which went very well indeed.

This, the Italian Grand Prix, started out as one of the most enjoyable races I have known. When it got under way, I think either Clark or Surtees or both shot away from the start leaving just behind them a whole pack of people including myself, Bonnier, Siffert, Gurney, Brabham, Ginther and Bandini. We had a splendid race together. It was really exciting stuff, all streaming along in close company like a pack of dogs after a bitch on heat and I am sure it must have been very good to see.

Halfway through the race, the bunch had thinned a little and three of us — Bandini, Ginther and myself were fighting it out about a lap behind the leaders, Surtees and Gurney. My car was going extremely well; the effect of the slipstream gave me extra speed, the six-speed BRM gearbox behaved perfectly well, and the roadholding improved beyond measure. As we went round lap after lap, I was sure that the man I had to beat in our little bunch was Ritchie Ginther, for Bandini was behind the two of us most of the time, At about the three-quarter stage of the race, I got a signal from my pit to switch over to the reserve fuel tank. This meant flicking a switch and allowing the petrol in the tank over my knees to drain into the main tanks at the side. This I did.

But within five laps of doing so I found the car beginning to handle like a pig. Whereas before I had been able to put it into a corner just so and know what was going to happen, I now had to cope with a relatively unstable machine. Naturally I lost ground to both Ginther and Bandini.

In the end, Bandini just pipped Ginther for third place, leaving Ritchie fourth and myself fifth some way behind. But it was so galling. The way the car had been running earlier, I felt sure I could finish ahead of both of them and might well have got third place. As it was, I more or less limped in fifth, although that was our best Championship result of the season.

However, having divined that the extra fuel tank helped the car, we decided to keep it fitted for the next race, the American Grand

155

Prix at Watkins Glen. It was rather a clumsy way of making a car stable and, of course, added to the weight. Nonetheless we did so and once more the car behaved extremely well. I was lying around fifth or sixth place after a couple of laps at the Glen and felt full of confidence. It was unfortunate that this Was the last race but one of the GP season, but it was something to have a car beneath me that felt as if It was really going places — and was likely to keep going!

Then the most infuriating thing occurred. The most stupid, piddling thing, and the last sort of breakdown I could have imagined.

The gear lever snapped off in my hand!

I had just overtaken Jack Brabham on the inside going into a bend, snicked the gear lever into fifth gear and found I had the gear lever in my hand, broken below the gate, so that I had no chance of changing gear again.

There was absolutely nothing for it but to retire.

I don't think I did it too gracefully, either, for it was just too frustrating for words. This was, in fact, the only time I could ever criticize the mechanics at BRP, for the same gear lever had broken off in practice for a race a couple of weeks previously and had been temporarily welded back. Somehow or other, the replacement of the thing had been overlooked, probably in the tremendous rush to get back from Italy and prepare the cars to fly to the United States. So, in due course, it had come apart again.

My last Grand Prix of the season was in Mexico City late in 1964.

It was really only remarkable for the fact that the car didn't go very well because the engine was affected by the high altitude — and for a most unfortunate TV interview, which I gave quite unwittingly.

During the race the car had been going terribly, and then on a corner where previously I had shed a wheel a couple of years earlier, something funny happened at the back of the car and I pulled into the pits next time round to have a closer look. Naturally, the first thing I had thought of was that the wheel was about to fly off. I came into the pits and took off my helmet, for I wasn't about to drive the thing any more.

Just then Stirling Moss came walking up to me and asked what was wrong. Obviously, as a director of BRP, I thought Stirling was just anxious to hear about it.

I certainly did not realise that he was interviewing me for live television, for when he put the question to me; I, in my fury at being stranded again, replied rather bluntly.

156

'What's the matter, Innes?' asked Stirling.

'Oh, I don't bloody-well know,' I said. 'Except that the... ing car is as rough as a bear's ass.'

Then I saw Stirling back off quickly, but then he came up to me again and asked: 'Well, why have you retired, Innes?'

Again, I was in such a stew that I did not see the microphone in his hand and I again replied in the vernacular.

'Oh, the bloody thing was wandering all over the... ing road. It's like a bag of ...'

By this time Stirling had vanished completely and it was only later that he told me how he had desperately tried to cover up my language and make some comment of his own!

However, I did get back in the car and had great difficulty in starting the thing. Only then did I notice a man with a television camera trained on me. I learned later that anyone with a slightest knowledge of the favourite English swear-word could plainly have seen it issuing from my lips repeatedly as I cursed the car for refusing to start.

As a matter of fact, there was nothing wrong with the car that anyone could discover and all in all, it was a most unsatisfactory last race — for it was indeed the last time I drove for BRP.

When this phase of Formula One racing came to an end, there was really very little more warning than there had been when I was tossed out of Team Lotus. There had been talk of BRP quitting at the end of 1962, when the team found itself without the support of the United Dominions Trust banking and hire purchase company, due to a change of policy in that firm. Again, at the end of 1963, there had been some talk of the team folding because it had made a loss on the year's activities. I am just a born optimist, however, and I felt that it wouldn't happen, that it couldn't happen to me, as it were.

I was in Switzerland, involved with my Snow-Trac venture when it finally did happen. A newspaper rang me up one day shortly before Christmas and asked what I was going to do now. I was a bit baffled until told that BRP had announced their decision to pull out of motor racing.

In some ways, it was a great shame, for it looked as if we were about to get the car to a pitch where it would have become competitive, if we could have been assured of a similar engine performance to those of the works.

I do not feel in any way that BRP let me down. After all, other people were paying for my racing and no one can expect those people to go on paying *ad infinitem.*

That was that. I decided to disappear to Switzerland to live in the mountains for a few months, staying with my very good friend David McLennan and helping him in any small way possible to develop his new ski resort — an incredibly fine venture — in the Lötschental.

A most pleasant change!

158

15

The team for whom I was going to drive in 1965 — the British Racing Partnership — had been forced to withdraw from the game because of the strangling financial closed shop which has developed in Grand Prix racing.

Motor racing has become such a money-conscious affair that for most people in it, the fun of the thing is but a minor consideration. For me, it was all-important.

The fact that I am racing again means I am driving for the fun of it. I am not interested, in getting back in step with the rest of the mice on the treadmill.

It is a thousand pities, but motor racing today is a rat race in which most individuals are chiefly concerned with screwing as much money out of the game as possible. I was probably always an idiot over money since I never felt it worth arguing about. Throughout my racing career, I always took what was offered and stuck to it.

I don't claim that being a financial idiot is a virtue, but I can't help it if the importance of money in motor racing sickens and disheartens me.

It is all made worse, to my mind, because this outlook affects not only many of the top drivers in the big-money bracket, but youngsters who are just now getting their breaks.

I remember at the end of last year, talking to one of these chaps — a driver who was having his first season in Formula One and had just been taken on as second-string to a works team. We had dinner together, at the Lion d'Or in Reims and he began to ask me questions about motor racing. While the subject remained on the lines of racing itself, the cars and the circuits, I was delighted to pass on anything from my own experience. Very soon, however, it became clear that his chief concern was money.

159

The questions came thick and fast: 'Am I getting enough start-ing money? How much more can I get out of So-and-so? Can I ask more from the X petrol company? Would the Y tyre company pay me more?'

In the end I got tired of it. 'Look,' I said. 'You have come to the wrong chap. I'm hopeless at screwing money out of people. I race for what I am paid and I'm damned glad to do it. You'd better go to an accountant.'

The driver in question will undoubtedly end up very well off. Yet, to my way of thinking, he will not have contributed a damned thing to the sport which gave him the opportunity.

To me, motor racing isn't a grabbing game for individuals. It's a team sport.

Personally, I like working with a team and racing with a team, but that aspect of motor sport has vanished. It's all very well talking about the tremendous, team behind a winning car and driver, but that usually only means that the mechanics work day and night and the driver gets in and drives it. Because, once the flag goes down for the start, the driver is on his own. There is no teamwork in the race. The mechanics might as well pack up and go home, for once you have to pull into the pits, in modem Grand Prix racing, that is the end of the affair ,for you — except in the unlikely circumstances when perhaps everyone else has to pull in too.

I am firmly of the belief that now is the time for the powers that be in motor racing to take a good, long, hard look at what they are doing to the game. Just now, they have formula'd the thing almost to the point of oblivion. I think many, many people will agree with me that this is a tremendous pity, for there is excitement in motor racing — or, there could be if the competitive element was once more injected into it.

As a suggestion, I would say that this might be done if the amount of fuel a car could carry was limited, or the races themselves lengthened.

If this were done, it would have the effect of forcing cars to make at least one pit stop, perhaps more, to take on fuel or to make running adjustments.

In this way, we would at least bring back the team work of the sport, since pit stops would again be matters of vital importance without necessarily being disasters.

Just now, of course, Formula One races and it is Formula One' on which I am concentrating in my assessment of motor racing — are just sprints. Cars are built to run at their maximum for two hours or so and I doubt whether the present type of car could go on much longer — many can't keep going for that long.

160

I think a tremendous amount of interest would be put back into the sport from the spectator point of view — mind you, I am only guessing here, since I have not been a spectator — if we had pit work again.

I am fairly certain that people who go to watch motor racing would find the whole thing more interesting if the lead in a race changed more frequently because of pit stops. I am also of the opinion that team-work between drivers and mechanics during a race would do a lot to foster a greater spirit of sport than now exists.

It would also be beneficial from that point of view I think, if manufacturers' championship points were awarded to both cars in a team.

That is another absurdity of this World Championship thing.

Team Lotus won the manufacturer's championship in 1963. Jim Clark's car never ever failed, but the second car in the team, which was Trevor Taylor's car, hardly ever finished. So you end up with a manufacturer winning the championship with one car.

This certainly doesn't prove that the champion manufacturer makes the best ears; all it means is that he makes one reliable car. To me, this is a rather absurd state of affairs. Taking 1963 as an example, we had Lotus winning with one car, while on the other hand, BRM, although not winning as many races, always had TWO cars well placed throughout.

Which is the best manufacturer? It seems clear to me that BRM that year made the more reliable motor-cars.

The present system, ordained by the FIA, is that manufacturers' championship points are awarded only to the best-placed car in each team. Hence, Lotus won.

I would like to see both cars in a team earning points and if this encouraged a manufacturer to enter more than two cars, so much the better for motor racing I should think.

As it is, a manufacturer is given a ready-made excuse for looking after only one of the two cars in his team.

When you tie this up with the financial agreements for starting money and so forth, you can see just what the temptations are.

Both cars in a team get equal starting money, so that in some cases the second car is virtually a Starting Money Special.

All it is going to the track for, it seems to me, is to collect the money. It just has to get to the grid and collect the starting money, which is up to £800 for each car in a team.

You could see the trend in 1965. Every leading team had one top-flight driver for its No. 1 car, whilst the second car was handed over to a comparative unknown. For all anybody cares about the No. 2 car, it might just as well be driven by the works tea-boy.

F   161

For instance, up until the middle of 1964, nobody had ever heard of a very, very pleasant fellow, an Austrian driver called Jochen Rindt. In 1965 he was 2nd driver to Bruce McLaren in the Cooper works team and now it looks as if he will be No. 1 for Cooper in 1967. During 1966 Cooper chopped and changed their No. 1 driver and although Rindt has shown that he is fast and courageous, to my mind he has not the experience required to lead a team. This is not surprising considering the short time he has been racing and perhaps 1967 will be a turning point for him.

This is only one of the ramifications of the Paris Agreement.

This agreement is an undertaking between the constructors and the organisers of Grandes Epreuves, the constructors being BRM, Lotus, Cooper and Brabham.

There is another major constructor in the forefront of motor racing — Enzo Ferrari. He refused to join this agreement on the grounds that he could always get the starting money he wanted just on the reputation of his cars, which is quite correct.

However, the other four went into this thing. The basic principles of this agreement are that each car in the teams would be given a basic amount of starting money — £800. That was for the car itself. The driver would then also get starting money on top of this, according to the number of points he had earned in the previous year's drivers' championship.

So, in the case of Clark or Graham Hill, the organiser has to pay something in the region of £1,300 for a Lotus driven by Clark or a BRM driven by Hill.

However, it does not matter a hoot who is driving the second car; it still qualifies for its £800.

The driver's part of this agreement is that the driver has to be paid a minimum of £150 — thereafter he is paid £25 a point for his previous championship points (provided he has more than six points) up to a maximum of £450.

For example, a driver with four points in the previous championship table gets the basic £150. A driver with twelve points get the basic £150, plus a further £150 — a total of £300.

What about those manufacturers outside the agreement? The pickings for them are meagre indeed.

Take the Dutch Grand Prix at Zandvoort in 1964.

The British Racing Partnership for whom I was driving were offered a mere £600 to take two cars, one driven by myself and the other by Trevor Taylor. Yet the second car for Team Lotus was getting more than that, with a driver who was only just starting in his first season in Formula One — Peter Arundel. A very good driver and a very able one, but nevertheless it was his first season at the top. And he was getting for his car more than the two cars of BRP.

BRP decided they could not possibly go for that sort of money. Their agreement with myself and Trevor Taylor would have meant them paying away about half the starting money, and they just could not afford to take two cars all the way to Holland, pay four mechanics, transport, hotels and everything else on £500.

So we could not go to the meeting. This deprived the team of income and it deprived Trevor and I of trying to earn points in the championship table — if that is what one races for.

Roughly the same thing happened at Nurburgring, when BRP did not go to the German Grand Prix.

In 1963, British Racing Partnership decided to start making their own cars. This they did and for the next two seasons they constructed their own vehicles. I think any observer, anybody who knows anything about the sport, and more particularly an engineer who would look at any of the five marques of car racing then — Lotus, Ferrari, Cooper, Brabham and BRM — and compare them to BRP's machinery would agree that the workmanship and care that went into BRP cars was certainly as good as any of the others.

Every drill-hole in the chassis, every weld, was precise, exact and beautifully finished. Everything about them was workmanlike and a precision job — which is more than you could say for some of the other cars racing. Obviously, they were all very good, but if you really went to town, you would find that the BRP was often a better made and a better-finished product.

Unfortunately, we all knew that it was not as quick and that the roadholding and the suspension were still being ironed out. Nevertheless the actual manufacture of the vehicle was frequently an improvement on the rest.

Now, Ken Gregory and Alfred Moss, Stirling's father, are both very, very experienced people in motor racing and they decided that, in the circumstances they must apply for membership of the Paris Agreement.

It was in the spirit of 'If you can't beat 'em, join 'em', that they took this step in my opinion.

They were manufacturers in their own right now, and they rightly enough thought they were entitled to join if they so chose.

Everything was done to prepare the way for this and, at Watkins Glen, during the American Grand Prix meeting in 1964, Tony Robinson told the powers-that-be of the Agreement that BRP cars would be open to inspection at the Glen for consideration for membership, so that, in the future, BRP would qualify for the same sort of starting money as the others and would in that way be able to keep racing.

163

As far as I know they didn't come to see the cars.

Shortly after that, the Paris Agreement people held a meeting, at which the subject of BRP's application for membership came up.

'BRP do not qualify for membership,' it was said. 'They are not really constructors. Too much of their car is supplied by other manufacturers.' With these remarks, someone carried the day.

BRP decided to examine this proposition. They checked up on other constructors already party to the Agreement. The car of one of these used roughly seven per cent of materials supplied by other firms, BRP estimated. He did not make his own engine, gearbox, nor front suspension uprights. He did make his own chassis, wheels and the rest of the suspension. In common with everyone else, he bought radiators, instruments and similar units.

Then, in the same detail, BRP analysed their own cars. The engine and gearbox they bought from BRM, the front wheels and front and rear suspension uprights from Lotus and the back wheels from Brabham. The rest was their own.

BRP calculated that they made all but ten per cent of their car.

So, we failed to make ten per cent of our car. The manufacturer mentioned failed to make seven per cent of his car — and at a very rough guess, I'd say that another failed to make about six per cent of his car.

Now, where is the dividing line between six, seven and ten per cent? I find it hard to see the justification upon which BRP were apparently excluded from membership of the Agreement.

Looked at the other way, one could say that the only people who are manufacturers entirely in their own right are BRM and Ferrari. Both make their own engines and their own gearboxes.

In the year of 1964, BRP were out of pocket. They lost something to the tune of £8,000 in starting money — from meetings they could not afford to attend and the low money they got from those they did go to.

Simply because they were not members of the Paris Agreement.

At the end of the year, the finances of the team were calculated and it worked out that the team had lost about £7,000 on the whole operation, And this was the second year that the team had lost money.

Had they been members of the Agreement, they would just about have broken even. If they had broken even — for that is all they wanted to do — in 1965, they would have gone on racing. Yet because they did not become members, they had to quit.

The British Racing Partnership was a private venture run by Stirling Moss, Alfred Moss and Ken Gregory. These three people took the loss on the team and, quite understandably, they decided they could carry the burden no longer.

I admire Enzo Ferrari for his attitude. He doesn't need the Agreement.

Personally, I don't really see why BRM have committed themselves to joining the Agreement. If am quite sure the Owen Organisation is well able to afford to keep out.

How ludicrous it is that a large and properly-organised outfit like BRP cannot afford to race.

I feel it is an indication of how much 'sport' is left within the sport when there is so little concern that a fine team like BRP had had to go to the wall.

16

If I had to sum up my outlook on life and my career in motor racing, I don't think I could do better than quote an old, well-worn adage, for in my case it has largely been a matter of 'Eat, Drink and be Merry'.

I live my life the way I enjoy it. I do the things I want to do — probably without too much regard for the people around me. I find that if I am not allowed to do what I want, I get irritated, frustrated and pretty impossible to live with. Perhaps this accounts for the undeniable fact that I have done a great many stupid things in my lifetime.

I know it has been said that I present an image of being a character on the motor racing scene, and it seems that I have made headlines of various sorts, for being arrested, for being involved in some pretty spectacular crashes and so on, and maybe some of the excitement, the glamour if you like, of motor racing has rubbed off on me.

I have never, however, consciously set out to create such an image — it is just the way I am. I detest anything phoney anyway.

I suppose it is simply that I have always lived for today and never thought too much about tomorrow. I know this is a selfish outlook, particularly since I am married and have a daughter, and I think this is one of the things that sobers me up a little. I have, in my own way, tried to make provision for my family so that if anything ever did happen to me, they would not be wanting.

This is my one contribution towards trying to live a normal life in the midst of the fairly hectic and perhaps dangerous surroundings in which I have hitherto made my living.

I myself have never thought of motor racing as being dangerous, though, only exciting. I went into it for the excitement alone and if I am a little disillusioned about the state of motor racing now, I will say that I still find the idea of driving a car fast in competition with other cars intensely exciting.

I certainly never regarded motor racing as a way of making money. It is financially quite rewarding, of course, and I will not say I have ever shied away from the money, but equally, I have never gone looking for it either.

One reads quite a lot about the fortunes which racing drivers make, and indeed the chaps at the top today are able to command something in the order of £50,000—£100,000 a year, which is not peanuts. Not so much, however, compared with the rewards picked up by pimply-faced pop groups, whose only dangers are that their electric guitars might fuse and burn their fingers, or that they may get their hair pulled by their fans!

No, it was never the money, nor even any particular ambition which drew me to motor racing. It was always the thrill of racing for its own sake. Of course, that is all out-dated now. Motor racing has changed tremendously since I began 9 or 10 years ago.

For a start, the social sphere of racing — all the whoopee and so on — was all so very much different then.

Today, it is very namby-pamby stuff, kindergarten type of fun. There are no really riotous times such as we used to have. Everybody seems to be frightened of making merry as racing men once did. I suppose this is the way motor racing is going. I think most drivers these days are a bit scared of the effect rowdy behaviour might have on their team managers. Consequently the so-called fun and games these days is a pale imitation of the things the chaps used to get up to in the old days.

I think this just reflects the difference between motor racing now and in the good old bad days.

I don't really know, in my own case, whether my getting out of hand now and again did any harm to my career.

Only one thing has definitely 'come home to roost', and that was about the time when I was asked to drive for BRM. Apparently this was under consideration at one of their board meetings and, I am informed, someone suggested at the meeting:
'Oh, we can't have him. He drinks.'

This, of course, is perfectly true. I do drink, but I don't really think I drink to the extent that it ever affected my driving, and I most certainly never turned up on race day with appalling hangovers. I would have thought that this would have been appreciated.

167

However, this is the only case which has come back to me. Maybe it did affect my career, but since I never did drive for BRM, I shall never know.

Not that it would have made any difference to me. I mean, if the BRM powers-that-be did not like the fact that I drink, that's fine with me. I have certainly never patterned my life around what I think other people are going to like or what they are not going to like. If people don't take to me the way I am, or if they don't want me to drive for them the way I am, that's also fine with me.

On the other hand, I think my general attitude to life might well have affected my being with Team Lotus. There again, only other people can say.

I think it is a great pity that most of the personality has vanished from motor racing. Today, one can only pick out a driver by the colour of his car or the motif on the crash helmet he is wearing. They all look the same, they all drive the same.

And although the cars may be interesting technically, inasmuch as they are almost as perfect as they can be, I think they are small and uninteresting. This was particularly true of the 1½-litre formula, and although I am sure the 3-litre cars will be much more exciting to drive, they will never present the same spectacles as the older generation of cars.

As to the performance of the present-day Grand Prix drivers there is absolutely nothing one can say about them. World Championships are not decided any longer on the skill of the driver, but go inevitably to the man whose car keeps going more consistently throughout the season. Anyone with a really competitive car is in the hunt, whether veteran or comparative novice.

This was pretty well demonstrated by the Grand Prix in South Africa at the beginning of 1965.

There you had a completely new driver, Mike Spence, who had not then had a complete season of Formula One racing, lying second to Clark until right near the end when he spun and lost it. Spence was obviously a very good driver but he must have had a limited reserve of experience. Nonetheless he did have a good car — he must have had, to lead the World Champion John Surtees at that stage in the race — and that is just about all you need in modem motor racing.

A few years ago, it would not have been possible for a brand new driver to go out and beat, say, Mike Hawthorn. Even Moss had to learn his skills the hard way, because the cars in those days were a great deal more difficult to drive, and one was matched

168

against the skill of the driver more than the impersonal factors which decide today's races.

I suppose it is small wonder that the outlook of a top driver in today's scene by and large, matches the faceless character of the sport.

I regard most of them as business men in overalls. I can't wait for the day when they begin to turn up at the track in striped trousers and bowler hats, carrying rolled umbrellas and brief-cases. This is perhaps taking things to extremes but if the act is not carried out in reality, it is in spirit.

The sport has become so commercial — I find it difficult even to refer to it as a sport any longer since it is becoming less and less so every day — that those who are making a success of it are those with a business man's approach.

The other chaps are prepared to accept that and to go along with it. I'm not prepared to. If I can't race motor-cars the way I like to race, or for what I get out of it in the way of pure sporting achievement, then I don't want to go on with it. I'm speaking, of course, in particular about Formula One racing.

If this all sounds like sour grapes, I am sorry. I don't think I am a sour sort of person. But I am speaking candidly and saying what I feel.

I think it is a great pity that the carefree, let's-get-out-and-have-a-go attitude has vanished in motor racing. Of course, some of the drivers of the old school never got home with much of their starting money they blew it all on parties and making whoopee and so on, paying the damages at the hotel or something like that. It is all obviously mixed up with this business approach to motor racing — just a sign of the times.

The greater pity, however, is that this has led to a decline in Formula One racing. Since it is not the spectacle it once was, the public don't bother to go and watch it as much. You can't really pin the blame for this decline on individuals, though; it is just the way the motor racing game has been organised by the powers that be — it's just a shame they have almost organised the thing out of existence.

I would like to see motor racing get back, somehow, to the standards where the World championship for drivers meant something in terms of driving skill.

These days it is a matter of luck, as was shown in the Mexican Grand Prix at the end of 1964. There were three drivers in the race who had a chance of the title, provided certain things happened. Clark could have won it; Graham Hill could have won it; or John Surtees — who eventually had the luck on his side.

169

It could be said that Surtees finished up as World Champion in 1964 purely because Lorenzo Bandini shunted Hill and put him out of the running and Clark's car blew up on the last lap. I am not denigrating Surtees when I say that. That is the way it happened.

Exactly the same sort of thing was true in 1962, when a broken oil line put Clark out and Hill in, although Clark won it fairly convincingly the following year.

Yet, I suppose, if pure dedication is the standard by which motor racing success has to be detemined, then John Surtees most certainly deserved his crown. He is, I think, the most dedicated and the most determined of them all.

Graham Hill, perhaps, would come next and then Jim Clark. These three, to my mind, think of very little else but motor racing. They are continually thinking about the technicalities of their cars, spending a lot of time in the workshops and so on.

However, the more and more a job it becomes, the less and less a sport it can claim to be.

The finance of motor racing has become so important that the sponsors of motor racing are probably only interested in having drivers who understand more about finance than they do about enjoying their racing, and who will be prepared to dedicate themselves totally to the whole business.

For these chaps, there is no room left and no time for considering motor racing as anything but a business proposition. For every hour they spend at the wheel of a racing car, they spend days negotiating contracts, starting money, bonuses, advertising deals and so on.

The whole climate of motor racing is that of a rat race. It is a treadmill for everyone involved in it.

That is the way motor racing is. In the olden days, you were paid on your value as a spectator attraction. Now, the fact that Clark or Hill or even Surtees is due to drive at a meeting would probably not attract an extra two thousand people to the meeting — and the drivers themselves know it. In my opinion the game can't possibly afford the fantastic starting money demanded by some of these drivers.

In any case, all these chaps are on view in some race or other every week-end of the year and the novelty of seeing them wears a bit thin.

Once, names like Moss, Hawthorn, Collins and their like were crowd-pulling attractions. You would get an extra ten thousand people turning up to a meeting if it was announced they were driving there, simply because of their personality and the exciting

170

spectacle that motor racing was in those hairy old days.

It is not like that any more.

Graham Hill summed it up pretty well in a film about motor racing in which we both appeared recently.

'Motor racing,' he said, 'has become a science.'

Unfortunately, I'm no scientist.

17

I started writing this book in Switzerland during the first four months of 1965. With the demise of BRP from the motor racing scene I felt a great emptiness, and more or less decided there and then to give up racing altogether. I had always been of the opinion that if an entrant, whether a Works or Private Team, wanted me to drive for them, I would be asked.

Since I was not prepared to 'hawk my services around' as is the present-day custom, and make all the correct 'social' and 'political' moves, I decided to call it a day.

This particular moment is, I feel, worthy of some passing comment. I had been having a Press Day for my Snow-Trac machine... a caterpillar vehicle for use in snow... and, after a day spent in glorious sunshine 7,000 ft. up in the beautiful mountains of the Lötschental, Jo Siffert and I successfully terrified our passengers by having a race back down the mountain track. It was only wide enough for one vehicle — with a sheer drop on one side — and the only place that one could get past was on the hairpin bends which appeared every half mile or so. At one stage I came round on the inside of Jo, but he was not of a mind to give up, and we went on edging each other until Jo found himself on the snow-covered roof of a hay-hut built below the road.

That night Adrian Cimarosti of the Swiss magazine Automobile Revue and Rico Steineman of Powerslide were my guests. We talked into the wee small hours about the changing face of motor racing to the background music of Trinez Lopez and the soothing effect of considerable quantities of Glengrant Glenlivet pure malt whisky. Somewhere about four o'clock in the morning a coin was tossed to decide my future in the racing world ... and racing lost. It is perhaps appropriate that Trinez Lopez was playing 'If I had a Hammer!'

172

Shortly after this memorable evening I had a letter from Tim Parnell asking me if I would drive in the GP events for him during 1965. After the tragic death of his father, for whom I had always had the most tremendous respect and affection, Tim had carried on where his father left off, running a team of Formula One racing cars. Remembering all my feelings and the tossing of the coin, I thanked Tim for his kind invitation, but declined to accept. Shortly after this the BP fuel company, with whom I had had a happy association for the past three seasons, asked me to reconsider my decision, since they had an interest in the Parnell team.

Since I did not really want to give up racing, and in the hope that it might lead to something else, it was not difficult for me to forget which way up the coin had fallen and agree to drive for Tim.

Once again I was being ruled by my heart and not my head, for the financial side was not at all attractive. My contract fee was meagre to say the least, and out of the £125 per GP that I received, I had to pay most of my own expenses.

The Team was using the Same Lotus cars they had raced in 1964, but which, of course, had been extensively rebuilt. Although they were the Lotus 25 chassis, the suspension had been updated to the type 33. The engines were the same BRM V8 units, again overhauled at the Works. 'My team driver was Dick Attwood, who was also the reserve driver for the Works BRM team.

We were plagued by a number of annoying faults, the most frequent in my case being the gearbox. As far as race results are concerned it was not an encouraging year, but it was great fun just to be racing again. I had some wonderful trips in my private plane, the most memorable being when I was going to race in Sicily. Never having been to Corsica before I decided to set off about four days early and spend some time in the sunny Mediterranean. This was a delightful interlude and I did nothing but lie in the sun on the rocks, swim, eat and sleep. After the race in Sicily I offered Jo Siffert and his wife Sabine, a lift to Rome, a journey which had to be done at about 1,000 feet all the way when we found that Sabine could not stand any greater altitude. We spent two or three hilarious days there, our greatest 'find' being a restaurant, in the old part of the city, called 'La Cisterna'. We quickly got to know the owners, and on one occasion I finished up singing with the musicians, who were one of the great features of this charming eating house.

En route to Austria, we stayed the night in Venice and before reaching Klagenfurt in the south of Austria, managed to

173

upset the Yugoslavian Air Ministry, by flying over their territory without giving written notice of our intention to do so.

I raced a GT Cobra at Zeltweg, but since the engine refused to fire on more than seven out of its eight cylinders at the one time, it was not a particularly successful day.

After some delay because of very bad weather, we left Klagenfurt, and by skirting round the mountains found our way to Vienna, back along the Northern side of the Alps to Zurich, down to Lake Geneva and then through the narrow and awesome confines of the Rhone valley to Sion, where we spent the night. After a quick trip by car to the Lötschental, we came back to Sion, and braved the rain and low clouds on our way to Geneva, where we were going to spend some time with Jo Bonnier and his delightful wife Marianne, prior to going to Monza for the Italian GP. The weather got worse and worse, and so, instead of flying to Milan, we went with Jo and Marianne in the Trans European Express. This was my first experience of the famous train, and I thoroughly enjoyed it.

Practice for the race went tolerably well and the car was handling all right, but unfortunately Monza is a circuit Where engine power is all-important. Without getting any sort of a 'tow' I could only manage a time of 1 minute 42 seconds, whereas the fastest cars were doing something like 1.36 and 1.37. In the race itself I was able to hang on to Ritchie Ginther in the Honda and keep in a reasonable position along with the works Cooper of McLaren. It is significant to note that my times were reduced, by the effect of the towing, to 1.38, proving once again that there is no substitute for horsepower.

As the race progressed one or two of the leading bunch fell out with mechanical troubles of one sort and another, and being in the second bunch it looked as if I might finish fourth or fifth. However, this was not to be, since, with some ten or fifteen laps to go, I joined the ranks of the 'retired' with mechanical troubles.

All in all 1965, was a year of some frustration and I came to the conclusion that racing around in the back half of the pack instead of the front half, with cars which were not really competitive, was not for me. One could find a satisfactory explanation by delving into one's innermost thoughts and mental processes, but here it will have to suffice to say that without a competitive car, the respect and confidence of a really competent management, I was, perhaps, unable to give of my best, for the end result would have been no different.

I decided that if I were to continue in racing in 1966 it would only be in GT racing if no opportunity with better prospects presented itself in the field of Formula One.

174

My first race of the season was in the Daytona 24-hour race in Florida, where I had been asked to drive a 275 LM Ferrari with Mike Hailwood. The car belonged to George Drummond, of the famous banking family, and the trip promised to be most amusing. We had rather a frustrating time during practice as our gearbox — a new one being brought over from the factory — spent its time flying between New York and Miami without getting off the plane in between.- Eventually we managed to get hold of it with very little time left to practice the car. It was of little consequence being a 24-hour race, and we managed to amuse ourselves in other ways.

I started the race in fairly good form, and without stretching the car to any great extent, managed to hold a fairly good place. I had almost finished my first stint when there was a nasty noise from the rear end and the crown wheel disintegrated. When I got back to the pits and told my story I was met by 'Oh, well! there goes another £800 gearbox' from George, and 'let's shove off and have some grub' from Mike Hailwood.

We left Daytona in high spirits, as George had asked us all to go down to his beautiful old plantation home on the island of Barbados in the West Indies. We arrived there after a night's stop in Miami, and a fairly long island-hopping plane trip. One of the guests was Viscount Fielding, now the Earl of Denbeigh, or 'Rollo' as he is better known. The islanders all seemed to think he was George Harrison, of Beatle fame, and I spent most of my time telling people that he was not, and they still did not believe me. Subsequently we met George Harrison, who was spending his honeymoon on Barbados, with his very attractive wife, Patti.

My next engagement was at Sebring, where I was going to share a GT 40 with Peter Sutcliffe, so, after Drummond had had to return to England, I went over to the island of St. Lucia, about 120 miles to the west of Barbados, to stay with friends who had a most lovely estate on the north end of the island. I think this must be the most beautiful of all the islands, for it had high, jungle-covered mountains, craggy rocks, little private sandy beaches and secluded harbours. I stayed there for about five weeks doing absolutely nothing other than lie in the sun, swim, fish and eat. As it was only February I did occasionally think of the fog and rain back in England, and looking at my ever blackening sun tan, felt better than ever!

After four weeks of this ideal existence, I spent a week in Texas with Tom O'Connor, before going on to Sebring. He arranged for me to take one of the family planes, a twin-engined Beech Queenair, so off I set on the morning of the first day's practice, on my 5½ hour, 1,200-mile trip.

I had to delay my take-off because of bad thunderstorms, and after a delay of an hour or so I was getting a little worried since practice started at two in the afternoon. However, I finally got off the ground, and by using the weather radar scanner fitted in the plane, managed to plot the thunderstorms and fly a course m between their centres. I finally arrived at the circuit about ten minutes after the session had started, only to find that Peter Sutcliffe had taken the car out to warm it up and on his fourth lap went off the road and bent the frame pretty thoroughly.

John Wyer, who was in charge of the team, did not arrive until about seven that evening, and we first saw him at the garage — where the mechanics were working flat out trying to get it all straight again. John looked as if he were in a pretty thunderous frame of mind and Peter and I kept out of his way as much as possible, as he seemed disinclined to want to talk to us. Naturally Peter felt awful about the whole thing and we both felt like naughty schoolboys waiting for the headmaster to summon us to the inner sanctum of his private office.

Finally my turn came, and in a fairly icy tone John asked me why I had not taken the car out first instead of Peter. I had to admit that I had been a little late for practice, and after getting my ears pinned back for the next five minutes I almost wished that I had shunted the car myself — Peter could not possibly get more of a telling off than I got!

The car could not be made ready in time for any training until fifteen minutes before the end of the last session on the last day of practice, in spite of the mechanics working in shifts day and night, so I did about five laps to make sure that everything was in working order. The wheels were not quite pointing in the same direction all round, with the result that the car went round left-handers all right but was rather tricky on turns to the right.

All the mechanics' hard work was in vain, for in the race I had only been driving for about two hours when the car blew up and I had to abandon it.

For the rest of the season I had an agreement with Colonel Ronnie Hoare to drive his GT 40 in all the major races on the calendar. He is perhaps better know for running Ferrari cars as he is the concessionaire for Ferrari in England, but since he had a Ford main agency also, I imagine there were political reasons for running a Ford GT as well.

My first race with this car was at Monza in the 1,000 kilometer race, where a combination of the road and banked tracks is used. This year a chicane had been introduced at the start of each banking in order to try to reduce speeds on the bankings as the surface was getting so bumpy. I had an exciting moment in practice time after I had left the pits and was braking to go into the first

176

(Photo: *R.C.A.Anvers*)

'...and there was I, milking the cow.' Talking to Dennis
Jenkinson at Nurburgring 1963.

(Photo: *Viki Lincoln*)

'The music goes round and round...and it comes out here!'
John Bolster Aintree.

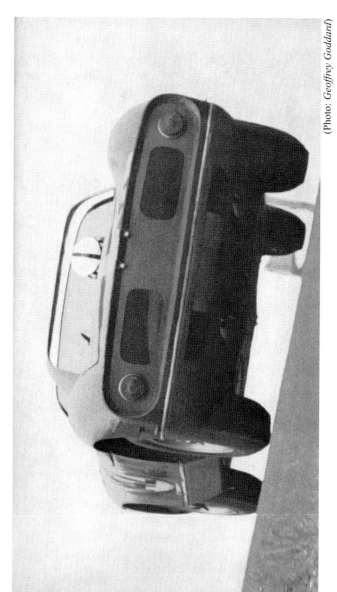

An exciting drive with a Ferrari at Nurburgring 1964.

(Photo: *Geoffrey Goddard*)

'If you'll ignore Trevor Taylor, lady, there I was...flat out...
when all of a sudden...'

chicane. I glanced in the mirror and was horrified to see that the rear engine compartment was on fire. I braked even harder and pulled in to the side of the track just inside the chicane. I opened the door and was in such a hurry to get out of the car that I nearly turned it over on top of me — I had completely forgotten to undo my safety harness! By a stroke of good fortune, there was a fire post within yards of where I stopped and a quick-thinking official put the nozzle of his extinguisher up the air intake and had the fire out before I had the release catches undone. Little damage had been done, and after adjusting a carburettor float, which had stuck down, allowing the petrol to flood all over the place, I was able to continue. We had various problems with the roadholding of the car and the brakes were very peculiar, so that we did not have a very good position on the grid — in fact, I think we were on the fourth or fifth row. Johnny Etheridge, a mechanic loaned to us by Ford Advanced Vehicles, and who I always called on when we had a particular problem with the car, assured me that the car would be much better for the race.

Apart from several other GT 40 cars, the principal opposition was John Surtees in a new Ferrari. As it was pouring with rain on race day I did not think much of our chances with my customary lack of enthusiasm for driving in the wet. At the drop of the flag I managed to catch one or two cars unawares, and by the end of the first lap I was lying second and only yards behind Surtees. This probably surprised my pit crew to some extent, but not half as much as it surprised me! For once the rain did not seem to trouble me and I managed to keep within a second or two of Surtees, although it was more like trying to keep up with a speed boat by the amount of water that was being flung up from his wheels. After about five laps he had the measure of the wet conditions and began to draw away from me, using the superior speed of the Ferrari to its best advantage. In my turn, I was gaining two or three seconds per lap over the next Ford GT 40, until I found the oil pressure fluctuating very badly. This was accompanied by some fairly exciting moments during cornering and braking, and I realised that I must be losing oil and that some of it was spraying over the rear wheels.

I rushed into the pits and quickly explained the situation to my mechanics. After what seemed like an age the leak was traced to a fractured oil line which went from front to rear inside the central tunnel of the car, and consequently was almost impossible to get at. A temporary repair was made by cutting the rubber hose at the point where it had been damaged and inserting a metal tube. By this time I had lost a considerable number of laps, but set off again hoping for a trouble-free run for the rest of the race — which

177

would have put us back in the picture again. This was not to be, however, and as I was half way round the banking before coming up to the pits the cockpit filled with smoke and I got very hot oil all over my left leg. I immediately cut the engine, as I knew what had happened, and did not want it to blow up into the bargain from lack of oil. I had to abandon the car on the circuit and walk back to the pits in the pouring rain — with the added discomfort of having to remove my oil soaked shoes and socks.

This was a year when the 'tyre war' hotted up considerably. The American companies of Goodyear and Firestone had made an inroad into the world of Formula One the previous year, but at that time they did not have the upper hand. Since they had so much experience in making tyres for larger and heavier cars, by 1966 their tyres were much better for our GT 40 than the Dunlops which we were contracted to use. I should qualify this by saying that Dunlops were still better in the wet and this had helped me considerably at Monza. During the entire season we were slower in practice than similar cars using the American products and naturally this was a source of considerable annoyance.

At Spa, where we ran in the 1,000 'K's', the same problem arose. We had the most awful trouble getting the car to handle properly, and in the end had to increase the size of the spoiler on the back of the car before it would even go down the straight without scaring me to death. My co-driver was Chris Amon, and neither of us could get the car below 3 mins. 58 secs. although another GT 40 was doing 3.53. The race was fairly disappointing for us although we did managed to finish — which made a change. It was also fairly uneventful, although I did have some lumps of rubber fly off the tyres and the pit crew spilled about two gallons of petrol into the cockpit during a pit stop when I was going to take over, which did not help my vision.

The proof of the pudding, tyrewise, came at Nurburgring, where we were having the same problem of bad handling. Eventually I managed to get a set of wheels with Firestone tyres and did a lap with those on the car. I was immediately ten seconds a lap quicker and the car was a great deal easier to drive. Having proved my point, it was perhaps easier to cope with the inferior handling on the tyres we were contracted to Use, for at least my entrant, Ronner Hoare, realised that the slower lap times were no fault of mine or my co-driver, Mike Salmon.

Once again our race really centred round other GT 40's as we could not hope to stay with the faster Ferrari entries which were in the prototype and sports classes, and the principle opposition was from the Essex Wire car of Scott and Revson, the Ford France one of Schlessor and John Whitmore's car, which I think was entered by Alan Mann. I got the most fearful shock during the first lap — we had not done any laps With full tanks before on this circuit — and going down a very fast, twisty section with a nasty left-hander at the bottom, the wheels were hitting the body-work so badly that great clouds of blue smoke were pouring out from under the wings. The suspension was bottoming in no uncertain fashion and I felt as if I was having a very nasty accident the whole way down the hill. There was one good thing about this, however, since the chap in the car behind me was so certain that I was about to fly off the road, that he backed off and I gained quite an advantage over him. At the end of that first lap I managed to overtake the leading Ford GT driven by Scott, and although he was right on my tail as we entered this particular section, by the time we got through it I had gained two or three hundred yards. so that although the cars antics were scaring me to death, they were obviously scaring everyone else as well.

On another part of the circuit, where a steep uphill straight culminates in a sharp crest followed by a right hand bend. I was getting the car so far into the air that it was travelling for about ten yards or more before the wheels touched the ground and just in time to take the right hander, all at well over 100 mph. After ten laps I was passing a back marker and estimated that he would have gone over the crest just as I got to it, so that I would overtake him just before the corner and would not have to reduce my speed. As I came up the hill I flashed my lights and he obediently kept over to the right of the road. Normally I went over the crest in the middle of the road, but because of this other car I went over on the extreme left-hand side. As I got airborne I was horrified to find that the car was sailing over to the right, towards the other car and of course there was nothing I could do about it. I was just waiting for the crunch as I landed, but by great good fortune it never came, and I was relieved to see the car in my mirror after rounding the corner, and that he was still motoring happily on. I found out later that I had paint from his car all along my door and rear panels!

With only half a lap to go until I handed the car over to Mike, the left front tyre burst and I went hurtling off the road. I was doing everything possible to keep on the road, but I finished up in the ditch and, as the mangled tyre caught in the side of it, the steering wheel spun to the left out of my grasp and in so doing bent my thumb back and cracked the bone. According to one of the spectators a car had just come round the corner, clipping the edge and throwing a shower of stones out into the road. I was unable to avoid them and one was sharp enough to rip my tyre and so burst it. It was in this race that the American built

179

Chaparrel, the brain-child of my one time team mate, Jim Hall, scored its first major European victory in the hands of Phil Hill and Jo Bonnier.

The rest of the season was one of frustration and disappointment with the car, including Les Vingt Quatre Heures du Mans, where we were out of the race within the first half-hour with a broken gudgeon pin. At another meeting, at Brands Hatch, I missed the first practice session because the car appeared with a new set of wheels which would not even fit on the car. I was also sent out to practice with only one brake pad in one of the front calipers, a fact which I discovered at the end of the straight when I applied the brakes and nothing happened in the braking department — with the exception of a dense cloud of blue smoke as the piston shot out of the casting allowing the brake fluid to go all over the disc. It was becoming apparent that most of the effort in preparation was going into the Ferrari cars which were being run in conjunction with the Ford, and naturally I was fairly unhappy about the situation. With the race in Austria coming up, I was anxious to have a good car, and was very pleased to be asked to go to Silverstone one day to set up the car find get it ready for this race well in advance. You can imagine my feelings when I discovered, about three weeks before the race, that the car I had set up so carefully was being given to Rindt to drive in Austria.

As I was determined to have something to drive in this race, I found a very good GT 40 that was for sale, and it was bought for me by Bernard White. I had previously met Bernard out in the States at Daytona and, in fact, he had offered me a drive in Formula One that year in one of the two BRM cars that he had bought from the factory. This never materialised as BRM failed to produce his second car.

The GT 40 was prepared by Ford Advanced Vehicles at Slough and four days before practice I set off towing the car on a trailer behind a DB 5 Aston Martin, intending to drive slowly across the continent going by Luxembourg and the beautiful scenic route through south Germany. It was great fun to be back 'to the old ways when I had my own cars, driving to meetings with the car behind and enjoying the trip in my own time.

As there was only one day of practice I was out on the circuit very early and soon recorded a time of 1 mm. 12.5 secs. This was soon bettered by Rindt, with something like 1 mm. 11.8 secs. For the first time my old team were using Goodyear tyres as I was, so at least we were on even terms. Gradually the times were reduced until Rindt finally came in with only 10 minutes left for practice. I was talking to the mechanics in the FAV transporter when one of his pit crew came in and very proudly told me that Rindt had

180

just done 1 min. 10.2 secs. I said something like 'How very interesting' whereupon he added that they had taken 15 gallons of fuel out of the car to help his time. I pretended to show no interest, but quietly slipped off and said to Rollo, my mechanic, 'Take 15 gallons out of the old charger, but quickly.' I only had time to do one flying lap, so with a certain amount of gay abandon I hurled the car around the track. At the end of my one timed lap, out came the chequered flag for the end of the session. I was fairly pleased to find out that I had done a time of 1 mm. 9.6 secs., which not only gave me pole position for the race, but broke Graham Hill's absolute circuit record of 1 mm. 9.8 secs. which he set up driving a BRM Formula One car.

There were two or three 'works' Porsche cars in the race which were going very quickly, and I felt that they would be a real threat. All the GT 40 cars were in a certain amount of brake trouble because of the heat. I had found that if I used the brakes to their maximum they would start fading badly after about ten laps. But this was not the only reason that I was not confident about the outcome of the race.

The Goodyear tyre people failed to get our new tyres to the meeting. Not only that, but the ones that they had given to FAV for our use turned out to be two dry weather rears, and two wet weather fronts. Since the rubber mixture for the two types of tyre is completely different, the car handles very badly if you are forced to adopt this combination. Knowing the year-long situation that Ronnie Hoare had been in I realised that Rindt would have to run on Dunlop tyres and he had, in fact, done a few laps on them in practice. Ronnie did have a complete set of new dry weather Goodyears in his transporter, so I asked him if we could have them. I was most surprised to hear that he had not made up his mind which tyres he would use, but he would let me know in the morning.

But when the morning of the race came along, he still had not made up his mind, although his car was all ready for the race and sitting on Dunlop tyres. He still would not give me a decision and when I at last asked him in some desperation, less than an hour before the start, I realised that I would have to start the race with new, unscrubbed rear tyres and the old fronts that had been on the car since we got it. This would necessitate a time wasting change of front tyres after only eighty laps, but since the new wet fronts would not last the full distance, we had no alternative.

As the flag dropped, one of the Porsche cars shot into the lead followed by a gaggle of GT 40's, the other Porsches and David Piper in his very familiar 275 LM Ferrari. With my unscrubbed rear tyres and the old worn fronts my car was an awful handful

181

and I had some trouble even keeping it on the road for the first ten or twelve laps, and I could only just hold on to twelfth place. As the rear tyres improved, so I began to press on, until finally I passed Mike Salmon, who was in fourth place behind the Porsches, and the leading GT 40 car. A few laps later I went into the pits for fuel and a change of tyres.

It was here that I lost the race, although it was unlikely that I could have caught the Porsche anyway. The front wheels were so hot that my mechanic was unable to undo the hub nuts to remove the wheels, and after some time I got hold of the hammer myself and laid into the offending nuts. Eventually they came off, the wheels were changed, the tank filled, and off I went.

A few laps later the passenger side door burst open, and being unable to close it, even when rounding the hairpin, I pressed on with the door swinging open on every right-hander. Once or twice I got a little close to the straw bales and the door hit them with a fairly convincing thump. I was black-flagged eventually and had to come in to tie the door shut. Within two or three laps it burst open again so back to the pits I went. By this time all hope was lost of a good position, and, as the car was handling like a bowl of soup on its funny tyres, I just motored on to the finish saving the car as much as possible.

The race at Zeltweg is perhaps not well-known for having a fabulous circuit, but the hospitality and the fun laid on by the warm-hearted enthusiasts who organise the meeting, are legend. That night in Knittlefield after the race was no exception. I was surprised to receive a cup for the fastest lap, but the organisers always seemed to find an excuse to give me a trophy. One year it was a broken, gold-plated bolt given as a hard luck trophy, since I had been leading the Formula One race until the last few laps when a cam follower broke. A great deal of wine flowed that evening, but the highlight for me was when I was carried all round the hall shoulder high, at the head of a crocodile of people all singing 'For he's a jolly good Fellow'. It seemed to me to be a spontaneous expression of friendship and goodwill to all the motor racing fraternity, and, not unnaturally, it warmed the cockles of my heart. When we finally took our leave, we left to the strains of 'Auld Lang Syne'.

The 1966 season ended for me with three Formula One races. I drove Bernard White's 2 litre BRM at Oulton Park, Watkins Glen in the American Grand Prix, and Mexico City in the Mexican Grand Prix. It was wonderful to drive once more in the type of car that I loved so well — and I finished 4th and 7th respectively in the first two races. In Mexico I had to start the race with a brake disc which I knew was cracked, so that I could do nothing else but motor quietly around. It was rather pathetic in a way that in this race which was to be my last drive in a Formula One car, that I could not 'have a go,' and retired when the gearbox lost all its oil and broke up.

I really wanted to hang up my hat after the race in Mexico, but after Watkins Glen I flew down to Florida with Bill France in his private plane. Bill is the dynamic personality behind the Daytona '500', the fastest race in the world. This is a race for Stock Cars, highly-tuned American saloons. He asked me if I would drive in the race in February, as this would lend an international flavour to the race for the first time, and he was most anxious to encourage this aspect. I eventually agreed to do this and so in February of 1967 off I went to Daytona.

The race was very different to anything that I had ever done before as the circuit is a tri-oval with very high bankings at each end. A completely new approach is needed to get the best out of these very large and fast cars, and, of course, this took some time to achieve. An indication of what I mean is that the fastest lap in the race was covered at an average speed of 182.7 miles per hour for the 2½ mile course!

My car was two years old and I had no great hopes of being able to keep up with the fast boys, but as the car was very highly geared I had great hopes of finishing. Since my practice laps had all been in the 174-475 region, I thought I would be well up after 500 miles, the incident rate being what it was. After about 350 miles, however, I was to become one of the 'incidents' when my engine blew up in the most spectacular fashion right in front of the pits. I was lying in eighth position at the time, and was well ahead on points to collect the 'Rookie of the Year' award given by the Chrysler Corporation.

It would have been a nice thought that in the last race of my ten years of motor racing, I could have collected an award for being 'The Rookie of the Year.'

The decision to give up racing has been the most difficult thing that I have ever done. Perhaps if I had not lived with the belief that Motor Racing was the 'Sport of Gentleman,' the decision would have been easier. The political intrigues — such as was evident at Zeltweg over the tyre situation — make it impossible for me to continue in racing with my outlook on life. With the very large sums of money floating about in the 'sport' from commercial interests, it has become necessary to have a 'bowler hat and rolled umbrella' outlook to stay at the top of the tree. I have never been able to equate money to motor racing, and the alternative of 'selling my soul to the rat race' is quite unthinkable.

I still have the urge and the desire to race cars — it seems

183

impossible to get it out of the blood — and even, now I find it hard to believe that I will never 'race' a car again.

At the time of Donald Campbell's tragic death, during his attempt to prove that a speed of 300 miles per hour was a possibility on water, I made an offer to carry on this attempt should another 'Bluebird' be built.

My sentiments at the time were of some patriotism, since land and water speed records are always claimed for one's country. Allied to this was the feeling that the final paragraph to this chapter of events in Campbell's life should be written, otherwise all the work, engineering, time and effort, and the giving of his life would be wasted, and in vain.

Should anything ever come of this, perhaps it would provide the excitement that my life and being seems to crave —who knows?

INDEX

185

188

Post Competition

Innes in his later years in all types of activities

C

In relaxed mood at Jarama in 1980, listening to a good story.

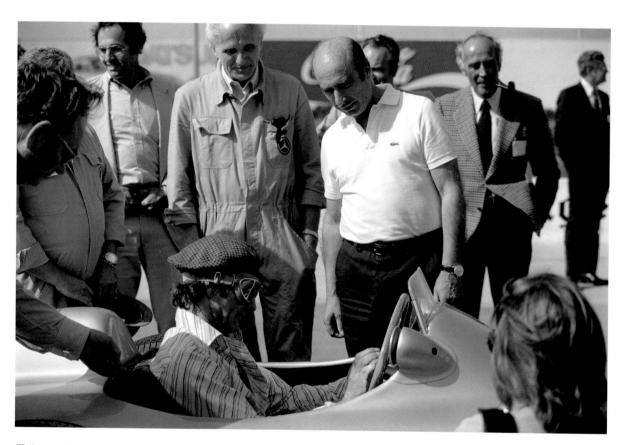

Taking advice from the 'Master' in one of the most succesful cars Fangio drove (Mercedes W196 GP car). Innes drove this car in a parade lap before the US Grand Prix at Longbeach, 1976.

On the pitlane with Frank Williams at the San Marino Grand Prix, 1986.

Innes as guest of honour a Clermont Ferrand in 1988. Innes was the overall winner in 1958 at the first race to be staged here.

Innes at Clermont Ferrand with his contemparies, 1988.

About to drive a Vanwall for the first time at Laguna Seca in 1989.

In the paddock with Jean and Christianne his daughter, posing in front of his Aston Martin DB6 Vantage at Silverstone.

In the car Innes had made.
Every part on the car was made to the original drawings. He was most insistant that the car was correct in every detail to the original specifications.

The Testarossa being loaded onto a trailer for its first visit to Silverstone leaving 'Kiln' cottage.

Here parked in his regular spot behind the BRDC building at Silverstone, which always caused problems with birds from above.

"Ask me again in the morning."

The happiest of brides. Jean and Innes leaving for their reception at Welford Park, Berkshire.

The newly married couple leaving St Gregory's Church at Welford, Berkshire.

Innes and Jean in his beloved Ferrari Testarossa at a classic event. Coombe Abbey n/r Coventry in the mid 1980's.

Here with his personnel hairdresser, the lovely Annie, and his favourite tipple at Sole Farm.

Innes enjoying one his favorite pastimes! New Years Eve at Sole Farm, Wickham, Berkshire.

At his computor (Kiln Cottage) drafting articles for "Road & Track" magazine.

Innes with his lovely step daughter Emma, sharing the same sense of humour always.

Innes and 'Ben', his faithful dog amongst the Autumn leaves.

President of the BRDC before leaving for an important meeting at Silverstone, 1993.

ROBERT MacGREGOR INNES IRELAND

1930 - 1993